Warwick Within L Memory

CW00693349

Compiled by the Warwickshire Federation of Women's Institutes

Published jointly by
Countryside Books, Newbury
and the WFWI, Royal Leamington Spa

First Published 1993
© Warwickshire Federation of Women's Institutes 1993

COUNTRYSIDE BOOKS
3 Catherine Road
Newbury, Berkshire

ISBN 1 85306 252 9

The cover picture shows Joyce, Betty and Sally
of The Women's Land Army
on a farm near Bascote

Designed by Mon Mohan
Produced through MRM Associates Ltd., Reading
Typeset by Paragon Typesetters, Queensferry, Clwyd
Printed in England

Contents

Acknowledgements

Warwickshire Federation of Women's Institutes would like to thank all W.I. members who supplied material for this project through their local Institutes. We are also grateful to Sylvia Gardner for allowing us to include material from the *History of Ilmington*.

Unfortunately we were not able to include extracts from every submission; to do so would have meant some duplication of content, and of course we had to take into account the total amount of space available in the book.

But all the contributions, without exception, were of value in deciding the shape and content of the book. We are grateful for them all.

Anne Allen
Co-ordinator

Foreword

Until the 1970s Warwickshire was a county of approximately diamond shape. When the county boundaries changed a lot of the land was lost, along with the two cathedral cities of Birmingham and Coventry. It is situated in the heart of the country and has some notable towns including Royal Leamington Spa, Rugby famous for its school, Kenilworth and Warwick with their castles and of course Stratford on Avon with its Shakespeare connections.

Sheep farming was the main industry in the Middle Ages. That declined in the 17th century and was much reduced by the 18th century, and when coal was discovered on our doorstep, industrial expansion took place.

Ways of life have changed vastly during this century. How often do we hear 'Do you remember when?', or 'When I was a girl'? These memories from the First World War, the twenties, the depressed thirties, the Second World War and post war fifties are part of our heritage and we in Warwickshire feel that they should be recorded for posterity. So our Women's Institutes around the county have listened to and written down the stories of the older folk. Special thanks must go to Anne Allen, who has done sterling work in co-ordinating this project, and also to Clare Emery who helped in the initial planning stages. We thank them all for their hard work and hope that you, the reader, will enjoy their findings.

Daphne Bradley
County Chairman

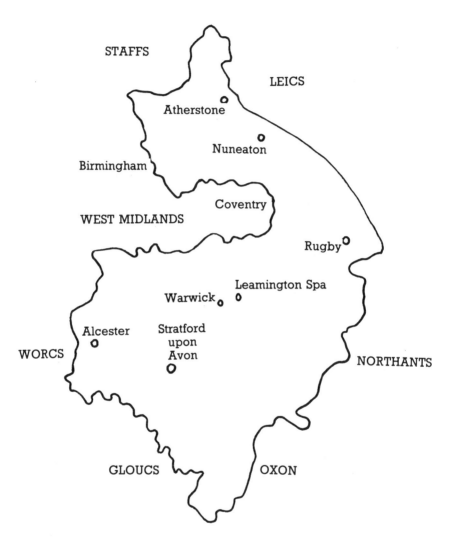

STAFFS

LEICS

Atherstone

Nuneaton

Birmingham

Coventry

WEST MIDLANDS

Rugby

Leamington Spa

Warwick

Alcester

Stratford
upon
Avon

WORCS

NORTHANTS

GLOUCS

OXON

County of Warwickshire

TOWN & COUNTRY
LIFE

SOME TOWNS AND VILLAGES REMEMBERED

The lamplighter on the streets of Kenilworth; Race Day in Warwick in the 1920s; trams clanging along The Parade at Royal Leamington Spa in the 1930s; villages where everyone knew everyone else and the whole village would be invited up to the 'big house' for the 21st birthday of the Squire's son. It seems like another world, but it wasn't really so long ago. Here are just a few 'snapshots' of life in the towns and villages of Old Warwickshire, as it used to be.

WARWICK IN THE 1920s

'I was born in Warwick in the 1920s and remember it as a small, busy market town, where we all knew each other and all the little shops were family owned and stayed in the same management for 30, 40 or 50 years.

My mother owned the draper's and milliner's shop in Coten End. She was 20 when she took over the shop with her sister, after she married at the end of the First World War. Houses were difficult to come by in those days so my parents made their home at the shop, and I was born there. My father was an engineer and had served his apprenticeship with Herberts in Coventry and afterwards joined the Rover Company. In the early days he used to walk from Coten End to Milverton station to catch the train, leaving home before six in the morning and returning about seven o'clock at night, a long day. My mother was 70 when she retired, and had been running the shop for 50 years.

On market days in Coten End all the public houses in the area were allowed to stay open all day, and the cattle drovers and farmers used to get a little the worse for drink. The cattle and sheep were driven down Guy Street from the railway station to the sale yard in Coten End. Many a time our garden gate had blown open and we had a herd of cows in the garden trampling the flowers down.

Lakin Road was then called Union Road, where the workhouse was. Here old men and women were well looked after and the tramps could have a bed for the night and a meal before continuing on their way. There was also a nursery for orphans under school age and often you would see the nurses taking the very young babies out in the town in a large square basket like a pram, which could hold six babies.

Another event which caused a stir in the town in the 1920s and 1930s was Race Day. There were very few cars in those days, so the punters and bookmakers all arrived by train and walked through the town to the racecourse, calling at various places for liquid refreshment. Smith Street and Jury Street would be full of people.'

STRATFORD ON AVON IN THE 1930s

'Living in Stratford 60 years ago was very different from today. It was very much smaller in those days and not quite the tourist attraction it is now. We had a picture house and a Hippodrome where social events were held. It cost about one shilling and sixpence for a downstairs seat at the cinema and the front row upstairs was two shillings and sixpence. We also had a good train and omnibus service which has fallen away very much over the years. On Saturday mornings it was possible to get a ticket on the train for Birmingham before 8am for two shillings return, known as the "fisherman's ticket".

We went to the theatre every Saturday night in the stalls for three shillings and sixpence throughout the season, which was considerably shorter than it is now. If you wanted to go in the gallery you had to queue in the morning, but later someone had the idea of putting out stools. We paid threepence for a ticket, which we fixed to the stool, and when the performance was due you went and sat on your stool until the doors opened. We then paid one shilling and threepence to get in.

The market was held on Fridays and this was down the centre of Bridge Street. Of course, there was not the traffic we have today. Mr Adams who owned a shop at 2a Bridge Street used to have a crockery stall more or less opposite his shop. He had crowds round him whilst he was auctioning his wares because he was so funny and made people laugh a lot. He sold good quality items at low prices.

On Mop days the main stalls were in Bridge Street too and of course there were the pig and ox roasts. During and just after the war, the Mops were very crowded because if you were lucky you could get blankets, carpets and lots of other things that were difficult to find in the shops.

Boys used to stand outside the paper works and collect papers as they were issued, about once an hour. They would run down the street as fast as they could shouting "Paper! Latest News!" or "Big Fire!" or perhaps the latest racing results. The ones who ran the fastest caught the trade.'

9

COVENTRY IN THE 1940s

'I was born in February 1940 in the Stoke Heath area of Coventry. My earliest memories are of air raids and being in the Anderson shelter that everyone had built in their back gardens, seeing searchlights and the light of flames. Shortly afterwards Dad was called up and my mother and I and my little sister were evacuated to Dad's home county, Berkshire.

On returning home after the war I can remember chatting to groups of Italian prisoners of war when I was out playing in the Sewall Highway/Blackberry Lane area.

On Saturday mornings I went to the Gaumont Cinema Club. Jordan Well then was still a very old area with medieval buildings and we walked in to the city centre afterwards. At that time repair of the bomb damage was just starting and I can recall the gaping empty cellars of buildings that had gone in the Smithford Street area and the groups of temporary shops near to the entrance to the Barracks Market Arcade. Unfortunately the old Arcade was demolished to make way for the new development.

At the back of Warwick Road Congregational church I can remember a wall with an advertisement for the Rover Company, which had previously stood at that site. The city was full of old motor factories and I recall particularly the old Siddeley factory in Parkside, the Lea Francis factory in Much Park Street and the Francis Barnett motorcycle factory in Lower Ford Street.

Several shops were full of ex-Service equipment and I remember the thrill of listening to strange languages and music on my cat's whisker crystal set, complete with big heavy headphones. The excitement was never the same with improved transistorised sets later. The arrival of our nine inch Murphy television set for the Coronation of Queen Elizabeth was my next great excitement – a picture so small that it needed a magnifying glass in front!'

RUGBY

'I was born towards the end of the First World War and lived with my parents and brother in a terraced house in Rugby. My father, a Rugby man, was the managing clerk to a firm of solicitors in the town. He was a keen gardener and grew all our own vegetables and fruit in a nearby allotment. In our small back garden there was a flock of hens, which provided us with eggs. We had a bathroom – just a bath and a geyser, a frightening thing with jets of fierce flames and noise. Few of our neighbours enjoyed this luxury, for them it was a zinc bath in front of the kitchen fire. The only lavatory was outside.

Warwick Historical Pageant

Warwick Castle Park
(By kind permission of the Countess of Warwick)

July 16th, 17th, 18th & 19th, 1930

Time Table, Order of Scenes and Principal Characters

(N.B. Names of Representatives of Characters are liable to occasional change.)

GATES OPEN TO THE PUBLIC—2 p.m. and 5.30 p.m.

THE PAGEANT—3.0 p.m. and 6.30 p.m.

PROLOGUE.

Principal Characters :—

COMPERE: Mr. COURTENEY BRANET, Wednesday, Thursday, Friday, Saturday Afternoon and Evening. (Understudy: Mr. GEO. SPRAGG).

COMMERE: Miss FLORENCE WALKER, Wednesday, Thursday and Friday Afternoon and Saturday Evening. Mrs. VICTOR HUMPHRIES, Thursday and Friday Evening and Saturday Afternoon.

(Full description of Prologue on page 14 Main Programme.)

TITANIA: LADY CYNTHIA ASQUITH, Wednesday and Saturday Afternoon and Evening. Miss JOCELYN HUBAND, Thursday and Friday Afternoon and Evening. (Understudy: Miss OLIVE HARRIS).

PUCK: Mr. GODFREY WINN, Wednesday, Thursday, Friday and Saturday Afternoon and Evening. (Understudy: Miss GLADYS GOSS).

(Full description on page 15 Main Programme.)

DUNCHURCH AREA.

Episode 1.—THE FOUNDING OF WARWICK BY CYMBELINE.

Principal Characters :—

Ancient British Chief	Mrs. TATHAM	Roman British Officer ... Mrs. LISTER KAYE
Cymbeline	Mrs. JOHNSTONE	

(Full description on page 17 Main Programme.)

COLESHILL AREA.

Episode 2.—ST. AUGUSTINE IN WARWICKSHIRE.

Principal Characters :—

King of Mercia...	Mr. TISDALE JONES	Priest of Thor ... ... Mr. F. T. KENYON
Queen of Mercia	Miss MARGARET PINNEY	Mr. H. PICKERING
		St. Augustine ... The Rev. W. R. WYLDBORE SMITH

Monks, Knights, Ladies, Attendants on the Queen, Assistant Priests of Thor, Crowd.

(Full description on page 21 Main Programme.)

BERKSWELL AREA.

Episode 3.—THE NORMANS IN WARWICK.

Principal Characters :—

William Rufus	The Rev. A. WHITTAKER	Edgitha, his wife ... ... Mrs. SMELLEY
Lord High Chamberlain	Mr. HARVEY	Clerk of the Market ... Dr. ORTON
Robert de Newburgh	Colonel BOURNE	Bellman ... ... Mr. GREENWELL
Thorkil, Sheriff of Warwickshire	The Rev. ASTON	Butter Woman ... ... Mrs. FREWING
Lady Levurunia, his wife	Mrs. COX	1st Mercian ... ... Mr. WARRINGTON
Edric the Saxon	Major HUGGINS	2nd Mercian ... ... Mr. KNIBER

(Full description on page 23 Main Programme.)

In July 1930 the Warwick Historical Pageant brought towns and villages together from all over the county for a hugely popular event.

11

One day at school, when I must have been about ten, we were all allowed into the playground to see the R101 airship fly over. Only a short time later it crashed in flames and that seemed to herald the end of travel by airship.

Rugby had an important cattle market and on Mondays farmers would bring their cattle through the streets. Irish drovers came over by boat and train and their animals would be turned into fields until the market was open. There would be chaos in the streets, with buses, cars, traps and carts all mixed up with the frantic cattle.

In the town's market place was a row of almshouses, and in the porch of each was a seat. On fine days the inhabitants would sit outside and watch the world go by. Outside was a line of taxis, and a motorcycle and sidecar, the latter with pretty curtains at the windows.

There were concerts to go to and in the summer a band in the park and fetes at nearby country houses, the proceeds going to political parties or to the local hospital. There were polo matches when Indian Maharajas would come with their strings of polo ponies and attendant grooms. The Prince of Wales, later Edward VIII, sometimes played in the English team at one time.

The railway had brought prosperity to Rugby. Two large engineering firms, the BTH Company and Willans provided many jobs and men came from all over the British Isles to work here or to be apprenticed to the various engineering trades.

I would go to the cinema with my mother, perhaps three times a week. There were the Regent, the Regal, the Plaza and the Scala – the latter dubbed the "flea pit". There was also a theatre used by travelling companies.

My parents had some friends who had a car – a "Bean". They were the only people we knew who owned one.'

ROYAL LEAMINGTON SPA

'Number 12 Milverton Crescent was my childhood home from the age of three, 1919, with its large basement kitchen, washhouse and backyard for drying laundry. A steep staircase led up to the rather grander dining room and drawing room, square hall and verandah with pretty front garden leading into the quiet tree-lined crescent. Those were the days of maids, and with hindsight how I blush to think of poor young Florrie carrying heavy trays up and down those stairs. Her mother, with a large family living at Rose Cottage, Whitnash, came every week for washdays – and how my small sister and I loved to see the huge mangle turning!

This was our grandparents' house, as our parents still lived in

Kenya where we were born, and we children slept in two small attic bedrooms with dormer windows that looked down on Strathearn Road at the back. I well recall watching the milk cart's progress with its docile pony, shiny churns and the farmer's name, "Clyde Higgs", well displayed. Folks, often the children, would come out of their houses carrying jugs of all sizes, and the milk was ladled into them from the churns by the driver. We could also watch the gas lamplighter man with his long rod, a very accurate performance!

There were few cars in those days, but many horse-drawn carts and carriages. We were horrified to see, one frosty day, a horse slither frantically and fall heavily in Grove Street; then a man quickly sat on its head to stop it struggling to its feet, until it had been unharnessed (or shot?) – but we were whisked away.

We loved to visit the Jephson Gardens on summer days, and then you had to buy an entrance ticket at the white lodge. Everyone dressed more elegantly then, grown ups were hatted and gloved, and children had to be tidy and well behaved! Another favourite walk was through the Guys Cliffe Fields to the working mill. In those days a golf course and farmland stretched across to Old Milverton, now mostly replaced by a school and residential estate, but the Dragon Cottage and railway bridge remain.

A local event which I distinctly remember is the opening of the newly built Princes Drive in the 1920s by the then Prince of Wales. Dressed in white frocks and holding tiny Union Jacks we were taken by an aunt to stand at the corner of Myton Road; there were crowds of people and it was a hot sunny day. After a very long delay a few open cars with bowler-hatted worthies drove by, but I think the Prince was hatless; after that we were able to walk back home along the new drive to Milverton station for the first time.

Shopping was a more leisurely affair than today, and goods were delivered to the house by cart or by an errand boy on his bicycle. And when you arrived by train there was always a willing man with a hand truck to bring your luggage home, after work, so you need not take a taxi. Leamington was a gracious, quiet, uncrowded town in those days, with quality shops like Francis, Burgis & Colbourne, Bobby's the Cadena, Englands and Frances'; also a splendid fishmonger, Colbrooks. Being a family without a car we made great use of the trams. They ran from Warwick and they were so numerous you never had to wait for one, even if you had just missed one. If only we had them now. But to get to Kenilworth or Stratford you travelled by train; I even remember being taken in the train to Kenilworth Common with some friends, for a day in the country – there were sand dunes then!'

In 1914 cattle still grazed on the village green at Long Itchington.

'My first remembrance of the Parade at Leamington Spa is of the trams clanging up and down. I suppose I must have been about five or six when I first rode on one in the 1920s. They used to start in Avenue Road, opposite the public library, and travel via Emscote to Jury Street, Warwick. The journey took 34 minutes. The trams were replaced in the 1930s by omnibuses painted in green and yellow, which later became part of the Midland Red Bus Company.

My first home in Leamington Spa was in Wathen Road. Mr Smith, our milkman, rode a tricycle with a large bucket of milk at the front and he would ladle the milk straight into your jug. He was a friendly man and the children in the road used to be given rides on the tricycle.

In those days we did a lot of our shopping at the door. The butcher came twice a week, a man visited the houses with fresh eggs and the greengrocer had a large well-stocked cart drawn by a docile horse. Our baker, Mr Plank, always seemed to do his rounds in the evening.

My family had a drapery business in Regent Street, Leamington Spa, from 1880 to 1963. I recollect at sale times I used to go down to help fold the catalogues. When a customer paid for a purchase the money would be sent in a "pot" at high speed along an overhead rail to the cashier's office. The change and receipt came back the same way. Stubbs got their first motorised vehicle in about 1927 which made things much easier. My father, uncle and other staff would cycle round the neighbouring villages collecting weekly contributions. Then on Saturdays the village people would come to Leamington Spa to spend their savings in the shop.

I remember in 1932 the river Leam burst its banks. It came up all over the Jephson Gardens and it was impossible to find the lake or the fountains. The river also rose above the Victoria Bridge on the Parade and steam rollers were brought in to hold the bridge in place while the water rushed beneath. The water then moved slowly up the Parade into Dormer Place and even into St Peter's church. It came to a stop outside Boots, opposite the war memorial.

The earliest illuminations I remember were in the Jephson Gardens. It was 1935 and the Silver Jubilee of George V and Queen Mary. Glass jars in different colours were hung on the trees and railings and each evening the gardeners went round lighting the night-lights inside. Later, electric floodlighting was used but I liked the effect of the twinkling night-lights better.

I am told I was carried to the Pump Rooms as a babe in arms and I certainly remember them from my earliest days. There was usually music by Jan Berenska and his trio. There was a very good atmosphere, quite high class, and it was the place to be seen in the 1920s and 1930s.

The Theatre Royal in Regent Grove was the town's leading theatre in the earlier part of the century. It had regular visits from touring companies, amateur drama groups and operatic societies. I once took part in a pantomime there called *Rumpelstiltskin*. We did a whole week of performances, myself, aged seven, as a gipsy and my three year old sister as a fairy.

Old Milverton then was a hamlet belonging to the Heber-Percy family. Tenants of the cottages worked on the estate farms or at the big house, Guys Cliffe. Lady Percy used to present the village girls with red hooded cloaks and the boys with blue pullovers to keep them warm on the long walk into Leamington to school. Mobile shops went out regularly. Barrs of Clemens Street, for instance, delivered pots and pans and other hardware, as well as oil for the lamps (there was no electricity until 1950). Mr Bradshaw, who had a basket shop in Regent Street, used to cycle out to collect rushes from the riverside. He made all his own chair seats and baskets.'

KENILWORTH LAMPS

'I was born in Kenilworth and have lived here all my life. When I was small, it was just a large village with many outlying farms and very lovely countryside. Today it is a busy town.

I was born in a small cottage with no mod cons, a sandstone sink and an outside toilet shared with our next door neighbours. In 1922, when I was six years old, we moved into a much larger house but less comfortable as the rooms were so big that the furniture looked lost. My mother was a very good home maker and did her best to make it cosy but it was a hard task and money was very scarce.

At that time Kenilworth was lit by gas lamps and I remember in the winter, about four o'clock, Mr Castle used to come round the road lighting the lamps with a long pole; he put this pole through a little window in the lamp and pulled a chain which ignited the mantle. As time went by the outskirts of Kenilworth were lit by gas lamps and these needed to be inspected at night to see that they were alight and hadn't been damaged or blown out by the wind.

My father worked for the Council and drove a green open-backed lorry with solid tyres. UE 37 was the registration number. The Surveyor asked him if he would do a nightly inspection of the outlying countryside to make sure all the lights were on. He was paid a shilling a night for five nights a week, very much appreciated in those days.

I often went with him after tea on those journeys in bitter cold weather and gales, with often a tree blown down. We covered all the outskirts from Rouncil Lane and the Castle, along Coventry Road to Common Lane. We could look through the bare branches of the trees to check the lamps in some roads, which helped to make it quicker. It was difficult at times for my father with cold fingers putting those little mantles on in a gale, but when we got home it was hot cocoa by the fire.

Kenilworth Common was a lovely place to play in those days. We used to spend hours there making fern houses. If we played outside Mrs Sharpe's house and were not too noisy, she would bring us some of her home-made lemonade. Delicious!'

BIRMINGHAM FOGS

'In Birmingham, prior to the war, we frequently got smogs. As the area was eventually turned into a smokeless zone, they do not suffer in quite the same way these days.

Our home was in the country on the outskirts of the city, which did not have footpaths and relied on gas lamps for street lighting. When the fogs were very bad the buses often had to stop running, but they would keep going as long as possible to get people home from work. We children should not have been out in that unhealthy weather, but always thought it was great fun, and we helped the buses to keep going up to the terminus and back. Collecting old newspapers, we stuffed them into the hedgerows on either side of the road to help the drivers to see where the edge of the road was. Some of us would run or walk in front of the bus, to help guide it, or ride on the back, hanging onto the upright pole. On the return journey we all changed places, so we all got a chance of a free ride. Our parents, who thought we were in the homes of friends, would have had a fit if they had known what we were up to.

I can't remember what time of day our letter boxes were emptied, but I do remember our pre-war bus postal box. At 9.30 pm each weekday evening, as the bus was heading back to town, it had a post box fixed just inside, on the back of the bus. Buses in those days did not have a door, and the entrance was at the rear. When the bus pulled up we hopped on to the platform, posted our letters and then jumped off again. A very handy service.'

NUNEATON

'My recollections of Nuneaton are of the time of the First World War. The market then was a cheerful noisy place full of the voices of traders shouting their wares. Some were great characters. Mrs Gee auctioned "crocks", knocking on an old tea chest with a broken battledore (a kind of badminton bat) when she declared the price. Goldberg sold cheap jewellery from his wooden box-like kiosk. Then there was the man who sold foot oils. He shouted "On the nails!" as he jumped barefoot on a wooden block studded with nails to demonstrate the efficacy of his product!

These were the days before general refrigeration. Palladino's in Abbey Street supplied fishmongers with blocks of ice, which they broke up and placed on the slab with the fish. Fish was sold cheap on Saturday nights and we often had a fish supper on Saturdays. Birch's cooked meat shop next to Coleman's sold pork dripping which customers fetched in their basins. On Fridays Moreton's the butcher's in Queens Road cooked tripe, cow heels, trotters and chitterlings in big coppers. People queued in the yard with their jugs etc.

Michael Palladino pushing his ice cream barrow was very popular with the local children – a halfpenny cup or a penny wafer. On Saturday afternoons there was a children's matinee at the Royal cinema in Stratford Street, a penny downstairs and twopence upstairs. In the interval those downstairs had a farthing stick of rock and those upstairs had a small bar of chocolate. Starmer's and Philimore's toy shops also provided great interest for the children.

Some time before Christmas the toys in Philimore's window would be marked at twopence, threepence or fourpence a week with twelve weeks to pay. These were times of very low wages.

Imported foodstuffs got very scarce during the war, particularly sugar. It wasn't until after 1918 that British farmers grew sugar beet. Queues would form quickly when people heard on the grapevine that a shop had a consignment of butter or jam, lard etc. A stallholder from Leicester sold bacon every Saturday. The queues got so long in the market place that the police moved his stall into Mill Walk.'

'I was born in Nuneaton in 1927 and apart from about 16 months during 1956/57, have lived here ever since.

We lived in a terraced house which my grandfather had built in 1906; the adjoining house was identical and the owner was a colleague of my grandfather's. They both worked at the local brickworks and both were foremen, this in those days being a "collar and tie" job.

It had, as most houses at that time, a toilet outside just up the yard, no bathroom or hot running water, but we did have two taps over the sink, one for cold water and one for "soft" water (ie the rainwater stored in a large tank in the coal house, next to the toilet). We always used the soft water for washing ourselves and our hair, you really could feel the difference.

There was a coal range in the kitchen, a black one that had to be cleaned with black lead – a very dirty job. There was also a copper for washing situated in the corner of the kitchen. This was heated by a fire that was lit underneath it. These were both used for Friday night's baths. The water was heated in the copper. It was really cosy in the winter but a bit warm in the summer.

I can remember the lamplighter cycling round with his bicycle with a long pole with a hook on the top to pull the switch down. I never saw him miss and thought he was very clever – as no doubt he was. Just before the war we had new lights as we lived on the main road. They were the first in the town and we thought they were wonderful – no lamplighter. They lit all the dark corners and it was a great improvement. Unfortunately they went out in September 1939 and we were in the dark again until the war ended.

We went to the local council school. It was a very good school, 60 children to a class but we learnt a lot and were happy there. At twelve I went to a new senior school that opened just before the war. It had everything but I'm not sure that we were any happier, or better educated.

I left school at 14 and was sent to work in the local offices of Armstrong Whitworth Aircraft Limited. There were several small factories in the town and we did all of the clerical work involved. The office was bombed out when we had our own little "blitz" when a lot of damage was done in the town and quite a few people were killed. I don't think we teenagers realized the danger we were in. We all used to go out in the evenings dancing the nights away. There were several dance halls and most of the church halls held dances on Saturdays to cater for our age group. We also used to "walk the town" on Saturday and Sunday evenings. This entailed walking in groups of boys and girls (separately) from one end of the town to the other. There was no traffic that I remember and certainly no trouble; no fights or anything like that.

We used to stop and chat to the boys we knew – or wanted to know and I guess more than one romance started there. At that time there were quite a few public houses in the town but we didn't go in those – only the milk bar, where you could stay for ages drinking a milkshake or glass of lemonade. We would disperse at about nine o'clock and go home.

On Sunday afternoons we did likewise in the local park. This used to be crowded – all of us dressed in our "Sunday best".

There seemed to be plenty of transport pre-war, the trains and buses went everywhere and stopped at every "tree"; but we mainly walked. Sometimes we were taken along the canalside. We had to dodge into the hedges to avoid the horses pulling the barges along. They were very busy places pre-war and just afterwards but of course we then became motorised and the horses were no longer used.

We used to have fairs come to town regularly – quite big affairs. They were owned by Pat Collins and stayed for a couple of weeks. These were held where we now have the bus station, but also used land on the other side of the road next to the cattle market, which was held every week and was a very busy place. My grandfather used to take me when I was a little girl and I used to take my own son until it closed round about 1960.'

ILMINGTON

'I was born in 1906 in Ilmington. My father was a woodman on the Foxcote estate. As a lad I used to fetch the milk to the Manor House and cream and cheese direct from the farm. Mother was the cook at the vicarage. The vicar owned three farms in the district and he looked after his parish on a horse.

My parents used to eke out their 14 shillings a week by bartering the wheat they grew on their allotment. There was one day in the year when a motorised thresher was hired for the village – they made a stack and divided it according to the amounts put in. They were boozy days! Horses had to pull the thresher, as many as nine to get it up Campden Hill.

There were three general stores in the village and three bakers to a population of about 600. The village pound was still in operation as animals often roamed round the village. The children collected manure off the road in buckets to put on the gardens. The lavatories were buckets. The big houses had three bucket lavatories – one for staff, one for family and one for visitors.

We had two blacksmiths, one at The Red Lion and one up Campden Hill, but one was killed in the war and that left only one. The horses were tethered to the tree outside The Red Lion. Lots of horses were used on the farms as well as for transport.

Most people worked on the land, though the big houses employed a lot of domestic staff. Entertainment included Ilmington Club Day on 14th October. The whole village was involved, with as many as 60 horses on the green. There would be stalls, coconut shies, rock, and a tent for the club members. Ilmington Band sat up on a waggon, and there were walking races from outlying villages and the show people brought roundabouts. We also had a bowling club with three rinks, and we drained the playing field ourselves and formed the Ilmington football league.

We never really knew the First World War was on, except that it took the men from the land and left it to children to work, some as young as twelve who had exemption from school. There was a lot of sadness at the deaths of those who came from the village.'

BARFORD

'This was a very pretty, quiet village in the early years of this century, when no juggernauts screamed through the main street. A horse and cart, pony and trap or even a few animals being herded to market in Warwick, or the house cow being driven to another pasture, were all that disturbed the peace.

With a population of around 500 everyone knew each other; the Squire's son played with the village children and joined in the dances frequently put on in the small room that passed as a village hall.

When the Squire's son reached his 21st birthday the whole village was invited up to celebrate the occasion at the house on Barford Hill. There was fancy dress, races and tea for the children, and probably dancing in the evening. Most villagers worked in some capacity for the owner of the big house.

Events of national importance were celebrated by the whole village; people liked to put on fancy dress and there was invariably a parade along the High Street.

The village was self-supporting with a number of shops, a bank and a post office. Gas and electricity were produced. There was even a mill. One resident can remember the days when her granny kept the main grocery shop and there were rows of measuring tankards hanging from the wall. These were for measuring vinegar and other produce, while sugar and rice were scooped up from large sacks or tins and weighed into paper bags. Half a pound of cheese was cut while you waited, and most other provisions were stored in large containers. Broken biscuits stored in large tins could be bought very cheaply and were a boon to those on small wages.

The church was the centre of village life and it was the custom for the children after attending a service on Good Friday, to walk to Hampton Woods – about two miles – to pick primroses. The Sunday school played a large part in village life and in the 1920s the outing took place to Edge Hill, the children having first eaten tea in the Rectory garden. Sometimes the children went to the Burton Dassett Hills, which was a novelty as most of the central part of Barford is flat. Adventurous boys, not used to the steep slopes there, spent time sliding downhill, sometimes at an alarming speed – and no doubt arrived home covered in mud, only to be chastised by mothers who had to scrub the dirty garment. No washing machines then – the scullery copper was filled, lit underneath and the boiling water scooped out for use.

The school still stands and teaches children until they are eight years old. Years ago pupils stayed until they were 14, sometimes 16 years old, and there were three teachers. No school meals then, with most cottages clustered in the centre of the village most pupils went home for the mid-day meal; for those too far away two ladies produced large pans of steaming soup. Milk was ladled out, also Horlicks, and one pupil recalls that although she disliked Horlicks she had the drink because she liked the design of flowers painted on the mug! These were the days of ink mixed from powder and water and poured into individual ink pots slotted into a hole in each desk; earlier pupils had slates on which to write.

There were only about twelve large houses in the village around 1920, and most of the cottages had bucket lavatories, many of them two or even three-seaters, with small squares of newspaper tied together in a bunch and hung from a nail on the wall or door. A daunting experience for the very young having to go a distance up the garden on a dark, cold night, to answer the call of nature. Even

21

at the beginning of the Second World War chamber pots under beds were normal. These things are unknown to children born since the late 1940s and one's grandchildren doubtless think it is positively awful to have lived under those conditions, yet no one gave such things a thought; they were all part of living.

The doctor came out in his pony and trap from Warwick, but before he would visit the patient had to be inspected by the resident Nurse Randle, who lived behind the church, and at one time had a small surgery in part of a nearby barn. More recently a cottage on Bridge Street served as a surgery and a doctor came out twice a week.

A saddler lived in the village and also repaired shoes, and once or twice a year a man selling shoes trotted up in his pony and trap to sell his wares. There was also a village taxi, a motorbike and sidecar, owned by George Taylor. There were no buses and when a service was started, there was opposition from a Blue Bus – the children who went on to school in Warwick were all told to wait for whichever bus charged a penny ha'penny instead of twopence.

During the Second World War, the Squire's house on Barford Hill was used as a hostel for Land Army girls, and with an Army camp in the village and two Air Force camps within a few miles, one can appreciate that there were jollifications and probably liaisons galore!'

BERMUDA

'I was born and lived until my marriage in a small mining village called Bermuda, just one road with rows of terraced houses running along each side. The village and nearby pits of Griff, Clare, etc belonged to Sir Francis Newdigate who lived in a huge hall on the Arbury estate.

We children had a large field with swings and slides to play on, and as there was no transport available walked everywhere on our very precious only pair of shoes. I had a poor but very happy childhood, walking in summer to "The Mill on the Floss", into the woodlands, through Bedworth and back through Collycroft, Griff Lane and home to Sunday tea of bread and cheese.

My mother had six children but reared only two, the other little ones dying before school age of influenza.

I left school at 13 and would help mind some of the many babies in the village until I was 14 years old and started a proper job in a local factory making silk and rayon. The money I brought in helped my parents as my father was no longer able to work down the pit through illness, and wages for working on the coal face were poor.

22

My mother walked round the villages selling milk from a churn on a cart, and taking in washing to help pay the rent and food.

I married when I was 25 years old at Chilvers Coton church which was bombed in the Coventry Blitz, and then rebuilt by German prisoners of war who were interred at Arbury Hall. After my son was born I would meet my mother at the brickyard once a week, when I would go shopping, Mother looking after my son who, if he got mischievous, would be placed in the dolly tub.

My husband was in the police specials in the early years of the war and then conscripted into the Navy, running the North Sea convoys, only complaining that "he couldn't swim one stroke".

Although not receiving the attention of the Coventry Blitz, many bombs were dropped over Nuneaton, causing a rush to the garden shelter when the sirens went off. We watched many crippled German planes trying to head for home.'

DAYS OUT AND AROUND

'I was a child in a village shadowed by the Second World War. Not that we children were particularly aware of it. There were evacuees at school of course and we didn't like them much – we resented the disruption of our parochial little lives by strangers from big cities with different accents who overcrowded our classrooms! We didn't appreciate how fortunate we were and that families from Birmingham came out every night to sleep in the fields, or in any shelter they could find around the village, to escape from the constant air raids. We did have bombs once – when Coventry was being raided. Poor Coventry. I do remember the night when it burned. I watched from the balcony of my grandmother's house and the sky was one huge red glow, although we were at least twelve miles distant. The village did have American soldiers too – only for six months, but they completely took us over. We children always hung around them hoping for goodies and gum, which we usually got. They loved our Warwickshire lanes and cycled miles, lured by flowery cottages and country pubs! Many came back after the war to visit and I know one young Canadian who fulfilled a lifelong ambition when he returned to cycle once more, with his wife, to Lowsonford and the Fleur-de-Lys Inn and was utterly overwhelmed to find it so little changed.

Of course they found their way to Stratford on Avon – as we all did on high days and holidays. Teenage days on the river Avon with the boyfriend and a picnic were so romantic – trips to Henley in Arden for one of those gorgeous ice creams were a great spree with the boyfriend too!

We used to go to Warwick on the train – GWR in those days – and all the stations on the line were so smart. Lapworth and Leamington Spa usually had the best displays of flowers but every stop was a delight.

Leamington Spa was another regular outing with my grandmother and aunt. What a *very* elegant town it used to be – all the shopping was "quality" and hats and gloves were obligatory, especially if one was visiting the Pump Rooms for tea to the accompaniment of piano, violin and cello. I loved the genteel bustle and the low buzz of conversation among the tinkling tea cups and dainty sandwiches.

The river Avon is for many people another abiding image of the heart of England, flowing through its market towns and gentle pastures, yet my own most treasured memories are of a much smaller Warwickshire waterway – the little river Blythe, which was the source of all childhood delight. Family picnics along its grassy banks were the highlight of our holidays during the war – grandmas, grandads, uncles and aunties as well as parents and brothers and sisters, everyone went. Children paddled and fished with nets and string-handled jam jars through long, warm, sunny afternoons while grown ups chatted. Teenage evening walks with boyfriends after church on Sundays invariably led down the lanes to the little river – and how searingly nostalgic to take one's own small children back to the same banks and suddenly to realise how time had flown!

Kenilworth was within cycling distance of our village too. The way led through Temple Balsall where we often stopped for a break, the ancient history of the hamlet so eerily present that we were always a little uneasy and when we eventually arrived at the gaunt ruins of Kenilworth Castle something of the same unease remained, even though we chased one another around and made a lot of noise to bolster our spirits. It was never a completely carefree outing and we were always quite relieved to be back in our own friendly living village!

Yarningale Common was quite another matter – this day out was part of the Easter Bank Holiday ritual, the whole of which I looked forward to, and now look back on, with tremendous pleasure. Good Friday was always really fresh, doughy, hot cross buns from the local bakery – one could smell them cooking all along the High Street, and then to church to augment the choir in Steiner's Crucifixion. Easter Sunday was a family gathering and Simnel cake, followed by church again, but this time with the bells ringing across the village and everybody congregating after the service for tea and biscuits in the Guild House.

On Easter Monday to Yarningale – picnics in saddlebags and full of high spirits to be doing our own thing. Whatever the weather the springtime lanes were lined with bluebells and we invariably scattered rabbits to their holes as we made our rather noisy approach, with hardly a car on the road. Not that we were alone when we arrived at Yarningale. The little tea-room at the foot of the common was a mecca for cycling clubs and lots of families were out for the day. We used to climb to the highest point of the common and eat our picnic looking across the countryside towards the Avon valley and the Welcombe Hills, and thinking how fortunate we were to be young, in England, in April, in a world at peace – and what wonderful times there were to come.'

LIFE AT THE BIG HOUSE

Most villages had their 'big house' nearby, sometimes exercising an almost feudal influence well into the 20th century. The extent to which the lives of the villagers were affected by the goings on at the Hall can be surprising to us today. These two accounts of life at Umberslade Hall come from a time when this way of life was changing for ever. The first was written by the gatekeeper at East Lodge, the second by a member of the family who lived at the Hall.

BEFORE THE FIRST WORLD WAR

'The main entrance to Umberslade Hall was the East Lodge, through an archway and a large wrought iron gate of ornamental design. A drive enters the park between two small spinnies of fir trees, then the drive to the Hall is bordered by large Wellingtonia trees and some very fine oak trees all the way to the East Front entrance. At the beginning of the century there was a herd of fallow deer in the park, which made a beautiful scene.

The large lawns in the West Front were mowed by a machine pulled by a pony with leather shoes on its feet. One of the gardeners did the mowing. The road from East Lodge to North Lodge is bordered on the park side by a narrow wood called the Bluebell Wood and a carpet of bluebells flowers in the early spring. Also the trees make a rookery for a large number of rooks nesting there in the spring. They would fly off each morning to feed in the fields in the surrounding country and return in the evening. They were named Muntz's Black Pigeons. When the rooks had nested and the young were ready to leave their nests, the Estate farm tenants were invited for a young rook shoot. This was to reduce their numbers.

The North Warwickshire Foxhounds used to meet at Umberslade on Boxing Day and on another day in the hunting season. At these meets the butler, footman and maidservants served drinks to the huntsmen – whisky and wines. Once or twice the meet was at the East Lodge. The gamekeeper knew where the foxes had their earths and would go and stop up the earths so the foxes had to lay out in the woods. Pheasant shooting was arranged on the estate during the season. Pheasants were hatched by sitting hens from the nearby farms during the spring. While the young pheasants were being reared, a gamekeeper kept watch day and night to protect them from hawks, jays, magpies and stoats and weasels. If any were shot they were strung up on a line of wire. When the pheasants were able to look after themselves for food, they were taken and released in the wood on the estate for the shoots in the season. The herd of fallow deer had to be kept at certain numbers, as a tax had to be paid on them. They were rounded up in the park and marksmen with special bullet cartridges would pick out the bucks to be shot; this was done in early autumn.

Mr G F Muntz was squire of Umberslade. At his expense he had Umberslade church built, a well built Baptist church of beautiful stone with a spire and a chiming clock. At each third hour it played a tune for three minutes; one was *Blue Bells of Scotland*. The woodwork in the church was beautiful, especially the pulpit and may I add that my father, Mr E Margetts built this and other woodwork in the church, this was in the year of 1878. Mr G F Muntz constructed a kind of microphone and placed one in the church and one in his study at the Hall so if he could not go to church he was able to listen in to the services. These two microphones were connected by a rope on small wheels, similar to telegraph poles, which were placed across the fields to the Hall. These poles remained in the fields for a number of years.

The maid servants at this time went to church on Sunday mornings, dressed in black with a small bonnet with lace and two pieces of long ribbon. Also on Sunday mornings the coachman would ride on horseback to the post office at Hockley Heath and collect the mail for the Hall.

F R Muntz Esq served in the Army with the rank of Major. He had three sons. The eldest, Lionel, was a Lieutenant in the Navy who lost his life at sea. The second son Gordon went on a holiday in Spain and caught a fever and died. His body was brought to

26

Umberslade for burial in the family grave at Tanworth-in-Arden church. For this funeral my cousin and I were approached by Mr Foster, the Head Gardener, if we would go in to Chalcot Wood, a mile away from the Hall, to gather some bunches of white anemones to line the sides of the grave. The third son, Douglas, was in the Naval Division Reserve and at the outbreak of war in 1914 was sent to Belgium. He took his motor car with him, an open car about 12 hp. He brought this car home when on leave with his servant and I was shown a sniper's bullet hole in the front seat where Capt Muntz and his servant were sitting, a narrow escape. After the war life went on but not just the same as before.

Now to Home Farm. Mr Jones was the bailiff in charge of the farm and a stud of shire horses, some of the best in the country. Two, King Forest and Dansfield Stonewall, won the championship of the Shires at shows. One morning Dansfield Stonewall was found dead in his stable; he had had a heart attack.

A blacksmith had a smithy at the farm and shod the horses for the shows. A cowman had about ten cows to attend to and hand milk, to make cream and butter for the Hall. A large area of the farm was grass for hay-making. For the last three years I was at school I had the job of going to the farm and taking a large can of milk and small can of cream to the Hall each morning and afternoon, about three quarters of a mile walk, and on Mondays a basket of butter made by Mrs Jones, wife of the bailiff. I was paid two shillings and sixpence per week for this job.

Each year two truck loads of sheep came by rail from Scotland and were placed in the park for the lambing season. They usually arrived in September, and were looked after by the shepherd. One afternoon I went into the park, it would be in September, I saw two buck deer having a fight for the King of the Herd. They clashed with each other until one dropped to the ground. I went to the buck that had lost the battle and found he had broken one of his front legs. I went and found the gamekeeper and he shot it. This buck had a good pair of antlers and I asked the keeper if I could have them and I have them now.

One year there was a heavy crop of acorns. The gamekeeper asked me if I would gather some to feed the deer in the winter. I filled 20 bags and was paid with two gold sovereigns. I thoroughly enjoyed my young days living at East Lodge Umberslade.'

THE END OF AN ERA

'I was not born in Warwickshire but my husband was – at Umberslade near Tanworth-in-Arden. He was born in 1928 amid great rejoicing and celebrations as he was the first male heir to be born since 1876.

Umberslade was a large stone Queen Anne house, with three storeys and a servants' wing. Built in 1690 to replace a medieval moated manor, it was set amidst beautiful undulating parkland designed by Capability Brown, with lakes and formal garden. Dev, short for Devereux, grew up surrounded by servants – nanny, nursery maid, housekeeper, butler, cook, parlourmaid, two housemaids, scullery maid, gardeners, groom, chauffeur and gamekeepers.

His father, known as the Squire, was a retired Royal Navy Brigade Officer, the youngest surviving son of a family who had bought the house in the 1850s. Dev was the eldest child of his second marriage. He was a landowner of an estate of 4,000 acres with tenant farms and large tracts of woodland.

Umberslade had many magnificent rooms, one for every occasion – dining room, drawing room, library, billiard room, study etc. Strangely enough there were only two bathrooms, though one was installed in the 1930s for the staff. The maids used to take cans of hot water to the bedrooms for washing and in cold weather, coal was carried up to the bedrooms. The story goes that a certain young housemaid met the master of the house while she was carrying up a bucket of coal. A spirited lass, she told her employer that the bucket was too heavy for a young girl, whereupon he gallantly carried it up for her!

Umberslade had its own fire engine and tender and a fire escape which was manned by the gardeners. It is not known if it was ever used for a fire. The fire escape is now at the Avoncroft Museum. Every evening a ritual would take place – all the shutters would be closed on the downstairs windows, a bar put across and a bell on a spring inserted in the bar. This took a long time, and was still being practised in the 1950s when there were no servants!

Dev saw little of his parents. Every day after tea he was brought downstairs by nanny for about half an hour before bed. Tea was taken in the large entrance hall which had a huge fireplace at one end. As a family they had simple tastes in food. They distrusted anything foreign or exotic with the result that the cooks seldom stayed long. The staple diet pudding-wise appeared to be rice mould and apple pie!

The servants' hall was in the basement; a little light filtered in through the windows, which were below ground level. Also in the basement was the kitchen, scullery, larder, pantry, wine cellar and housekeeper's room. A wrought iron spiral staircase led from the basement to the servery adjacent to the dining room – a lift had been installed so that the meals could be hoisted quickly from the basement.

Every consideration was given to Dev as a child. When the local carpenter was installing shelves in the library, which was just below the nursery, his father used to come in with a newspaper every day, telling the carpenter to take an hour off while the baby had his sleep. He was not quite so fortunate in later years, as when at the age of seven he had chicken pox he was banished for weeks to the top floor in case he should give it to his parents – who had very inconsiderately not had it themselves as children!

Although the estate provided every opportunity for pheasant shooting in the winter, the whole family plus a contingent of servants used to de-camp in August to an island off the Isle of Skye, for grouse shooting, fishing and deer stalking. This was a major undertaking. A reserved coach would be loaded at Dorridge and attached to the London Inverness train at Rugby station. It was said that the family alone had around 26 items of luggage including budgerigars in cages, all of which had to be counted at each change.

It seems that the family had little to do with the village life. Dev's father was the patron of the living and appointed the vicar, who the

The Muntz family of Umberslade Hall at the turn of the century. The way of life for such families was to change forever with the First World War.

29

story has it was chosen because he was a cricketer and enjoyed hunting and shooting! Father was a churchwarden and always sat in the front pew, much to the discomfort of young Dev who disliked it intensely and felt very self conscious. Father, in common with most of his generation, believed that God was a White Anglo-Saxon Protestant! He was a staunch Royalist and always stood to attention whenever he heard the national anthem, particularly when the King broadcast on Christmas Day.

A certain local worthy built a village hall during the 1920s and it was said that Father objected to this effrontery and promptly built and presented to the village a cricket pavilion and playing field.

He also sat on the local Tanworth Charities which provided funds for the church school, and funded local children when they needed it for further education.

Dev and his younger brother Reggie progressed from nannies to nursery governess and from there to prep school and Eton.

The Second World War changed everything. Umberslade was requisitioned and the family moved up to the Scottish island where they stayed for most of the war – though the boys travelled to and fro to school. The deer park was ploughed up in the drive for home-grown corn. The servants were called up. After the war, the family moved back – living at first in the servants' wing, then into half the house. The other half was piled up with furniture which had been stored there since the beginning of the war. Dev, or Fred as he now called himself, did his National Service 1946-1948.

His father died in 1947 and with him disappeared an era which had changed little since Victorian days. Fred's father was born a Victorian and carried his Victorian values and principles halfway through the 20th century.'

THE VILLAGE INN

No electricity or mod cons, and rats in the cellar – perhaps we should be grateful for our modernised village pubs!

THE BOOT AT LAPWORTH

'I came to Lapworth when my parents took over the tenancy of The Boot Inn, a favourite old hostelry for miles around. In those pre-war days we had no electricity, no mains water and no toilets. We had to manage with paraffin lamps, pumps and buckets. I suffered from chilblains from standing in the damp and cold kitchen, where we had to use a water pump on the kitchen sink.

We also had a thermometer which was marked "cellar temperature" and had to be kept at 55 degrees to make sure the beer kept properly.

As far as the cellar was concerned, it was a haven for rats. Every Sunday morning the rat catchers would call with their little Jack Russell terriers. They would drive the rats up the cellar steps with the dogs, standing at the top of the steps to catch them one after the other as they ran up. There was apparently a Rat Catchers Club which had its headquarters at The Bluebell pub in Henley-in-Arden.'

THE MALT SHOVEL AT GAYDON

'Prior to the Second World War our grandparents, Mr and Mrs W H Terry, retired from being master bakers in Birmingham and became the licensees of The Malt Shovel in Gaydon.

Grandad's sister, Mrs Leonora White, had previously been the licensee of The Gaydon Inn, where it is alleged that Cromwell stabled his horses at the time of the battle of Edgehill. As children we regarded the mounting-steps outside the inn with great awe, imagining all the important persons who may have used them in years past.

It was in this inn that Great Aunt "Lol" served a dish with custard sauce, remarking to the customer, "This is real custard made with eggs, none of your Bird's Custard Powder." On the departure of the clients Auntie found a card under the plate, on which was printed: "With the compliments of Sir Alfred Bird"!

When we knew Great Auntie Lol, she kept a tea house a few yards down the road from The Gaydon Inn. What a spotless kitchen – white wood, scrubbed kitchen table and plate racks. The storage canisters were all highly polished. Earlier in her life, Auntie had been the local midwife and district nurse. Our mother used to tell us of her visits to patients in the pony and trap.

The Malt Shovel was a 16th century inn with not one single level wall and few level floors. We are sure that one of the attic rooms, into which we were forbidden to venture, was haunted. Granny had it sealed up.

It was an adventure to go to Granny and Grandad's – no electricity and no mains water. We still remember the smell of those beautifully elegant paraffin lamps and also the big pump in the yard for water, with the smaller one at the stone sink in the scullery.

After closing time Grandad always let out the pigs from the sty, for their wander round the yard and their scrub with a bass broom under the water pump. Those pigs could tell the time as well as any dog! In due course these pigs, who were all known by name, were sent to be slaughtered and the bacon cured. How we remember that rather fat and very salt bacon. We also remember the pigeons, the pheasants and the rabbits which Grandad brought to our home to supplement our rationed food.

On Sundays we were not allowed skipping ropes or balls to play with, only dolls, quiet games or books were acceptable. On special occasions we could use the old wind-up gramophone. Grandad sometimes allowed us to take home a clay pipe, from the smokers' bar, to blow bubbles, using soapy water. Oh, how those clay pipes could take the skin off your lips! I suppose the old seasoned smokers knew how to pre-treat them before smoking.

The toilet at the far end of the yard was an earth closet, with a twin seat. This toilet was always scrubbed snow-white and never smelt objectionable. At the other side of the hedge from the toilet, in the inn's private garden, grew a magnificent egg plum tree. Nowhere else were such huge, juicy and delicious plums to be found – I wonder why?

There were wonderful characters in the old village. Old Sarah had never been out of Gaydon in her life, her longest journey was up the road to gather firewood, complete of course, in her white bonnet cap worn under a tall hat. We never saw her without that tall black hat and shoulder shawl. It was rumoured that she had never ever washed her hair! Granny took us to her cottage to visit her. Here you could stand in the fireplace and see the sky out of the top of the chimney. When she eventually became ill, it terrified her to have to go to hospital by car. We felt that she died of fear and a broken heart.

The war brought a great change to Gaydon. The airfield was built just outside the village. We always remember how polite the airmen were to Granny when she went into the bar to say "Time, gentlemen, please". We wonder if any of those airmen who returned after the Second World War remember her. She was a remarkable woman.'

THE MOTHER HUFF CAP

'Although there were once two public houses in Great Alne, The Boot and The Mother Huff Cap, only The Mother Huff Cap has survived. Its name is derived from the froth on a well brewed pint of beer. A rhyme goes as follows:

"Twixt Michaelmas and Martinmas old dame began to brew,
First she brewed some old beer and then she brewed some new.
The first to pull was cloudy beer but then there came the
    crystal clear,
And so she brewed some more like that and on the top was
    huff the cap."

Drinkers used to blow, or huff, the froth off to see if the tankard was full, as unscrupulous landlords would let the beer froth up to increase their profits.'

CHURCH AND CHAPEL

At the heart of every village was the church or chapel, in the times when Sunday was a special day and most families went to services at least once and often twice, while the children went to Sunday school. The Sunday school outing was an eagerly awaited treat when days out or holidays were few and far between.

THE HALL AND THE RECTOR

'I was born in 1911 and attended a small school intended mainly for children whose fathers worked on the various farms belonging to the Elmdon Hall Estate. Mrs West, who lived at Elmdon Hall, took a great interest in the school and was very kind and generous to us children. She gave a large field called The Lawn to the school for the use of the children and for a maypole among other things.

We were ruled over by Canon Hayter, who took care of our spiritual life. We were expected to attend Sunday school from half past nine to eleven o'clock on Sunday morning, when we marched to the church for matins. Then we crossed the drive to the kitchen at the Hall to collect two enormous rice puddings spread with a good layer of jam or golden syrup. These were carried back to the school by four of the biggest boys. After tucking in (there was never any left) and washing up the plates and spoons, we were ready for afternoon Sunday school, again taken by the rector. The reward for regular attendances was a red hooded cloak and a black straw hat with red ribbons for the girls and a navy blue reefer jacket and a white scarf for the boys. I never achieved this as I never managed the required number of attendances in the year.

In later years when the Hall was partially closed and Mrs West had moved to the Isle of Wight and only visited Elmdon occasionally, these customs ended and books were awarded for school work. Mrs West always came to see us when she visited and instructed her head gardener to send us big hampers of apples, pears and any other surplus fruit in season.

Mrs West gave a huge party for everyone in the summer of 1919 for the Peace celebrations, and over the years we had fetes on the lawn in front of the Hall, when we schoolgirls wore pretty dresses and sunbonnets and danced around the maypole.

We girls were taught to curtsey and the boys to take their caps off and bow to Mrs West and her sister Mrs Smythe, as well as to Mrs Hayter, the rector's wife. Mrs Hayter came twice a week to the school to inspect our work. She was very critical. I remember once I had written a composition on "Who I would like to be". I chose the Viceroy of India. Mrs Hayter read it and said, "I think a woman's place is in the home." I was eleven years old at the time.'

THE VICAR'S WIFE

'My first meeting of Stoneleigh friends was a very happy occasion. We were returning to our new home after our honeymoon, in an antique car, a "Swift". In those days, 1910, it was considered modern. It had no bonnet in front and the body was rather like a waggonette. The Abbey hill scared me as I thought our car might run away into the bridge at the bottom. The hill having been safely manoeuvred, we arrived by the blacksmith's shop to be stopped by a concourse of parishioners who gave us a great welcome. There were speeches from the churchwardens and we were showered with flowers.

With regard to the church, Mr Spiers, a venerable figure, was the verger. Standing by the font he kept an eye on the congregation and welcomed them. I was told that the Vicarage pew was opposite the Abbey pew directly under the reading desk. As I felt that I could not face this alone on the first Sunday, Mr Spiers allowed me to sit halfway down the aisle for Matins. When I went to Evensong and asked if I could sit in the same pew, Mr Spiers said, "No – they expect you to sit up there (pointing to the vicarage pew) and you must go."

The farmers drove to church in their "gigs" or horse-drawn carriages. They were regular attendants – dressed in their Sunday best and all with top hats. A weekly service was held on a Wednesday morning to which the five old gentleman and five old ladies from the almshouses regularly came, ushered in by Mr Flint. A branch of the Mothers' Union was started in 1911. It could always be relied upon to help in any church work and back up any organisation. The MU members did the tapestry work for the kneeler at the altar rail. Every single member did a bit, even the oldest. The Church Lads Brigade had a strong branch which met regularly and commanded great respect. When the First World War was declared every one of those "Lads" who was old enough volunteered for service.

Stoneleigh parish was a wonderful place of friendship and happiness from 1910 to 1948. There were many gatherings on the vicarage lawn – all so friendly and a very happy home. One incident shows the friendly spirit. When my first baby was born the church bells were rung. When the vicar asked why this had been done he was told that it was in honour of the first baby to be born at the vicarage.'

THE BELLS

'At Brailes in the 1920s the Angelus bell was rung daily at twelve noon and the curfew at eight o'clock in the evening.'

'In the 1930s I belonged to the church youth club at Coleshill and during the winter months we took it in turns to go up to the church and ring the curfew; the bell hung down at the back of the church, in the porch, and we would toll the strokes for the day of the month, and also the month.'

SUNDAYS WERE A SPECIAL DAY

'On Sunday morning Dad used to clean our shoes and we put on our Sunday best. We were not allowed to play and we walked to Tredington for morning service, then again in the afternoon to attend Sunday school, and then we went to the village chapel at Blackwell at night.

My eldest brother bought a gramophone player with a large red horn and we used to sit around the table, as quiet as mice, and listen to music. On other evenings we played cards but not on Sundays. On Sunday evening, at supper time, Dad would draw some wine out of a barrel and let us taste some; we had little barrel-shaped glasses about the size of an eggcup.'

'Sunday was a special day for many. The old couple in the nearby cottage would never prepare vegetables on Sunday. Had they forgotten to pick peas or sprouts on the Saturday, they went without them for Sunday lunch. Special clothes were worn by most villagers in Church Lawford. B, who worked for us for over 20 years, always wore a clean shirt collar and tie for Sunday afternoon milking.

Many women refused to knit or sew on a Sunday and certainly we were encouraged to play only indoor games. My parents would never have played cricket with us on a Sunday. It may not have been only for religious reasons – it was the only day they had a few hours off work. On sunny summer evenings we frequently walked around the farm together viewing animals and crops, and if we did not have a sing-song we would perhaps read a book together. All who were able to do so, read a chapter each. I remember *Black Beauty, Lorna Doone, The Mill on the Floss* and *Tom Brown's Schooldays* as joint ventures.'

'On Sunday evenings a great number of families from Alcester took the train to Wixford station and then walked back down the Roman Road to Oversley Hill. Some called for refreshments at The Fish or The Three Horseshoes on the way back, but we never stopped. On we walked back down the main Evesham road, past the haunted spring, scuffing our shoes through all the leaves on the footpath before Rapley Gates.'

LONG VICTORIAN SERVICES

'What the present generation would think of the two-hour long service I can't think, but we took it in our stride, and made up our own interpretation of the long words, which might have startled our elders had they known. The Sutton under Brailes schoolchildren were taken to church by their mistress, named Miss Binns, and sat just in front of us, so we could watch her disciplinary methods, which consisted of a sharp tap on the head of the erring one, followed by a freezing stare. We practised this on one another, calling it "Binnsing", but somehow it didn't work with us.

Another member of the congregation we watched with interest was our washerwoman, who was much afflicted with hiccoughs, which she controlled by placing one finger firmly on her lips. Again, even with much practise we never made this a success. She was most devout and followed the prayers in a sibilant whisper which had great carrying power. She came dressed in poke-bonnet and shawl, and carried with her book a clean hankie and some sweet-smelling flower, such as lavender or a moss rose, which she sniffed at intervals. In the winter she wore pattens over her shoes. The sole was wood with leather straps and toe-cap, and underneath was a ring of iron which lifted the foot out of mud and wet. These pattens were much used to keep the feet dry when walking or doing such jobs as washing or dairywork. If you have never walked in them you don't know what a feat of skill it is.

There was the clerk, a tall handsome man with a voice like a corncrake on a summer evening. He always looked immaculate, and no wonder, as his wife would have washed him from head to foot seated before her on a stool (in summer out of doors), and finished by combing his hair and shaving his face. This was what all good wives in the village did, and if we could escape and watch, it made our day.'

AT LEAST ONCE A DAY

'On Sundays we would go to church at Tiddington at least once a day, each dressed in our Sunday best – panama hats in the summer, brown velour for winter. We each wore black patent ankle strap shoes, which had to be cleaned with cream from the top of the milk to keep the leather supple.'

'We were expected to go to Sunday school in the morning and then on to church at Coleshill. We marched in crocodile from Sunday school (then held in the local day school) to the church, where special pews were kept vacant for us. One source of interest during the service was watching the organ blower pumping the bellows. He was partly hidden from view in a little square box, but now and again he would peer out and pull faces to make us giggle.'

'Maids employed at the Manor at Radford Semele had to attend church at least once on a Sunday. Failure to do so was noted by the vicar and their employer was informed. These same girls had to get permission from their employers to attend village dances – they did not finish their duties until ten o'clock and had to be back from the dance before midnight!'

CHARITY AND GIFTS

'I belonged to the Young People's Union, attached to Coleshill church. This would have been in about 1928 to 1930. Early in the summer we would have a card each, marked with 60 small squares with the value of a penny each, making five shillings. We would collect from friends and neighbours, pricking one square with a pin for every penny collected. Each five shillings would pay for a child from a Birmingham parish to come and stay with a family in

Coleshill for a week's holiday during the month of August. In the winter we made and collected gifts, and took a Christmas tree to children in Birmingham, one year to Ashted and alternate years to Aston. This I think was supposed to be a charity for poor children, though on reflection I have no doubt we were no better off than they were – but it did instil in us the desire to help others.'

'Long Itchington has various charities connected with the church and school. Tommy Loaf Day (St Thomas's Day) bread and florins are still handed out. I remember blankets being given to young couples who had got married that year, handed out in the school.'

'Among the local charities at Radford Semele was one called the Greswolde-Williams Charity which had been set up to provide flannel for old women and beef for old men. The value of the charity gradually diminished and was changed to a hundredweight of coal and later to £10 each.
During the 1930s one vicar's wife used to knit a matinee coat for all the newborn babies in the village. Her successor gave each baby five shillings; as the village grew this custom stopped.'

DIVISIONS

'People were much more class conscious in the past than they are today. Our parents were very careful who they let us fraternise with. We were not allowed to play with the farmworkers' children, and although we went to Sunday school, the annual treat was considered not quite the thing! There were three churches in Brailes parish – Church of England, Roman Catholic and Methodist – but they did not mix in any way.'

'In the 1920s there was a great deal of poverty at Willoughby but I don't remember it clouding our lives unduly. One family of a farm labourer lived in a two up, two down house and there were ten in the family. The children slept top and bottom of the beds and the eldest boy in the "parlour", as it was known. Their shoes were often without soles and the toes hanging out but for all that we played together and were happy. Mother didn't like this very much but we met on the way to and from school. There was then a great consciousness of the local social ladder. At the top were the people who lived at the big house, who had nannies, grooms and servants. Next were the people at the manor house, who had servants and a few farm workers. The vicar was held in very high regard, and he kept two servants and a groom-cum-handyman and a gardener. The schoolmistress also held a revered position. Farmers were, I think, on a par and were of the upper or lower hierarchy according to the size of their farms or houses. After that were the tradespeople and then the labourers. The church and chapel were very much a part of this village life.'

SUNDAY SCHOOL

'We went to Sunday school at Dordon morning and afternoon and the Sunday school Anniversary was the big spectacular. It was held in the village hall and a platform was erected on the stage for the children to be seated. The choir sat in front together with the musicians. It was attended by 200 to 300 people and was always a happy and memorable day.'

'The Roman Catholic school at Ilmington in the 1920s was held at Foxcote Manor at the top of the hill. Converts were eagerly sought – one source of temptation was the annual tea party which was held not at the Manor but on the village green so that non-participating children were very jealous. The Anglican Sunday school took place in the schoolroom and one mark was given for attendance and an extra mark for going to church, but they were not allowed to leave before the sermon! The vicar played a very lively part in life, even travelling with the local football team, the Ilmington Rovers.'

'The owners of the estate at Little Wolford allowed a Nonconformist family to start a chapel in the banqueting hall of the manor house, while the rest of the house was divided into four cottages. The hall had an open fireplace, a minstrels gallery and muskets hanging on the walls. Dedicated people came from Stow and Moreton each Sunday to take services.
  The Sunday school had a party in the summer when a local farmer would hang ropes from beams in his barn for swings, races were held and a picnic tea and scrambling for sweets. On occasion, at Easter we joined with other Sunday schools in the North Cotswold area for walks, a picnic and games, and sometimes a GWR train would be hired to take the children to the seaside.'

'In the 1920s we used to go on Sunday school outings at Ufton by horse and waggon to Stoney Thorpe Hall, when Mrs Chamberlain lived there. We went into the main hall to watch lantern slides, and then came home again.'

'Sunday school treats at Stockingford were great days for the

39

children. Scholars from the church and chapel schools would parade the streets with flags and banners, preceded by a band. After the parade we had tea and afterwards went into Mr Burdett's field for races. At nine o'clock we went home with a penny bun, but the older people stayed behind until dark for the game Kiss in the Ring.'

'In the 1930s the Methodist chapel at Welford on Avon was enjoying something of a revival and attendances at services were good, as were those at Sunday school. The latter had two outside attractions. A pantomime was produced each winter in the Memorial Hall; one memory is of the little girls who, having been made up and dressed for their parts, were put up on a shelf so that they had no opportunity to undo this good work before they went on stage. The other annual event was an outing to the seaside, usually to Weston-super-Mare. One year two little girls found they were lost and men with loudhailers walked the beach calling their names. When duly restored to the party they tearfully said they would never get lost again. One certainly has not.'

'We attended the Congregational chapel at Kenilworth and at Whitsun the "treats" were special. We paraded through the town on Whit Monday in a procession of witness and then had a tea back in the Sunday school rooms.'

'The Sunday school treat was the highlight of the six and seven year olds who attended Sunday school at the Congregational chapel, Stratford upon Avon.
    The Big Treat started when Mr Wyatt's horse-drawn furniture removal van (which was fitted out with benches for us to sit on) arrived outside the chapel. Once loaded we set off for "Welcome" – the home of Sir George and Lady Trevelyan who were there to welcome us on the front lawns. Also on the lawns sat two life-size bronze stags and the story goes that when they heard the clock in the courtyard they got up and walked around! After games and a few races we had tea – a slice of slab cake and a drink. To end the afternoon sweets were thrown into the air and everyone scrambled for them and then it was back in the van for the two mile journey back to the chapel and home.'

'Sunday school at Lapworth was held in St Chad's wooden church. We all dressed in our Sunday best clothes, and in the summer the girls wore very large panama hats. After arriving home, the Wall's ice cream man came along on his tricycle and we were allowed to buy a water ice or ice cream. This was a wonderful treat. We had an annual party at Christmas, and during the summer children from Birmingham Sunday schools came to Lapworth on the train. Kingswood House opposite the station hosted a day of races, competitions and a large tea, and Lapworth Sunday school also joined the celebrations. All went home with a bag containing an apple, orange and chocolate.'

'Along with everyday schooling, I was also sent to Salem Baptist Sunday school, which was pleasant and we enjoyed each other's company. Longford in the 1940s-1950s was very much a village community; every family knew nearly all the other families in the area. Every late spring/early summer, Salem Baptist chapel held what was known as The Sermons, when a visiting preacher of note would be invited to attend and address the congregation both at the afternoon and evening services. Several weeks before the event, the children of the Sunday school would begin rehearsing and practising the songs and anthems to be sung. Naturally, we all had to have new clothes for this event – if only the outer garments. But this was wartime and clothing was rationed. We had clothing coupons issued and these would be saved up for special occasions: "BUX are 4, BUY's are 2, L's are 1, and M's are 2, G's and J's are 6" (this was a rhyme my brother composed to enable us to remember the different values of the coupons). Mother overcame the clothes problem by asking my dressmaking cousin to make my Sermons dresses for me. But long after the war ended, I still used to wear dresses, skirts and blouses passed to me by older cousins and friends. My brother's school uniform for the grammar school he attended had first priority.

So the great day would arrive, and my new dress, clean new white socks, short white gloves, sometimes a straw hat and my shoes brightly polished would be laid out on my bed ready for the afternoon service. The chapel would be full of doting Mums, Aunts, a few Dads and Uncles – not a spare seat anywhere – and we girls very proud in our best frocks. And in between the afternoon service and the evening one, we did all we could to prevent our clothes becoming soiled in any way, or there would be trouble!

A special tea would sometimes be held at one of my aunts' houses, theirs being much larger homes than my own, and treat of treats – sugar sandwiches! One of my uncles grew his own vegetables and his speciality was tomatoes, so cucumber and tomato sandwiches were always on the table during summer and early autumn.

The Sunday school outings I remember were walking from Salem chapel, carrying a little bag in which were an enamel mug and plate, a few sandwiches and a small bottle of water, all the way to Corley

Rocks; this is an outcrop of sandstone to the northwest of Coventry on the road to Fillongley village. It must have been a day's outing as the distance each way was about six miles. The other outing was on the canal barges as the canal was only a few hundred yards up the Longford Road from the chapel. The barges would arrive cleaned out (they used to carry coal) but even so you still wiped the bench with your hankie; and we all hoped for a dry day as there were no overhead covers to them. After the war had finished, we went one day to Wickstead Park in Northamptonshire by charabanc – what a treat.'

GETTING ABOUT

At one time we walked anywhere we wanted to go, unless we were lucky enough to have a pony and trap or were able to afford a lift on the carrier's waggon. Horse power was still many people's main method of transport right up to the Second World War. By then, though, the bicycle, motorbike and, of course, the car, had appeared on our roads – even if cars were still a rarity. Local bus and train services were fully used and are still affectionately remembered.

VILLAGE WALKERS

'Our village of Sutton under Brailes has had some wonderful walkers in the past. One of the outstanding was William the Mason who helped build the Rhaiplir reservoir for the Birmingham waterworks, walking home the mere 102 miles at the weekend to get a clean shirt and see his numerous children. When I knew him he was a handsome old man, very knowledgeable in repairing the mud walls with their thatched or tiled tops which were a feature of the village. He used to say, "You must watch the swallows a'buildin' their nests. They does a bit and lets it dry and then does a bit more; and they allus puts 'um under a roof to keep 'um dry. Let the rain get in, and they be gone." Alas, that happened to most of the walls and no one has the patience and time to rebuild that way now. He also helped build the suspension bridge over the Avon at Bristol, walking to and fro the 73 miles. The son who told me this said that as a young boy he would walk about five miles with his father on the return journey and then be given a penny and told to go home and look after the family.

A shorter walk, but one that must have needed "guts" was that of a man with one leg and a wooden peg in place of the other. He daily stumped ten miles to work as a farm labourer for a matter of 20 years. Nor were men the only people to use their legs!

Mary Ann, a great friend of mine, used to walk to do her shopping at Stratford and once when halfway she remembered she had forgotten her purse. Nothing daunted, she retraced her steps and started afresh, making a total of about 20 miles. A mere bagatelle! She was a small spare woman, always dressed in black dress and girded with a beautifully white apron and she wore a black straw sailor hat with the remains of an ostrich feather at the side which looked more like the back-bone of a fish than a feather.

She told of planting wheat by hand with a stick, grain by grain. She became a most loyal and outspoken member of our Women's Institute and once when a demonstration of miming was being given, and arms and legs were going up and up an imaginary staircase, a high senile voice was heard to say, "What ever be 'um a doin' now?"

Of course her funeral was a wonderful subject to discuss. She said, "If you puts any flowers on my coffin, I hopes the Lord will send a wind and blow 'um all away – such a wicked waste as it be."

Alas before that happened she became almost blind and, fearing she might burn herself if she attempted to cook, I used to take food for her. Once thinking it might be a treat, I took chicken, but she remarked, "I'd rather 'av a bit of a pig's behind."

Dear Mary Ann, so self respecting and independent. How I admired you!

Family reunions such as weddings and funerals, club and wakes, to say nothing of courtings, gave occasion for walks by even very young children of distances incredible to us poor, puny, car obsessed moderns. One woman told me that as a child about five or six years old she walked hanging on to her mother's skirt, while she pushed the primitive springless pram of those days with two smaller children in it up a two mile hill and then four more miles to spend the day with her grandparents, and then walked back to get her father's tea.

What might be called ritual walking was practised by the aristocracy when their friends died. They would walk in top hat and frock coat for 40 or 50 miles to attend the funeral, scorning to use horses or carriages on an occasion when all men are equal.

But the one I like to think of most was our Musical Miller. On Sunday he led the music in church by playing his bass viol in the gallery at the west end. He recorded in his beautifully written diary dated about the 1850s that he always attended the Three Choirs Festival wherever it was held. He walked to Worcester 31 miles, Hereford 54, and Gloucester 35 miles. Starting at dawn he would get there in time to enjoy the music, then return walking through the night to begin his work as miller the next day.

Think of it! With the music of the masters still ringing in his ears, with all the scents, sounds and beauty of the summer sky, what reward beyond all price!

Such were some of the walkers of the past from one – then – quiet little Warwickshire village.'

BATH CHAIRS AND CARRIAGES

'In 1917, when I lived in Leamington, my mother used to hire a Bath chair to bring us back after visiting friends for tea in the winter evenings. I remember the cosy feel of sitting on her knee, protected by a glass panel from the cold winds or rain.

In that summer my grandmother had been very ill and as she recovered my grandfather would sometimes hire a Victoria carriage so that she could visit us and enjoy the fresh air and sunshine. I remember being taken for several rides, but was always afraid I might fall out, as the sides were so low.'

PONY AND TRAP

'There was no bus service through to Ufton until the late 1920s, so we had to walk the five and a half miles to Leamington Spa and back when we needed any special shopping. We did sometimes have a lift on a carrier's cart or pony and trap, one way.'

'We used to travel quite long distances from Brailes to visit relatives by pony and trap. My father was a very enthusiastic horseman and once had a mare which he bought at Stow Fair. She was very fast and could cover the distance to Banbury in record time – but she had an unfortunate tendency to kick the front of the trap in.

The story goes that when my father first bought a car, when he came to a gate he pulled the steering wheel and said, "Whoa!"

We used to cycle many miles, and enjoyed visiting the picture house at Shipston, and taking picnics to Traitors Ford.'

CARS AND BIKES

'In about 1913 I remember running up the village at Leamington

The early cars, such as this Clyno owned by a farmer at Church Lawton in 1928, were a source of great pride to their fortunate drivers.

Hastings to see the first motor car from the Manor House coming round the bend.'

'My husband used to have a Model T Ford which had to be turned round and reversed up Crabtree Hill, near Merevale Hall, so the petrol could travel to the engine.'

'Although my family had a car in the 1930s it was used only for business, ie trips to market or to sales and a very occasional visit to relatives. Not many women learnt to drive in those days and my mother had to cycle to the village shops at Bidford on Avon, returning home with large bags of shopping hanging from the handlebars of the "sit up and beg" old-fashioned bicycle.'

'In the late 1920s, at the age of 16, I rode a motorbike. Trousers for women were unthinkable then, so I wore my ordinary clothes plus a leather jacket and a leather helmet. When I decided to abandon the motorbike in favour of a pushbike, I left home at Brinklow at half past six in the morning to cycle to Rugby and arrived home again at about six in the evening.'

'I well remember going with my father to Warwick to buy a new car, a Citroen Tourer, one of the first cars in our village. We were driven back to the nearest town and my father took us home from there, never having had a lesson or driven a car before.

All roads were repaired with stones in those days. Heaps of large stones were delivered to the roadside and stone breakers would sit and break them up using hammers with long handles, a steam roller coming along to roll them in later.'

BUSES, TRAMS AND TRAINS

'During the First World War there was no local organised transport in Nuneaton. On Saturdays, horse-drawn milk floats fitted with seats lined up in Queens Road outside the gasworks, the drivers shouting "Round Towers" and "Old Lane", waiting to take people to Stockingford who had been shopping in the market.

Sidwell's at Bermuda had a horse-drawn waggonette used for group outings. It was also used to carry Coton Sunday school infants to join the procession on "Treat Day". Deacon's also had a horse-drawn closed cab, used to take travellers to the station. It was not until after the war that motor taxis were used.

After the war local businessmen bought small buses and started regular services. The Lucas family and Mr Williams used the two routes to Stockingford, the Kitely family ran a service to Ansley Common and Galley Common, and Monty Moreton to Hinckley.

About 1929 the Midland Red came to the town. The first of their buses had solid tyres. Eventually they took over from the local services, although Monty kept his service to Hinckley factories for many years.

All this time, people depended on the railways, then separate companies – LNWR and Midland. Out of town pupils attending the girls high school and the grammar school in Nuneaton travelled each day by train. Those from Longford, Exhall and Bedworth on the Coventry line, those from Whitacre, Shustoke, Arley and Fillongley came on the Midland line.'

'In those days, when you went away on holiday you used to send your luggage in advance to your holiday address. It would be there when you arrived. It took about three days on the journey, and would be delivered from the station by a horse and dray. In those times the trains were very full and if you couldn't find a seat it was possible to ride in the guard's van and sit on the luggage. There used to be excursions to seaside places on cheap tickets, for about six shillings return – same day of course. Very popular at holiday times.

Trams were popular in most large towns. They were electric and ran on lines in the middle of the streets, and had overhead electric cables. When the tram reached its destination it could not be turned round like a car. The conductor had to pull the connector off the electric wire and swivel it round to the other end of the vehicle and connect it to the cable again. The driver then went to the other end of the tram and drove it from there. The mechanics were very simple – a couple of hand wheels, one for steering I suppose and the other to apply the brake, and a bell in the floor which the driver stamped on if anything got in the way. He stood up all the time whilst he was driving. On special occasions such as Coronations and Jubilees there would be a decorated illuminated tramcar, which was run always when it was dark and usually late at night and our parents had to get us up to look at it. It was beautiful and we were fortunate to have the trams passing our door so we only had to get out of bed! As time went on and traffic got more, we had trolley buses which could pull up alongside the kerb and pick up its passengers. With a tram, which was in the centre of the road, traffic had to wait whilst passengers were getting off or mounting the tram and this upset the flow of traffic.

The trolley buses ran on wheels with rubber tyres and a connector to an overhead electric cable. They were much more flexible.'

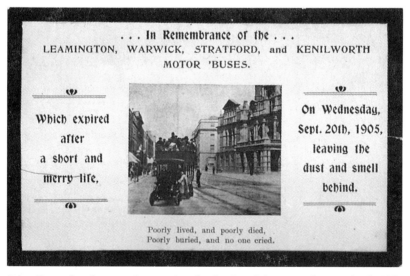

A locally produced postcard regretting the demise of the motor bus service in 1905. They would soon be back on the streets, however.

'A bus came through Radford Semele at regular intervals run by a Mr Edwards from Bishops Itchington. He had started with a twelve-seater van and then bought a bus. The fare was threepence ha'penny return to Leamington in the 1930s. The Midland Red Bus Company later ran a competitive service which eventually took over Mr Edwards' run.

A railway line ran through part of Radford heading for Rugby. There was not a stop in Radford but some of the train drivers did stop on the way, to collect mushrooms in their caps.

The canal was used to transport heavy goods like coal or grain.'

'The LNER used to run through Derby and as a child my parents would put me on the train to visit my cousin in Aylesbury. The guard would keep an eye on me. He also had the responsibility of delivering our duck at Christmas time, which was put on the train at Aylesbury and we collected it at Rugby station.

Everyone in Rugby seemed to have a bicycle to go to work or school. It was not unusual to see cycles parked all along the kerbs in town so that it was difficult to cross the streets.'

'Buses were rare at Tanworth in Arden but there was always a train service. There was what was known as a "Workmen's Return" costing tenpence if you travelled before eight o'clock and returned before five o'clock.'

THE SNOW BUS

'Well over 50 years ago when the snow fell deep over Warwickshire, the little village of Ashorne could be cut off from the rest of civilization. Even its sister Newbold Pacey was an arctic adventure away.

In those far away days there was no salting or gritting of the highways and byways, but at least we did have our little village shop and the public house. Above all we were a tough and resourceful lot, and in such times the village became even more of a "big family".

Many of us worked in Leamington and I well remember a deep fall of snow preventing cycles and even motor cars leaving the village. But all was not lost. We had Spicer's lorries! For several days Bill Spicer's lorry became an open-deck bus for all and sundry. Bill did not stand on ceremony, nor did this excellent driver take fares; "Get up on the back," he said. The double rear wheels of the lorry were decorated with rope wound over the tyres and through the spokes in order to obtain extra grip.

In a few minutes the strong had clambered up and the weaker

pushed and hauled aboard, and we were ready to move. No doubt the weight of the passengers helped traction and they were useful to push and shovel should the faithful Fordson become snowbound.

So off we went, looking rather like refugees. It must have been a cold ride – but I don't remember any discomfort!'

THE COFFEE POT

'The Coffee Pot was the name given to the train that ran through Great Alne, plying its way from Bearley to Alcester to join the Great Western and Midland railways. Its chimney was in the shape of the spout of a coffee pot – hence its name. The crossing gates were manually operated and the station was manned by a stationmaster and two porters. Most villagers loved the train and could tell the time of day as it passed through the village. Farm work revolved around its good timekeeping, as the morning train would take the milk churns, the midday signified lunchtime, the afternoon train picked up such commodities as sugar beet for the refinery at Kidderminster, and the five o'clock meant home time. This timekeeping was occasionally spoiled when the driver got down to pick mushrooms.'

FRIENDLY STAFF

'In the 1940s I travelled into Birmingham each day to work on the train from Earlswood Lakes station, which was about five minutes walk from my home. There was a very good train service at that time. The trains on the Stratford line all went into Moor Street station. When my future husband used to come home on leave from the RAF and he was in his uniform, the friendly guard used to lock us into a compartment so that we could be left on our own!'

'Stechford station was an important one before the First World War. Engines were filled with water from a long floppy leather tube at the end of the platform. The waiting rooms were beautifully kept with leather seats and shining woodwork. In the winter cheery fires were kept burning by the porter, who saw that no litter was about.

When the train to Birmingham arrived, ticket officer Colin Watson would chase down the steps and close the large iron gates at the bottom while he collected tickets carriage by carriage. This would take some time and for the late passengers on the wrong side of the gate it was very frustrating.

When we were going on holiday our black leather trunk had to be collected two weeks in advance.

One Christmas we were taken to Birmingham to see Sandy Powell in *Cinderella*. When we came out of the Theatre Royal there was a thick yellow fog blocking out everything. At the station we were told that no more trains would run that night and a railway official who lived in Stechford agreed to lead us through the tunnel and along the lines to Stechford station. I was fine, asleep in my father's arms, but my brother, three years older, had to walk with my mother, striding over the sleepers.'

'There was a very good train service from Lapworth, with wonderful steam engines. There were trains to Birmingham, Leamington Spa and Stratford on Avon. Businessmen would be brought to the station usually by their chauffeurs or wives, and in latter years would leave their cars in the station car park. Most people either walked or cycled to the station. In those days the staff included a stationmaster and porters who were always most helpful. There was always a roaring fire in the waiting rooms, and it was a pleasure to travel by train in those days.

At weekends hordes of fishermen came to Lapworth by train to fish on the canal. Just before the public houses opened there would be long queues waiting to be served. They would then have to rush to catch their train. Other visitors included many ramblers and cyclists.'

LIFE AT FLECKNOE STATION

'The Flecknoe railway line ran from Weedon to Leamington Spa. The line was a by-pass from the busy central line, which ran from Northampton to Rugby and down to Leamington Spa. There were six trains a day passing through Flecknoe station. Some were short passenger trains taking local folks shopping in Leamington Spa, while others were "chalk trains" carrying limestone from Stockton cement works, and freight trains bringing cattle from Scotland and Wales. Mr Andrew Baine bought many dairy cows in Scotland and transported them by train to Flecknoe. The cattle pens have now been removed.

The timing of the trains was so accurate that the locals could use them to tell the time of day. The first train of the day was at 7.30 am and the time-table followed with the 10 am, 1 pm, 3.30 pm and 7 pm, with the last train at 9 pm. The 3.30 pm train meant tea-time for the farm workers in the fields. There were no trains on Sunday.

Two porters manned the Flecknoe station with a stationmaster. The first porter would open up the station at 6 am and work until 2 pm when he would be relieved by the second porter, who worked from 9 am until 5 pm.

The dairy farmer at Lower Grandborough Fields Farm, Mr Andrew Baine, used to take his milk churns to the station every morning to catch the 7.30 am train going to Leamington Spa. The 17-gallon, steel churns were carried by horse and cart to the station. Cows were brought to the station from Scotland and they would often arrive late at night. After being unloaded, the cows were run along Dead Man's Lane to the farm. The cows had endured a two-day journey and were very thirsty, so the Baines children had to line the watering pond and herd the cows into the parlour, where they were milked, fed and watered. They could have drowned by going into the pond.

The ganger's hut still stands today alongside the quiet, disused railway. It was used as a shelter for the gangers and a place to keep the tools and wheelbarrows.

During the later summer, many a freight train driver would stop his steam engine alongside Lower Grandborough Fields Farm, hop off and pick mushrooms growing in the pastures.

Jeff Bygraves kept a flock of hens at The Cottage. These hens loved to scrat along the railway line, to the enjoyment of the train drivers, who hoped to run them over.'

POST-WAR TRAFFIC

'Few people in Coventry had cars, and for several years after the war new cars were in limited supply. People went to work on the bus, or by bicycle – even people in quite senior positions cycled. Most school teachers used bicycles.

Most people went on holiday by train, or increasingly by coach. There were always huge crowds at railway and bus stations at holiday times, especially those stations which were departure points for the popular holiday resorts of the West of England. Birmingham, Snow Hill was one such. There would be a constant stream of trains on summer Saturdays to Devon and Cornwall.

Though there were far fewer cars and lorries on the roads than there are now, the main roads were congested, especially at weekends and holiday times. There were no motorways, and not many dual carriageway roads. Consequently journeys were slow. Most places could be reached by train, though several changes might be necessary. Coventry, however, was somewhat of a backwater as far as train services were concerned, and apart from the direct service from London (which took about two hours), most journeys of any length involved changing at Birmingham, Rugby or Nuneaton. Leamington Spa was well served by the Great Western Railway from Paddington, and more were through services to Wolverhampton,

Shrewsbury and Birkenhead. Rugby was an important rail centre on the London Midland and Scottish Railway, but there was also the London and North Eastern Railway line from London Marylebone to Leicester, Nottingham and Sheffield; all those expresses stopped at Rugby Central.

There was a great deal of freight traffic on the railways in the 1940s and 1950s. The LNER line through Rugby carried coal trains from Nottinghamshire to London, and the CWR line through Leamington saw coal traffic from South Wales. Most other freight went by rail, but canals were still used for coal. The Oxford and Grand Union Canals pass through Warwickshire and at Brinklow the main railway line from Euston to the North of England and Scotland ran alongside the Oxford canal for some distance. Brinklow was a favourite place for train spotters in those days (Coventry being uninteresting because of its not being on the main line). Despite the previously faster transport of freight by rail, there were many barges laden with coal to be seen on the canal at Brinklow.

Locally horse-drawn freight traffic was still quite common. Most houses had open fires – central heating was a rarity until the 1960s – so coal merchants were numerous and busy. Although by 1945 most coal was delivered by lorry, there were still many horse-drawn coal drays. Milk carts were often pulled by a horse. Local freight from the railway was delivered by little articulated trailers pulled by a three wheeled "locomotive", usually made by the Karrier Company. These were always to be seen coming and going around the goods yard at Spencer Park, just outside Coventry station. Bread was often delivered in little three-wheeled vans.'

HOUSE & HOME

THE WAY WE LIVED THEN

Our way of life has changed enormously within living memory, and whether we lived in a small terraced cottage in town or a thatched cottage in the country, we shared the lack of amenities, the cold and the damp, and the lack of frills! Furniture was basic and bought to last a lifetime, carpets were practically unknown, and for some people a new council house seemed the very height of luxury – running water and all.

INCENSE AND ROAST BEEF

'I was born and brought up in an old farmhouse, reputed to date from the 13th century. It had a priests hiding hole in the attic and was joined to the Roman Catholic church. On Sunday mornings the smell of incense mingled with that of the roast beef! The house was very primitive, the water supply a pump in the scullery. There was no bathroom, we had a tin bath on the scullery floor, and the loo was a three-seater up the garden with newspaper for toilet paper. There was no electricity and we cooked with an oil stove, which made excellent pastry, better than anything I have used since. We had oil lamps, and the Aladdin lamp gave a good light and also a background warmth to the room. The sitting room was warm, but the rest of the house was freezing, especially the bedrooms.'

A 16th CENTURY COTTAGE

'I remember, how well I remember, the house where I was born, as were my seven sisters and three brothers, and where I lived until I was nine years old. It is still there, where it has stood since the 16th century, a solid half-timbered cottage, with thick walls and small windows. In summer it was dark and cool, and in winter it was warm and cosy. There was only one door, and this opened directly into the large living room.

This room was the heart of the house, and the heart of the room was surely the big black range which provided heat, the only means of cooking and hot water. The constant hot water was supplied by a huge black kettle which sat on the hob and sang a gentle, soothing song as a wisp of steam bore testimony to the heat within. A black cast-iron "arm" with pot hooks could be swung over the fire to bring pots quickly to the boil, when they were returned to the hobs to simmer gently. There was an oven to one side of the fire in which all baking and roasting was carried out.

In the centre of the room was a large pine table where both food preparation and consumption took place, and when neither of these activities was in progress it was covered with a dark green chenille tablecloth, an ideal surface for games of tiddleywinks, cards, dominoes, and many other family pastimes. In the centre of the table at night stood a tall oil lamp, a brass column with an opaque glass container for the oil, surmounted by a beautiful pink glass shade which cast a soft glow, and combined with the firelight created a very special feeling of security and well-being. There was a pine dresser with drawers and cupboards where the more mundane items of everyday usage were stored, and there was a mahogany sideboard with a high back in which mirrors were set. This contained the best china, and displayed the most cherished knick-knacks of the period. A set of eight Edwardian dining chairs, a lady's and a gentleman's upholstered easy chair, and a sofa (today called a chaise longue) completed the furnishings. The floor of red quarry tiles was softened by the strategic placement of pegged rag rugs, the making of which was a further pastime for winter evenings.

In addition to the living room there was a sitting room, also quite large, but due to the size of our family this had to double as a bedroom for the boys. It was reached along a narrow inside passage, which also led to a scullery-cum-pantry which had shelves along three sides on which were kept foodstuff, pots, pans and crockery. There was a single cold water tap above a large stone sink, and a thrall (a raised brick or stone platform with arches underneath). On the thrall stood a large brown glazed crock which held the bread, and barrels containing home-made wine or beer. Food which needed to be kept cool such as butter, milk etc, was also stored there. Underneath were bottles of home-made wine, and pickles. The shelves were filled with jam and preserves, and even runner beans in layers of salt. Although we were well served for dairy produce, there being four farms and a smallholding among the 18 dwellings which made up the hamlet, as well as keeping our own hens, there was always a large bucket of eggs in isinglass, which were put down when the hens were laying well, and used during the winter when eggs were scarce.

A very necessary item in the pantry was a "safe" – a wooden cupboard with an open front covered by a fine wire mesh, where meat and other items of food could be kept cool but protected from flies and dust. Although there were no refrigerators, and sanitary arrangements left much to be desired (outside privies were the order of the day) we never seemed to suffer the stomach upsets and viruses which are so prevalent today. We fetched our milk straight from the farm, chickens were killed for the pot as required, and our own pig was killed just before Christmas with its attendant curing of hams, making of pork pies and sausages etc. Once again, with no ill effects.

A ritual which accompanied the pig killing was the taking of a plate of "fry" to friends in the village – portions of meat from the pig suitable for frying, such as liver and kidney.

I used to go upstairs and hide under the bedclothes when the pig was being killed.'

THE ROADMAN'S COTTAGE

'When the boundary changes took place in 1929, the very picturesque and charming villages of Welford and Weston became part of Warwickshire. They had many old thatched cottages and larger houses together with St Peter's and Weston churches.

One such cottage was Woodbine in Chapel Street. Standing for 400 years in its grounds, it was clearly visible from the maypole. Thatched and lightly coloured, it was constructed in wattle and daub with a small brick extension. Behind a large hazel bush a separate timber thatched building was used as a bedroom. Its inner walls were stained olive green and a large window overlooked fruit trees and grass. On the roadside a thatched motor shed held the County maintenance tools. In the rafters the bat fouling nets were kept, while tea chests made space for cats and kittens. The whole shed smelt of Laxton apples which stood there. At least 20 yards down from the main building was a pigsty, coalhouse and earth closet. The nearby gardens were cultivated with vegetables and a few flowers. The main areas were grassed with many fruit trees. During the war fowl were kept in a high wired pen. Hedges of various types surrounded all sides and in season violets blossomed beneath them.

Through the arched gateway, covered in honeysuckle, stood the well in its rock garden. The well was deep with cold clean water. Around the door and on the cottage more honeysuckle grew and so the name "Woodbine" was taken. Entering through the white front door, the living room with its stone flagged floors, dark beams and lightly distempered walls and ceiling could be seen. Over the inglenook a large beam carried a heavy brass chain whilst above, a shelf carried ornaments. Two small windows looked over the fields to Weston and between them the Welsh dresser stood, adorned with blue willow patterned china. Each end had a presentation bowl and a china spaniel dog. The family box of papers stood in the centre. A decoratively tiled fireplace had a small stool at each end of the fender. In a dark recess a rifle was concealed. To the front a casement window looked out to the street.

The top of the built-in three-cornered cupboard contained glasses, fine china and sewing materials with below, old papers. Furniture included a table and chairs, two straight backed armchairs, settee and a wireless run by an accumulator. The floor was partly covered with matting and a handmade rag rug lay before the fire. Coats were hung by the front door. An adjacent black door opened to reveal the stairs. On the landing an orange curtain hid a bedroom whilst the main room was behind a door. Both had a window and sloping ceilings. Down this another small door led to a passage and kitchen. Vegetables, fruit, sacks and sundry tools were kept in the understairs cupboard. Opposite and down a steep step the old kitchen was now a larder. Here the barrels of home-made wine were stored with everyday crockery and foodstuffs.

The small brick kitchen had a range and a brick-fired copper. Opposite the window a door above a high step stood the washhouse containing a sink and mangle. The heavy timber door opened to the garden. A table and chairs filled the kitchen. On the wall a picture *The Steps of Jericho* looked down. Curtained shelving provided space for daily essentials. In the hearth sticks, boots, kettles and irons were kept and on the mantlepiece a small paraffin lamp resided. The shades and wick were daily tended. A bowl of water on a table was used for daily washes and a tin bath provided for a washdown.

My grandfather rented the cottage from a Scottish gentleman at Weston House. He was employed as a road man by the County Council. His area covered several miles and sometimes meant a long walk pushing the handcart loaded with scythe, sickle, broom, picks, shovels and forks. Hedging and verges were cut by hand whilst litter was swept up and disposed of. He maintained the maypole greens and kept an eye on the chestnut tree, planted by Mrs Watson in 1937. His hobbies included fishing and bowling, making home-made wine and smoking a pipe of baccy. This was twist and other people found it obnoxious when lit. He was a good shot and beater for the local farmers' shoots.

Grandmother washed clothes etc for ladies of the village. She used Oxydol in the copper and of course, the mangle. It was usual to see the gooseberry bushes covered with drying hankies, whilst the main items blew in the breeze beneath the trees. Ironing was by flat irons heated on the range and was carried out on the front room table. She was in great demand for sitting with the sick and laying out the departed. Both were small jolly people and they had many visitors.'

Picturesque cottages at Radford Semele in the 1920s — but without running water, electricity or indoor plumbing.

TERRACED COTTAGE

'I grew up in the 1930s in Cubbington, where our home for six was a two up, one down, back to back terraced cottage in an enclosed yard – rent two shillings and sixpence.

The living room had a blackened fire range and a gas cooker, which were polished daily; hard and dirty work. In front of the range was a fender, fitted with a box at each end; one held sticks for lighting the fire, the other shoe cleaning material. The boxes were also used for seats, a warm place to sit on cold days. The coal fire was otherwise the only form of heating. The chimney was swept at intervals but occasionally we did set it on fire.

On the floor was a rag rug made from old clothes, while under the window was a sofa and opposite a sideboard. There was also a fireside chair and four wooden chairs. In the centre of the room was a scrub-top table, which was used for literally everything, from rolling pastry to washing up. Waste water was thrown over a wall into a field adjacent to the cottage. Children then had to be helped over the fence to retrieve cutlery accidentally left in the dishwater!

The three doors in the living room led to a small pantry, upstairs, and outside. Gas was only supplied to the downstairs room, upstairs candles were used.

Toilets were shared and a short distance from the house. They were very primitive. In the early 1940s buckets were supplied. Washday meant an early start at about half past six, when everything had to be taken to a communal washhouse which was allocated one day per week to each household. It was usually mid-afternoon before the washing was completed and the washhouse cleaned.'

NO LUXURIES

'Wharton's yards (closes) with their small dwellings have virtually gone, though a few remain, much improved. With horror one hears of black beetles crawling out of the wallpaper at night, toilets shared (two between four houses), outside cold water supply, coal cellars, candles to bed, blackleaded cooking ranges, baths in front of the fire in a tiny kitchen, uncarpeted stairs which were scrubbed daily leading to the bedrooms – parents and six children in this crowded accommodation! A bed on the landing for one child, or perhaps two, and school clothes washed and dried overnight ready for the next day. Yet, despite its shortcomings, the people loved the place.'

'In the early 1900s at Lapworth most families had four or five children, but one family who lived in a barrel-roofed cottage along the canal numbered 15. In those days the canal water was so clear that all the children were bathed in it.

Most houses had a blackleaded fireplace with a trivet and dutch oven. The saucepans were black due to smoke from the fire as they sat on the hobs; they were given an extra good wash on washday by being soaked in the soapy water. Permanent in our memories from those days are the horsehair-filled sofas and chairs covered with leatherette and plush, chenille tablecloths, and large walnut sideboards from floor to ceiling, some with mirrors.'

'There was no such luxury as carpets, but cold lino or mats and quarry tiles in the back kitchen. No such thing as easy chairs either, but high-backed wooden armed chairs for mother and father and ordinary kitchen chairs for the rest of the family.'

'I was born in a farm cottage in 1920, which stood in fields off the main road. The only way to the cottages was a cart track. The cottage was red brick with a tiled roof. All the downstairs floors were red quarries which were washed every day and scrubbed well once a week. The rugs were shaken outside every day. The bedroom floors and stairs were white wood and were scrubbed every week. Upstairs the only floor covering was home-made woollen rugs.'

'In 1937 I bought a house in Coventry for £450. This had three bedrooms and a bathroom.

In large families it was quite common for children to sleep at top and bottom of the bed. If we were to have the luxury of having the bed heated, this was done with a stone hot-water bottle, or the solid oven shelf warmed and wrapped in a piece of cloth.'

VICTORIAN HOUSEKEEPING

'Housekeeping was a very different thing then to now. The grocery came once a month and one of my joys was to help unpack it and pour the coffee beans into a jar to be ground daily for breakfast. Soap was in bars about a yard long and was cut into cubes by a half-moon blade with a handle on top. It was then hung to dry in a home-made net. Candles were of two varieties. Wax for use in the house, and tallow in bundles tied together by the wick for stables and cow-house use. These were hung up and doled out as required. Salt was in huge blocks which were sawn into bricks, some rubbed together and sifted for table use, the remainder put in the salt chest by the kitchen fire for use in cooking and dairy. Paraffin came in bulk in a barrel and was stored outside. Bath-brick was used for cleaning the knives by the house-man cum groom cum gardener who rubbed them on a leather-covered board sprinkled with brick-dust, aided by the same hissing noise he made when grooming the horses or polishing the boots, and such things as steel fire tongs, pokers and fenders and so on. None of the easy work polishes and detergents of today. Elbow-grease and wood-ash were the chief ingredients for many purposes and the home-made polish of beeswax and turpentine, castile soap and rainwater produced a polish on the furniture second to none.

Then another ceremony was looking through the household linen to see how many new sheets or towels must be bought, and what turned "sides to middle" or mended or cut up for use in the dairy.

Then there was feather-dressing. All feathers from poultry were put into paper bags and placed in the oven after baking. This was to kill any life they might be harbouring. Then would come a day when Mother and her helpers would disappear into an upstairs room, with heads well wrapped up, and on no account were they to be disturbed. They began by rubbing the feathers in a wire sieve to free them from all "foreign" matter. With scissors the hard stalk of each feather would be cut off. When sufficient had been accumulated they were made into beds or pillows or cushions. The down from the breasts of ducks, geese and turkeys was kept separate and made into eiderdown quilts. Another ingredient in bedding, chiefly mattresses, was wool. Before shearing a sheep, the soiled wool round its posterior was cut off and this was then washed (the water was highly prized by the gardener as liquid manure) and carded by wooden hands stuck with metal pins. Horse hair too was all saved for mattress making. Yes, they were thrifty days. Now thrift is almost a dirty word.'

SO COLD!

'Snow in February! How that brings back Coventry childhood memories of the 1930s. It was during the month of February that I had measles and well remember looking out of the bedroom window at the deep drifts on the other side of the road and watching the girls who worked at nearby Cash's ribbon factory making their early morning journey to work. Later on the children played on their way to Pridmore Road School, and I couldn't join in the fun.

Winters always seemed extremely cold for most houses had only coal fires. We had a range-type fireplace in the front room of our house, which had a hob; an oven at the side of the barred fire and a kettle hanging over the fire on a pothook. The grate had to be blackleaded to keep it in shining condition, and the ash-preventer, fender, and poker handle which were made of brass had to be cleaned with Brasso and polished weekly. We also had brass stair-rods and the task of cleaning these fell to me when I was older. There was no central heating and all hot water had to be boiled in a kettle on the fire or gas cooker. We had no bathroom – only an outside toilet (or lavatory as it was always called). A paraffin lamp was kept alight in this outhouse to prevent ice forming in the cistern and in the pan, and the cistern was well covered with old matting as an additional precaution. As our house was an "entry" or end house and the floors were red quarry tiles covered with linoleum (later on we had carpet squares) my feet always seemed to be cold, and chilblains were an expected winter condition. How they itched and ached! Rubbing them in snow was an old-fashioned remedy. Of course, we were always well wrapped up when we went out to play and to journey to school. Scarves were pinned right round our bodies, hats and caps were a *must* and the girls normally wore fleecy lined liberty bodices and green, navy or brown knickers which stretched nearly to our knees. These were accompanied by black or brown woolly stockings. In many cases children had camphor bags pinned onto their vests to protect from colds and chills. These were made of cotton or linen about two and a half inches square and a piece of camphor was placed inside. Whether they did the trick I cannot remember!'

IT WASN'T EASY

'The house where I first lived was close to the railway in Rugby and consisted of two rooms upstairs and two down. There was no bathroom, bathing was in front of the open fire in a tin bath, no electricity or gas. We had oil lamps and cooked on a range using coal or wood. The toilet was outside in a yard. We were comfortable but not luxurious. Fridges and washing machines were unheard of. Hardly anyone except the well-to-do had cars and it was many years before my parents had a carpet square. Floors were covered with lino and rugs. My father made rag rugs – old clothing cut into strips and pegged on to hessian. He drew a pattern to follow and used different colours to make it. The end result was quite attractive.

We moved near to Bilton when I was seven. The house was newly built and cost £500. There was just a few of these semi-detached houses surrounded by fields in a narrow country lane. After living near the railway it was heaven. There were sheep in the fields behind us, a brook at the bottom of the hill and wild cherry trees along the hedgerows. Now, alas, the lane has been widened and all the fields have become housing estates. We now had two rooms and a kitchen downstairs and three bedrooms upstairs. There was still no bathroom but we had a bath in the kitchen covered by a board which served as a worktop. There was no hot water supply and we filled the copper to get hot water to bath. The toilet was outside. Later my parents converted the smallest bedroom into a bathroom and installed a hot water supply. We had washstands in the bedrooms where we could wash in privacy. There was a gas supply to the house and electricity. We had a gas stove but no plug-in points. My mother had an adaptor in the light socket into which she plugged her iron and many years later when we acquired it, a radio. This would be seen as highly dangerous now.

My next house was a council house. We married during the war; no iced wedding cake available, clothes and food all on coupons, only a weekend leave from the forces for a honeymoon spent in bomb-scarred London. To us the house was heaven after living with parents and in-laws with our two children until allocated a house. We had all mod cons in the council house but limited furniture as we had to apply for dockets to buy what we required. There was no choice as only what was called "utility" furniture was made. You made up with secondhand items, which were at a premium. We again had lino and rugs and I never had a fridge in that house although I did eventually have an electric washing machine. I still had to rinse by hand and use a mangle.

Both our subsequent houses which we purchased needed renovation. My husband is no DIY man and we enlisted the help of relatives and friends as well as reliable tradesmen. We had many trials and tribulations. To the young I say, press on with life – you will get through.'

WATER, LIGHT AND HEAT

The mod cons we take for granted today, such as running water, light at the touch of a switch, a bath in a proper bathroom, indoor plumbing and effective heating, were all unheard of luxuries for most of our grandparents – and perhaps even for our parents. How did we ever manage in those good old days?

FETCHING THE WATER

'A feature of Withybrook is the many freshwater springs to be found. These are fed by underground streams and the overflow from the springs drains back into the brook. One special spring in the centre of the village has never been known to run dry, no matter how severe a drought has been. It was the main source of drinking water throughout the centuries until mains water was brought to the village in the 1950s. There are still some of the older generation who maintain this water is purer and more beneficial than "town" water.'

'When I was young at Radford Semele, no one had taps or sinks in their homes and we had to go at least twice a day, carrying two buckets at a time. Now every time I turn on a tap I think how lucky we are.'

'In the 1940s I lived in a cottage at Earlswood with my parents. When we first moved in it was a one up and one down affair, but my father managed to get a bathroom installed and a partition upstairs making two bedrooms. The kitchen was basic, to say the least. The sink was a crock one built on legs of brick with a pump handle to bring the water up from the well outside in the front garden. The water was beautiful to drink and so lovely and cold in the summer, but it did awful things to the electric kettle.'

'Our drinking water supply at Ryton on Dunsmore in the 1930s came from a well in the field at the bottom of the garden and supplied approximately ten houses. The ram which pumped the water to our houses frequently went wrong and my father was always involved in getting it working again. There was a large soft-water tank on the roof over the back porch, coalhouse and downstairs toilet. My mother always used soft water for washing clothes, and my grandmother used to say that it was ideal for hairwashing.'

'Our house at Napton was by the canal, so water was carried from there to fill the copper for washday. We had a well, and soft water tubs which we used for washing our faces and hair. There was a pump in the yard for drinking water; we had to tip jugs of water over the top first to prime it, get it going and often when it was icy in the winter it would freeze up and need to be thawed out with hot water from the kettle. We stored two or three buckets of drinking water in the dairy.'

'One day in 1939 my husband, then a boy of nine, called to visit his grandparents in his dinner break from school at Bidford on Avon. Grandad had made a new wooden cover for a small well and Geoff was invited to test the strength of it by jumping on it. Unfortunately the cover and Geoff fell into the well. It only contained a few inches of water but the shaft was about eight feet deep. Grandad pulled Geoff out with his walking stick. Aunt Lucy was sent to the village shop to purchase new socks and Geoff returned to school, complete with letter to explain why he was late, and luckily none the worse for his adventure.'

BATHNIGHT

'Bathnight at our cottage in Shilton was always a Friday, when the tin bath was brought in from outside and placed in front of the fire. Water was carried from the pump in the garden and heated in saucepans on the black kitchen range. After bathing, the water was baled out and the bath thoroughly dried to prevent it rusting.'

'I remember pumping water into the tank by a hand pump in the kitchen. It took about 100 pumps for enough water for a bath.'

'Bathing in the tin bath with the clothes maiden around to act as a screen. I was always the last one in the bath, being the youngest!'

'Hairwashing and bathnight was a great operation, with nine children to process and just a galvanised bath on the hearth in front of the fire. Our hair was washed in the sink, then we were put into the bath to be washed by eldest sister, then it was a good rub down and a warm drink and off to bed.'

AT THE BOTTOM OF THE GARDEN

'At Mappleborough Green in the 1920s villagers used earth closets, emptied by the night-soil man once a week. Before that, waste had to be dug into a ditch marked out in a field.'

'The loo was outside and across the yard. In summer with light nights this was fine but on dark winter nights we had to have older brother to hold our hand to go past the yard pump and washhouse. Then we would sit shivering and our imagination running away with us, not being helped by our brother outside making weird noises to frighten us more.'

'Toilets at Radford Semele were in outhouses or privies. They were treated with chemicals and they were emptied by the council workmen, who arrived in the "Lavender Van" to carry away the effluent.'

'The loo at Welford was down the garden. The seat, or seats, was kept well scrubbed and the bucket emptied periodically onto the garden – which is why so many cottage gardens have soil as black as peat.'

'The outdoor closets at Middleton were often way down the garden, where two people could sit companionably side by side and there was a small hole for the little ones to use.'

'Our lavatory at Coventry in the 1940s was situated in the garden; it was therefore necessary to take some form of illumination after dark – usually a small torch, but if the battery had run down then a candle would suffice. My mother and her family had lived at the same cottage from the early 1900s. On one occasion, as a very young girl, one of my aunts forgot to take a candle with her to the lavatory, and on sitting on the seat felt "something soft and feathery against her nether regions". It was their cockerel, gone in there to keep warm!'

EVERYONE BURNED COAL

'The row of terraced houses in Waverley Road, Kenilworth is still there where the first of my childhood memories began. In those days there was a coal-yard and a station behind: I used to stand with my face through the railings, watching the coal merchants loading up their carts and leading their horses to the weighbridge. The big hooves would clatter over the metal weighing platform as each cart

The village pump at Shilton c1918. Many villages continued to rely on pumps or wells for water for another 20 to 30 years.

was brought to rest squarely on it, while a man in the office watched through the window. When he was satisfied that all four wheels were correctly positioned, he would disappear for a minute and then hand out a chit. With a click of the tongue and a slap of the reins, the driver would climb up on his cart and set off on his rounds. I can recall those sounds and the smell of the coal to this day.

Everyone burned coal in those days. We had a large cellar under the house, and the coal man would open a metal cover in the front garden and shoot the coal down into it. My mother would have to light a fire under a built-in copper in the scullery before she could do her washing, and there were fireplaces in all the rooms. We mostly lived in the room with a black range, with an oven at the side, because that fire was always alight and that room was warm. What hard work it must have been! All that coal carrying and blackleading the range until it shone.

The rooms were lit by gas, as indeed was the road; in the winter I would sit in the window and watch the lamplighter come along with a long pole with a hook on the end and light each lamp in turn. It seemed like magic to me because we had to use matches. Mind you, that was sophistication compared to my aunt in the country, who only had oil lamps and candles.

On summer evenings after the coal-yard was closed, the wide sweep of the station approach was a marvellous place to play "whip and top"; we children could buy plain wooden tops for a few pence", and we coloured them with crayons. When we whipped them they made pretty rainbow patterns.

But best of all for me were the horses. I've mentioned the big gentle carthorses that pulled the coal-waggons. On May Day they would be all decked out in coloured ribbons, their manes and tails beautifully plaited, and their brasses polished. The baker had a horse too, and that animal knew which house to go to and where to stop. The baker would have a break outside our house and would give "Dobbin" his elevenses . . . a nose-bag of oats. Every now and then there would be a loud snort and a cloud of chaff would fly out. The sparrows soon got wise to this of course and as soon as the cart moved off would fly down and clear up!'

CANDLES AND LAMPS

'Oil lamps and candles were used for lighting. This was dangerous and at least one family at Radford Semele perished when their cottage in "The Grassyards" was gutted by fire.'

'Electricity became available in Welford gradually from the late 1920s, but before that light in house and cottage alike was provided by oil lamps and candles. The task of filling the lamps with paraffin, trimming the wicks and washing and polishing the glass chimneys was a never ending daily chore. Possibly, in the homes of the better off, the ordinary lamp might be replaced by an Aladdin lamp. This had a mantle, which in spite of the whiffling noise it made gave a much better light and had the added advantage of no wick to trim. With the introduction of electricity, the post office, pubs, shops and larger houses were among the first to be connected, but many had to wait until 1939.'

'Paraffin lamps were used at Middleton before electricity was installed throughout the village in 1935/36. At first each house was allowed only four electric lights. As one householder was holding out for more money for a piece of his land on which to site the transformer, another resident gave permission to the electricity company to use her land. On the night the supply was finally switched on, she opened her house to the villagers to come and celebrate, with her home-made wine and food.'

WASHDAY

Once a week, always on a Monday, washday came round with horrible regularity. It really did take most of the day in those days of soaking and boiling, mangling and blueing, starching and wringing – and that was after you had managed to fill the copper with water brought from pump or well.

WASHING FOR THE BIG HOUSE

'Washday in our cottage took all of three days of hard, demanding toil. This situation arose when my grandfather died, leaving my grandmother to bring up six young sons. He died just as she had given birth to a much longed for baby girl, who sadly died within a few weeks. The Squire owned most of the tied houses in the village, in which lived his employees, so when Grandfather died, being a tied worker, his widow legally had to leave her house. For whatever reason, compassion or village concern she was eventually allowed to continue living in the cottage provided she did all the laundry for the big house, quite a daunting task.

I can write of the later years, after Gran's family were grown up, and I myself was brought up by her. On Monday mornings the handyman from the big house delivered a large hamper to her, full of the washing to be laundered. The cottage washhouse was a cold outside building, containing the old brick-built copper and stone sink. The copper fire had to be lit with dry kindling wood, and "slack" used which had been sieved from the coal all the week. This fire had to be lit early on Monday morning to bring the water in the copper to boiling point. Water had to be carried to fill the copper from a tap erected in the lane at the bottom of a long garden, bucket by bucket. Before I went to the village school, each Monday morning I ran to the village shop for a "packet of Persil and a packet of Sunlight Soap". Gran came down the lane to meet me, in her snowy white apron, I went off to school, she to her laborious task.

The whites, sheets, tablecloths, best towels, handkerchiefs etc were washed in the first boil, the coloured things next, and the more soiled clothes lastly. Each lot of washing had to have three cold rinses, the latter for the whites needing a squeeze of the "blue bag" to whiten them. The worst of the dirt was first removed by soaking clothes overnight, then further removed with a large scrubbing brush and the Sunlight soap on a scrubbing board, big articles being put in the dolly tub and pummelled with the dolly. All washing was put through the rollers of the mangle several times to squeeze excess water out to assist drying. I loved winding the handle for this job! All this work was spread over all day Monday, Tuesday, until Wednesday midday; and in wet or wintry weather clothes hung all around the house to dry, encouraged by the heat from coal fires and the old cooking range, steam filling all the rooms. Then the copper was emptied, the fire raked out, all utensils cleaned, floor scrubbed ready for next time. Wednesday afternoon Gran went shopping, and many times I cleaned and polished the kitchen for her return, to help her.

On Thursday began the ironing, the range fire in the living room having to be lit early to get the top red hot to heat all the flat irons. Back and forth went Gran to the ironing board as the irons cooled, continually having to put more coal on to maintain the heat. She must have walked miles, and spent hours standing to iron. Irons must not be too hot for the delicate garments, but had to be hotter for the heavier materials. Gran had a set of flat irons ranging in size from very large to very small for the tiny sleeves and garments. I still have these irons. A special "sleeve" board was used for small things. Some of the lovely underwear laundered was delicately perfumed, and Gran had to use the goffering iron (like curling tongs) to replace all the fine pleating after washing, like the nylon pleating today. I was allowed to do this after much practice, and also to iron the fine white huckaback towels with the blue borders and fringes, which I felt so proud doing well.

Needless to say, everything had to be handled with such care, not creased, and packed back in the hamper so carefully, big things at the bottom to light garments on the top layer, all ready for collection by the handyman at 12 noon on Friday, ending a week of dedication to the onerous task Gran had to do to keep a roof over her head. I believe she received the large sum of ten shillings, even after providing all the coal and heating, the soap and powder as well!

What dutiful tasks Gran undertook to keep a home going, looking after me as well (she was not young to do this) and others of her family. She never refused help to anyone, worked hard for all organisations, made the family's clothes, and was a keen church goer, washing all the white surplices of the church choir (and starching them) every Easter. They really were "whiter than white". Apart from her big washing commitment, she did many other people's "wash", including the vicar's! The latter regularly asked her in a loud voice before Evensong, "How much do I owe you?", much to her embarrassment.

Washdays will stick in my memory for ever – how did you do it all, Gran?'

BUCK-TUBS AND BOX MANGLES

'On our farm at the end of the 19th century the buck-tubs were huge round wooden affairs with a tap at the bottom. The whole wash was put to soak in lye-water which was made by soaking wood ashes and then straining the water off. The following day when the lye-water was supposed to have done its work of bleaching, it was run off through the tap at the base of the tub, and washing began in earnest. Everything white was boiled in the big copper alongside the open hearth in the back kitchen which was separated from the house by the paved courtyard, so laundry work didn't interfere with the house. The day started with the elder of the two women who did the washing drinking a glass of neat gin, and ended with another when she went home.

Ironing was done in a room over the back kitchen which had a stone-flagged floor. A stove stood in the middle to heat the twelve or 14 irons of varying shape and weight, and round three sides were trestle tables for ironing on, backed by horses where things were hung after ironing to air. At the end of the room on a platform was the ancient box mangle, which consisted of a big box about six ft by four ft filled with huge slabs of stone. A kind of bridge across the platform had a winch which was worked by turning a handle and a strap of leather attached to the box was wound back and forth over wooden rollers round which such things as sheets and towels were wrapped. When the box got to the end of the platform it was tipped up and the finished roller taken out and another inserted. Once I remember the strap broke, and the whole box of tricks was shot over the end – to, of course, our great amusement.'

THE WHOLE VILLAGE

'On a Monday in the 1940s the whole of the village of Ilmington was devoted to the weekly wash. The midday meal was always cold cuts from the Sunday roast with baked potatoes or bubble and squeak. The first chore of washday was to fetch the water and to fill a large copper in the outhouse or "brew'us". Then firing had to be brought in to light a fire under the copper. A bowl of starch and a bowl with a blue bag in it were put to hand. Everything that could be boiled was boiled; a white wash and a coloured wash accounted for everything except woollens, which were always done in Lux flakes. A mangle stood outside, underneath the verandah in case of rain. On rainy days the children came home from school to find the kitchen festooned with strings of wet washing. Ironing was done on the kitchen table on a blanket with a white sheet as cover. Soap smoothed the bottom of the flat iron, heated on the range, and the clothes were sprinkled and rolled to prevent them drying out.'

WORKING AT NIGHT

'I am the second daughter of a family of three girls and we all well remember washdays (or rather washnights!) when we were children.

Dad always worked on the farm, mainly as cow-man, and was poorly paid. He had a succession of moves and each time, of course, a tied cottage went with the new job. One cottage we lived in for a time had no stairs and the bedrooms were reached by a ladder. Our next move was little better, the cottage being situated right by a river. The smell was dreadful and the rats would keep us awake at night with the sound of their gnawing.

My mother had to work hard in the fields all day, so the washing started when we were all in bed. We can still recall the thump-thump of the dolly in the tub, the scrubbing on the zinc board and our poor mother sweating away at that awful wooden-rollered mangle. Once the copper was up to the boil the kitchen doors and windows would be opened to let out the steam – and one of us would have to get out of bed to close our windows to keep the steam out! Apart from her field work, our mother used to take in washing and the money she earned from this task was used to keep us children nicely clothed.'

FOOD AND DRINK

Mastering the art of cooking on an Aga, going to the dairy for fresh milk and butter, making wine and cider – all memories of days when we were far more self sufficient. Food may have been plainer, but it was usually home-grown or home-cooked!

THE BLACK JEWEL

'In 1943 my father was delivering coal to a farmhouse not far from the Fells, near to the small village of Quernmore, where they had just installed a new cooker, and outside in the yard was an old black kitchen range, complete with steel fender, poker and tongs. It was waiting for the scrap iron man, and so Father made an offer and brought it back on the empty lorry. It came to Nineveh farmhouse kitchen in July 1944, just before we all left for Warwickshire in August 1944.

It had an enormous oven and a big grate which devoured fuel greedily and at an alarming rate. Fortunately there was wood galore to sate its appetite. The food it cooked was wonderful. Delicious home-cured bacon fried in a tin in the oven bottom, plus duck eggs for breakfast. Hotpots, rice puddings, fruit pies, cakes, bread, to say nothing of the joints of pork, cut up at pig-killing time by none other than Tom Blunn, a native of Tysoe and the chief pig-killer in the district. Many's the time I helped to scrub the pig outside in the little orchard. Tom was a good encourager. Food cooked in the fire oven tasted far better than food cooked by gas or electricity. In any case we had neither – it was "no mains water" and lamps and candles. This great "Black Jewel" was blackleaded daily; it was my aunt's pride and joy and no one else was allowed this privilege. Dante's inferno had nothing on it for heat. However, in due course the oven began to give trouble, after being in use for many years. In December 1962 it got really bad, and we were very worried as to how we should manage to cook the turkey. We had an electric oven, but it meant hacking the bird to accommodate its great bulk, as we had to do the previous year, and Father disapproved since he deemed it his privilege to provide and carve the bird. He therefore decided that it might be a good idea to try to cook something in the old oven, as a "test case". I did. I cooked some liver in a tin in the oven bottom. It took four hours. Father said he thought the flues were blocked, so we had the sweep, to see what he could do.

Meanwhile we nearly didn't have a bird at all! Oswald, as he was nick-named, must have had a premonition, because the previous Sunday he got out of his pen and decided to head for Brailes, via Aylesmore crossroads. He was spotted by our children as we drove out of the farm gate, en route to chapel. There he was! Well-nigh running, flapping his wings. He had been a troublesome creature all along and had made one or two attempts to escape before. He was caught and put back in his pen and his wings clipped, and the stakes supporting the wire-netting hammered in more securely.

When Christmas Day dawned the bird was put into the big roasting tin at 7 am. The fire had been lit at 6 am and seemed to be going well. We had a large pile of wood in the outhouse and we stoked up for all we were worth. Dinner was to be at 1 pm prompt, Father having gone, as was his custom, to Idicote church to the morning service. By 11 am we were fed-up, hot and bothered and "ratty" because we had burned nearly all of the wood cut. We had toiled and sweated and the wretched bird was only just warm and the fat only gently frizzling. It was really all too much for flesh and blood to bear. So I got the carving fork and jabbed it in the parson's nose, and out spurted three sprays of fatty juice, as if in defiance. Oswald was determined to be difficult to the last. The pudding was boiling on top of the electric stove, the sprouts were ready to go on, and the jacket potatoes and the sage-and-onion stuffing (no packet variety, the real thing) were doing nicely below in the oven. I played with the idea of slicing some of the meat and cutting off the legs and transferring it to the electric oven, and then thought better of it, for fear of the wrath to come. We dreaded it.

At 12.50 pm one of our youngsters – who had been posted as look-out in the back kitchen window – shouted, "Grandad's coming up the track," and sure enough there he was, driving up in his car. What a day to remember! Talk about panic-stations. He came in and he never said a word. He just sat down, made himself at home, waited a while, and then carved a little off the bird, just to say we'd had some, and Oswald was returned to the oven to finish off. We had our dinner at 2 pm, and the bird was ready to come out at 5 pm. Father just smiled and said nothing. What we didn't know was that he had been very concerned about this old oven, and had seen a secondhand Aga in a nearby farmyard for sale and had bought it, and it was duly installed before the end of the week by a Tysoe man. So, the four hour vigil with the liver, plus the perverse behaviour of Oswald the turkey, resulted in Nineveh Farm kitchen having its first Aga cooker, and it remained there, in good working order, until only a very few years ago.'

IN THE DAIRY

'Ann Pad ruled our dairy at the beginning of the century with a rod of iron. Woe-betide anyone coming in with dirty boots or children bringing dirty jugs for milk. To them she would say, "Take that filthy jug to your mother and tell her I don't put my clean milk into stinking jugs, she must wash and scald it." The dairy was a sight for sore eyes with its spotless cleanliness. You might have eaten off the flagged floor. The shallow leads round and across shone like silver with their daily scouring with hot water and wood ashes. Into these leads the cowmen brought the milk in wooden buckets. When the cream had risen to the top, it was skimmed off by hand with a tin saucer-like skimmer which had a handle and holes all over to let the milk through. The cream was accumulated in a wooden trough lined with lead, till churning day came. It was then poured into a two-handled revolving churn and two men worked it round and round, until a sound told them that "butter had come". It was strained from the buttermilk through a piece of muslin, then washed and salted and made up into pound blocks, each with a strip of boiled linen rag, ready to go to market. Of course, there was no such thing as greaseproof paper invented then. Besides these blocks, rounds were formed and with a mushroom-like wooden contraption a pattern was imprinted on it – maybe a flower, or a thistle or a cow. To do this was one of my childhood delights. All dairy utensils were washed and then boiled in a copper in a penthouse attached to the back kitchen across the courtyard. This copper was always kept hot and provided water for all domestic requirements. It also gave the warmth crickets loved. Their cheerful chirping is yet another sound rarely heard now. But think of the conditions of working in an open-sided shed when it was wet or cold, and the labour of carrying all water into the house and upstairs.

I must tell a bit of the mistress of the dairy for she was a remarkable woman. She was not only an expert dairywoman, as shown by one wall of the dairy being covered by prize cards from shows all over the country, but an excellent cook and nurse. Left a widow with five small children to bring up on the meagre parish allowance, she knew only too well how to make two ends meet. One of her thrift sayings was "Never begin to eat new bread, new butter, or new bacon", the staple diet of country people. She was a pillar of strength to my mother in all family crises and by some mischance she was the only person to help when my youngest sister was born. So from henceforth she was always "my babe" and allowed liberties in the dairy accorded to no one else.

Her special drink when people were ill was "tea-kettle broth" which was made by pouring boiling water on diced toast, pepper and salt, chopped parsley and a lump of butter. She always came to help with parties and took part in all family festivals. Once a year we went to tea with her and had cakes which, we told Mother, were much nicer than we got at home, which seemed to cause rather a funny look on her face. This was explained long after when we found she always supplied them.'

'One of the tasks I enjoyed most as a child at Hartshill was fetching the milk from Moorwood Farm. As soon as the cows had gone from the fields to be milked, Mother would hand me the milk can. It was a white enamel one with a lid. I went to wait in the dairy, watching the pails of creamy milk being poured into the cooler. Auntie Margaret gave me a mug of warm milk to drink while the churns filled with the cooled milk. Father would tell us when calves were born in the spring, and when we went to admire them Mother

Feeding the poultry at a Newbold on Avon farm in 1920. Chickens were kept in even the smallest cottage garden, and eggs preserved for winter use.

would say, "Ask nicely if you could please have some beastings." That was a special treat for we all loved the custard she made with this milk from the cows that had calved. Sometimes she would bake it in a pastry case and at other times we each had our own beastings custard in a small dish, with nutmeg grated over the top.'

'My friend and I worked at Haselor Manor Farm before the 1920s, helping with the milking twice a day. The milk was normally sent to Birmingham, and we had to take the 17-gallon churns to Alcester railway station on the float. The churns had to be heaved over on to the other side of the track. The dairy did not want the milk at holiday time so then we learned to make cheese.

The milk was put into a very large tub and while it was still warm, rennet (which was taken from a calf's stomach) was added, turning it into curds and whey. The curds were nice to eat, but the whey which was drained off was not very pleasant. The curds crumbled up, and then salt was added and it was all put into a cloth and pressed, and stored for future use.'

FROM FIELD TO LOAF

'At Ilmington flour was frequently obtained by growing corn on the allotments, the corn being sent to the mill nearby at Halford to be ground before being baked by the local bakers into bread which was stored in earthenware pans (pancheons).'

WINE AND CIDER

'Cook's favourite apple was the Souring, whose name describes it. My word! it was sour – but what apple sauce and apple pies it made! It was also the mainstay for cider making. Another variety valued for that was the Devil's Dessert apple, which was purple all through which was its chief value as it added colour to the cider. But the Devil had no rivals for it as dessert. It had an astringent quality. We children treated it with a measure of awe; the same feeling of superstitious apprehension we had if we walked on a grave in the churchyard. Would something really dreadful happen to us?

A few pears were grown. Huge trees bore reddish brown fruit known as iron pears and they certainly were hard. They were chiefly used in cider-making but were delicious stewed. They were not peeled – just cut in half and packed in big brown jars with the addition of brown sugar, spice and water, and slowly cooked in the bread-oven. A few weather-beaten trees bore small brightly coloured pears which were highly prized by children, and delighting the eye of all when autumn set the leaves a blaze of colour. No pruning except the removal of a few big branches here and there which, with the trees blown down by winter gales, provided logs for burning that filled the house with their delicious scent.

Cider making was done with a very primitive machine for pulping the apples which was powered by a poor horse going round and round in a circle. The resulting pulp was shovelled with a wooden shovel into frames covered with hair blankets, and they were piled one on top of another and then a huge beam of wood put across and screwed down with long poles as levers. The thick muddy looking juice was taken down through a hose into the big empty ex-wine barrels in the underground cellar and left to ferment, and the result was a lightly coloured highly alcoholic drink which you needed an acquired taste to enjoy. The men came into the kitchen for their dinner, and we peeped through the glass partition that divided the kitchen from the hall to see them place all the food in the middle of the table, and from there each person helped himself with his own knife and fork or fingers. Their name was Jarrett, so this method was known as Jarretting and we used it on occasions when grown-ups were not present!'

'I can remember cider and perry being made at the cider mill at Walcote. The drays came through the village loaded with apples and pears, and the children ran alongside picking up the fruit which fell off the waggons.

The horse pulled the grinding wheel round and round and the first crushing pressed out the juice, leaving a thick pulp behind. The juice ran into the barrels and the pulp was shovelled into oblong canvas troughs. These were put in the press. After the second crushing, the juice was barrelled and the residue pressed into solid blocks called puggins.

The puggins were stacked at the back of the mill and dried to be burnt as fuel in the winter, the same way as peat blocks. They burnt beautifully, with a strong, pungent smell of apples.

Although the mill still stands at Walcote, the cider making finished after the Second World War.

Our next door neighbour made cider himself and always told us he put in a dead rat to improve the taste, and when it came time to clean out the barrel, there would be only a skeleton left!'

'Ilmington was well known for the brewing of home-made wine and for cider making. The town band and the bellringers were often entertained by the households that could offer this refreshment.

A cider press "put up" for two or three days at a time at various

78

locations in the village and the families nearby took their apples along to be pressed. Although to nothing like the same extent, cider making is still carried on in the village.'

'My parents were both of the opinion that to go to a pub for a drink was sinful, as were my aunt and uncle, but they were both avid makers of home-made wines. Some of these, like potato wine and wheat wine, were almost as potent as whisky, and they were thoroughly enjoyed. At one period I joined the Band of Hope, signed the Pledge and joined with the rest in singing a song which began "No drink I take but water pure . . ." – one pledge I have not kept!'

'My father in law's special brew was rhubarb wine and there was always a large bed of rhubarb in the garden. The sticks of rhubarb were beaten and smashed on a board then dropped into a large wooden barrel about three ft high. Hot water from the copper would be added, sugar and baker's yeast placed on a piece of toast and floated on the top. When fermented the wine was drawn off into small wooden barrels with a wooden tap, not bottled as now. It was very potent!'

'Our Gran excelled in making the most refreshing dandelion pop. As soon as the long meadow near our cottage was golden with dandelions, my brother and I were sent to gather the heads. It always seemed to be sunny and dry when we filled our baskets – as it always was later in the year when we picnicked on the hills, quenching our thirst with Gran's pop.'

COLD TEA

'The men would return from their day's work on the farm or the estate to eat their tea and then go to their allotments to work until dark. They took tea to work in a bottle and drank it cold during the day. Coffee was rarely drunk except on a Saturday when it was a replacement for pudding.'

HIDE THE KNIFE!

'Chickens were kept for eggs and for eating. When one was to be killed, my grandmother would approach them with the carving knife behind her back so as not to upset them.'

KILLING THE PIG

Many families kept a pig or two at the bottom of the garden, an essential part of the diet when other forms of meat were rarely affordable. Pig-killing day was an important event, and the start of a great deal of hard work to preserve the meat and to make sure that every part of the pig was used – all except the squeal!

EVERYTHING BUT THE SQUEAL

'I used to come home from school to find that during the day Smith, the local pig killer who lived on Church Hill in Shustoke, had killed the fat pig. This was done while we were at school because we did not like to hear the squeal. Smith used to stick the pig and catch the blood in a milking bucket. The blood was stirred until it went cold so that it did not clot. We used the washing stick to stir the blood which was afterwards made into black pudding by adding groats and lumps of rough fat from the pig. The best lard was the leaf. If it was a 20 score pig you would expect to have 20 pounds of best leaf lard ie a pound per score.

The pig would hang in the back kitchen for 24 hours. Then the pig killer would come back and cut the head, feet and hams off and cut the pig down the middle. Then the two sides would be laid on the red brick thralls in the pantry for six weeks. After three weeks the sides would be turned, the bottom one on the top and vice versa and rubbed with more salt. They were then hung from hooks from the ceiling of the kitchen to dry. Occasionally the saline water would drip from the bacon onto the kitchen table!

The tongue was boiled and skinned and rolled and put in a stone jar with straight sides with a weight on the top. We also made brawn from the pig's head; we used the ears to make the jelly for the pork pies, as well as the pig's feet. Sausages were made from odd bits of meat put through a mincer, covered with the intestine of the pig for skins. This was first cleaned with the back of a knife and then turned to do the other side. They were kept in salt water until they were needed. Faggots were made from the liver minced and seasoned with sage and onions and wrapped in the "curtain" (skirting). This was very thin membrane with small globules of fat attached. The bladder was used for making jam pot covers when it was dry. The remaining intestine was taken to our neighbour, Mrs Simmons, the wife of Peg Leg, the road sweeper, to deal with.'

'Pig killing was always a very busy time. A large block of salt was delivered by the local baker to be crushed down and put into large stone jars ready for the butcher to salt the sides of bacon and the hams on the stone thralls. These were turned at intervals, and after about three weeks were wrapped in linen bags and hung up to dry and cure. The leaf of the pig was rendered down into snow-white lard with a sprig of rosemary. The meat trimmings were made into pork pies. I felt very grown up when my mother let me pour the stock into the pies which, when set, formed the jelly. Daddy always said that the only part of the pig that wasn't used was his squeal.'

EVERYONE KEPT A PIG

'Everyone kept a pig at Radford Semele in the 1930s, or even two, one for pork, the other for bacon. Old Mr Timms used to kill the pigs. He had his tools attached to his belt. When he arrived the pig was brought from its sty onto the street "screaming blue murder". There it was killed. Straw was lit to burn the bristles off the pig. It was scraped and salt and water were used to cool it down. It was hung on a beam in the scullery where it was opened. Chitterlings were used, lard made from the fat. Some of the chitterlings were taken to a large family in the village. At Mr Timms' cottage sides of bacon were hung on the walls. In the barn was a large pulley on chains where a newly killed pig would be hung for a few days until it was butchered. At the back of the house was a large walk-in pantry which faced north and was always cold. It had a stone sink in which a side of pork would be covered in salt to cure it before being hung on the wall. Bacon had thick fat.

Pigs were fed on kitchen scraps – some people went round collecting other people's scraps for the pigs, and small potatoes, which were boiled in a home-made copper. Pigs were killed when they reached 20 score in weight – never before that.'

'Nearly every family in Ilmington had a pig in the back garden that played a large part in the domestic food supply. The local folk-dance hero, Sam Bennett, was also the local pigkiller. The families of course got rather fond of the pig, and I remember my mother sitting with her hands over her ears while it was killed. Almost as heartrending were the pig's squeals through the night preceding the slaughter, because of course it had not been fed. The bristles were burnt off the pig and the whole family turned to making bacon, faggots and lard. The bits of the pig which could not be preserved were shared around with other families, secure in the knowledge that they too had pigs which would be shared out in turn.'

IT FED US THROUGH THE YEAR

'All our vegetables were home-grown and the root vegetables were harvested in September. We had to help pick up the potatoes, then they were sorted and the small ones were kept to feed our pigs. Dad used to put a black pot on the hob and they cooked ready to feed the pigs in the evening. We were allowed to eat two or three of these potatoes, having first skinned them and dipped them in salt.

Dad used to have two pigs killed every year, for the house. Mother would have the hams and flitches of bacon hanging up and drying either side of the fireplace. This helped to feed the nine of us through the year.'

SHOPPING AND CALLERS
TO THE DOOR

Even the smallest village was likely to be self sufficient in the past, with its own general store and other retailers. Traders were keen to woo customers away from rivals, and most housewives had commodities such as bread, meat, milk etc delivered to the door. Other things came to the door too, such as paraffin and salt, and there were the travelling services such as the knife grinder to watch out for.

SELF SUFFICIENT IN THE VILLAGE

'Born in Tanworth in Arden in 1926, the second child in a family of five, I recall many happy memories of my childhood. We lived in a cottage in the centre of the village, next door to one of the shops which had rows and rows of large bottles of sweets. The village was almost self sufficient. Mr Hicken, the farmer from the end of the village, walked round every morning with his small churn of milk, with his one pint and half pint measures hanging on each side of it. He ladled out the milk into our large white jug, always dipping his measure in for a second time to give us that drop extra. At the other end of the village was Mr Brettell, the shoe-mender; Mr Tibbles, the tailor, who made everyone's Sunday suits; Mr Hemming who kept the shoe shop, with the smithy next door so he could tend to the horses' shoes when he was not selling footwear to the villagers.

C. Taylor & Sons was the grocery store. Someone came round in mid-week and sat for about 20 minutes taking down Mum's order and then delivered it on Friday by horse and trap – all very leisurely – no rushing off to Tesco's or Sainsbury's. In the shop most goods were weighed out by hand – bright blue bags for granulated sugar, purple ones for caster, butter cut from great slabs and carefully wrapped in greaseproof paper. The butcher's shop, with strings of sausages and whole carcases hanging up was opposite the church. Next door was the post office – Mr Rollins sold everything from press-studs to magic painting books. Right next door to the school was Mr Fullwood's sweet shop. We could buy ten aniseed balls or ten spearmint balls for a halfpenny. I liked the spearmint ones best. They lasted for ages, changing from pink to white to green as we sucked them. We were always taking them out of our mouths to see what colour we had got to. Mr Summers kept the garage. He was a wizard with anything mechanical, and carried out repairs from bicycle punctures to the workings of the church clock. Now all we have is a garage, an off-licence and thankfully the post office with its very useful village stores.'

'My childhood in the 1950s was spent in Corley Moor. We had two local shops, one of which was very cluttered. The lady who owned it used to keep such items as butter, cheese and bacon in large pieces on her living room table, no fridge or anything like that, and she just cut what you wanted with a knife. The bacon would be rather thin in some parts of the slice and thick in others, and quite often there would be traces of lard on the cheese where she had used the same knife for both. I dread to think what the health authorities would have said if they had seen it. We also had a butcher's shop which was open three or four times a week, but again there was no fridge and the meat was just put out on the counter.'

BARGAIN BUYS

'Few shops had cold stores or fridges in those pre-war days, so on Saturday nights the perishable goods were sold off cheap. My mother used to do some shopping on Saturday morning, but always went to town again at night for her meat and other things. I can still remember how my shoulders used to ache on Sundays, after helping to carry the heavy shopping bags on the previous night.

Somehow there always seemed an air of excitement in being down the town at night, with the lights, the smells, and the shouting of the stallholders. We went first into the butcher's shop, with the thick layer of sawdust on the floor, again with its own smell. I stood at the back, while my mother got to the front among all the others looking for a bargain. As the men behind the counter chopped away at the meat, throwing it on the scales, and shouted out the prices, it all seemed very hectic to me. When my mother had got her Sunday joint, perhaps also a pig's head to make brawn, some sausage, and brains for breakfast and whatever else she required, we made our way to the fish market, for we always had fish for Saturday supper. Then we purchased all the other things, like soft tomatoes, specked fruit, cracked eggs, cream, and fresh cream cakes. One shop sold reject biscuits and damaged, but to my eyes almost perfect, chocolate marshmallows and other kinds by the pound.

With our big bags loaded we struggled to the bus, sometimes not getting home till about half past ten. Then we had to get into the kitchen and get the sprats or herrings, or whatever we were having, prepared and cooked.

Mrs Bailey and her pony Molly would have travelled in to town at a spanking pace. This photograph was taken in 1907 but horses continued to be used for family transport and for tradesmen's deliveries until the 1940s.

My mother had been a cook in her younger days and always fed us well. Visitors, seeing fresh salmon or some other good thing on the table, got the idea that my father had a good job and that we were well off, but these things were only there because my mother knew a bargain, was a good cook, and also went shopping at the right time.'

'In the 1930s at Stratford you could buy a loaf of bread for fourpence, a quarter of tea for sixpence, and ten Craven A cigarettes for sixpence. Sugar was threepence a pound, pikelets were a halfpenny each, biscuits fourpence a quarter and milk threepence a pint. Best cuts of meat were about one shilling and sixpence a pound and you could get a small joint of silverside for three shillings – delivered to your door too! The poorer people used to buy butcher's pieces which he had scraped off the bones, for sixpence a pound. Vegetables were cheap by today's standards but you did not get things out of season. You only had lettuce in the summer.

To put this in perspective, labourers at the factory where I worked were paid £2 a week, and a foreman would get about £5 a week, which was considered a good wage. Unemployment pay was about ten shillings a week.'

COVENTRY SHOPS

'In the 1920s and 1930s people living out of the city any distance relied on corner shops (open all hours sort) for casual shopping. Our corner shop was a place of assorted smells, sweet, spicy, aromatic, oily, pleasant and unpleasant. Large jars of sweets sat in a row on a long shelf behind the shop counter, tins of slab toffee were propped up on the counter. The shopkeeper broke the toffee into irregular pieces with a little hammer before putting it into a paper poke-bag. Banana split, treacle toffee, "troach" rock and mint toffee for your choice.

On other shelves were tinned foods, but nothing like the variety we have today, boxes of furniture polish, shoe polish, cottons, bootlaces, pins, needles, tape, jams, marmalade, fly papers, matches, cigarettes, tobacco, treacle in barrels – bring your own jamjar, vinegar also in barrels – bring your own bottle, and hanging on hooks or shelves and door posts were mops, brooms, dusters and carpet beaters. All of this was in a room which had at some time been the front room of the house.

Nearby was a Co-operative store, a very good one, very neat and clean with pleasant assistants. On her way to town, one and a half miles away, Mother would leave a list of her requirements and pick it up on the way back; a parcel neatly wrapped in thick brown paper and tied with strong string. The brown paper was carefully folded and stored away to be used to cover my school books when I went to secondary school; that was in 1925.

There were no buses to the city in those days, at least anywhere near where we lived, so we walked to town – it never seemed a hardship. When I was very young I relished that walk with Mother who was very observant and interesting to be with.

Shopping was fun in those days of no supermarkets. The Maypole, for instance, was a source of delight, the assistants in white coats while little bands with "'Maypole" embroidered on them kept hair in place. They were always polite, walking backwards and forwards behind the long white, grey veined, marble counter to get each article requested. Tea, currants, raisins, sugar, brown sugar, tinned pears, peaches, pineapple, tinned milk, cake cut from a large piece, cheeses, all English ones, and butter. I was fascinated watching an assistant slice off, with a wooden spade, the amount required, snipping off a bit if too much, adding a bit till the correct weight lay on a rectangle of greaseproof paper on the scales corresponding to the polished brass weights on the other side. Then pat, pat, pat into a real oblong, deftly folded into the paper and added to your little pile of goods.

The milliners' shops were a delight for any young girl's eyes. Lovely velours, straws of many shapes trimmed with ribbons, bows, feathers, flowers.

Your money was put into a small cylinder with the bill, fixed on to an overhead trolley and at the pull of a handle whizzed along the wire to the cash desk, checked by a cashier, change and bill returned by same route to the counter. A farthing change was given as a packet of pins.

The market in Coventry drew me like a magnet. Stalls of glowing fruit, vegetables, groceries in West Orchard. In the Market Hall more stalls of sweets, plants, pots and pans, haberdashery, hats, dress materials in rolls galore, a lovely smelly cheese stall where a sliver of cheese was offered for tasting before purchase. A lace stall with lace of all kinds festooning the uprights of the stall. On Fridays the lace stall usually offered bags of remnants; I loved to be given one of these as a treat, the contents to be sorted and gloated over and later used to trim my dolls' dresses and undies, sewn with great care, but rather large stitches by my tiny hands. Longer pieces were used by my mother to trim my knickers and petticoats – I still love lacy undies.

There was a fish market under the same roof, a cool airy place, each stall a huge white tiled, sloping surface on which the fish was laid out carefully, often in intricate designs. Scattered among the fish were heaps of broken ice to keep the fish cool and fresh. There were great blocks of ice in a store at the back of stalls – no refrigeration in those days.

In the open market square was a sweet stall where sweets were made while you watched. A wonderful gadget turned ropes of sticky, gooey stuff, pink, white, brown into harder, thinner ropes from which were snipped with scissors little three-sided satiny sweets, flavoured with lemon, vanilla and peppermint.

The eggman had no proper stall, just a stack of wooden egg boxes containing loose eggs. The eggs were handed to the customer in brown paper bags. When, in my teens, I did a great deal of the shopping when my mother was ill, I dreaded buying the eggs, so afraid they would get broken on the way home. Boots and shoes were sold from a stall nearby and there was a stall for patent medicines, when if you believed the stallholder you could cure anything from a broken leg to a sore throat.

I enjoyed shopping between the two world wars much more than I do now.'

'Gosford Street was a very busy area with lots of shops, one of which sold pigs' trotters and peas. The trotters used to be kept in a large tin bath at the back of the shop in the yard. Garnier's pie shop was a great favourite of the area, and Frenchies who made ice cream and delivered blocks of ice to local fishmongers etc.

In the old grocery shops the butter was patted together, and sometimes made into shapes like Lady Godiva.'

RABBIT SKINS

'Children at Ilmington jealously guarded their self-appointed rabbiting areas. Trespassers (other boys) were warned off with the help of the catapult that was always to be found in a lad's pocket. This habit led Tom into trouble one day when he despatched a rabbit while wearing his best five-shilling worsted Sunday trousers and got blood on them. His father, however, quickly forgave him when the rabbit was collected! Rabbit skins were much in demand and could be sold or bartered – on one occasion Tom received a kipper from a travelling tinker in exchange for his rabbit skin. These tinkers and rag and bone men regularly toured the village, selling whatever they had managed to buy as a job lot.'

'Grandfather had a greengrocer's shop at Dunchurch where he sold rabbits. He reckons his first car, a Rover, was bought from the proceeds from selling the rabbit skins. Many of the rabbits he had shot or caught himself. They hung in rows over the front of the shop, along with chickens and bananas. Customers would make their choice and then my mother would proceed to skin and clean them. The shop was wide open to the elements and very often bitterly cold.'

DELIVERING THE MILK

'The milk for Alcester in the 1930s was collected from the farm about two miles away in a horse and trap and brought to the dairy in Swan Street, sometimes having to wait until the cows had been milked and the milk put through the cooler. This had to be done twice a day as milk could not be kept fresh, some customers having only half a pint in the morning and another half pint in the afternoon. Morning milk was never delivered in the afternoon. The daughter of the dairyman when only a schoolgirl had to help with deliveries, starting when she was ten or eleven, by taking some on her way to school. At 13 to 14 she had two buckets on her bicycle, one on each handle to help balance, and a one pint and a half pint measure. If the customer was out a jug would be found and the amount left as she knew every customer and their needs. Spilling milk made extra work as if she got nearly to the end of her round and was short she had to go all the way back to the dairy. Sundays and Christmas Days had only one delivery; there were no days off and no holidays.

After bottles came into use they were washed in hot water and soda, as were the buckets, a bit primitive by today's high standards.'

'The milkman in Coventry always wore a khaki coloured "cow-gown" and seemed to have a permanent bend to one side from carrying his milk churn. Hanging inside were two measures, one pint and half pint, and he would transfer the milk into our jug. As we had no refrigerator the milk was put in the pantry on the thrall (a large stone shelf which ran from wall to wall at the end of the walk-in pantry). Later we had milk delivered in bottles and to keep these cool they were covered with terracotta clay covers in the shape of the bottle.'

CALLERS TO THE DOOR

'Although there was little or no public transport at Great Alne, an abundance of tradesmen would visit by horse and cart. The baker would spend all day delivering round the neighbouring villages, not arriving in Great Alne until ten o'clock at night, and would have

88

paraffin lamps on his cart. The milk would be delivered straight from the churn, a knife and scissor grinder would call, as well as several ironmongers, a greengrocer and someone to pick up the rabbit skins from the local lads. The grocer would take our order on a Monday and deliver the next day. If you could get a message to the Co-op in Alcester, clothes would be sent up "on appro".'

'There were plenty of tradesmen who called at our house in Tanworth in Arden. There were at least three butchers, four bakers, two or three coal merchants, a grocer and the Co-op to choose from. You could even order a selection of shoes from the Co-op rep and choose the pair you wanted. Even a wine merchant called selling beer, wine and (oddly) seed potatoes. A tailor would visit on a monthly basis.'

'Best of all the callers at Coventry was Mr King with his vegetable and fruit cart. This was a flat dray drawn by a placid horse with lovely feathery collars above its feet, which loved the many offerings of apple, sugar and bread crusts Mr King brought his cart from the wholesale market to our streets several days a week, carrying a big variety of good quality vegetables and fruit at reasonable prices, saving the housewives carrying heavy loads from the town one and a half miles away. Mr King was a cheery fellow in trilby hat and a large dark blue and white striped apron with its huge pocket to hold his money. He always had a happy smile and chatted as he deftly weighed out the vegetables and fruit. For me the special fascination was the row of rabbits hanging head down from hooks along the end of the dray. At your request he would weigh a rabbit and skin it with a few quick flicks of his very sharp knife, wrap it in newspaper (!) and take his payment with a cheerful "Thank you little Miss Brown," and I would run back to Mother bearing the precious parcel, knowing I would have my favourite dinner next day – rabbit stew.'

'At Studley horses were still seen daily on the streets in the 1930s. Milk, bread and coal were delivered by horse and cart. Growers from the Bidford area came, walking by the horse's head as they called "Cherry-ripe", "Strawberry-ripe", or "They're lovely!" – and a great shout of "Pay-o-ah!" meant they had green peas to sell.

One man came pushing a handcart. He waited outside the school to sell the children goldfish or balloons in exchange for rags or old clothes. One boy wanted a goldfish so much he took off his blazer and gave it to the trader for two fish. Soon a very angry mother ran up, demanding the blazer back – or she'd fetch a policeman. She got it.'

'All the callers used a horse-drawn cart – the fun it gave us kids when a horse bolted! After each visit it would be a race to go out in the street armed with a bucket and shovel to collect the manure for the back garden.'

'Once a month in the early years of the century, a man came from Leamington by horse and cart selling huge bricks of salt, priced one shilling each.'

'Itinerant traders would visit Brailes and repair china by means of rivets. This would be done as they sat on your doorstep.'

'Earlier in the century at Ilmington, the grocer's van came from Shipston with special sweet biscuits, the fishwoman in her cart on Thursdays to this partly Catholic village, and the watercress man. The old man with his "five oils" called once a year, and another with peppermint cordial.'

'Living down a long drive, the tradesmen used to grumble incessantly about the potholes. Twice a week the butcher, the fishmonger and the baker called, and the groceries arrived on Fridays from Burgis & Colburne of Leamington. They always sent items not written down on my mother's list or the wrong varieties, it was never right!'

FROM THE CRADLE
TO THE GRAVE

We were much more likely to be born, to suffer our illnesses and to die in our own homes in the past. Home remedies were often preferred to seeing the doctor – if his fee could be afforded, though sometimes, as at times of epidemics or when more serious illnesses struck, professional help was the only remedy. So many young children suffered the trauma of being separated from their parents for weeks on end during the scarlet fever and diphtheria epidemics between the wars.

FEW WHITE WEDDINGS

'Marriages followed the reading of the banns for three weeks running during morning service at the local church. There were not many "white weddings" until after the Second World War, they were considered too smart and expensive for working folk.'

'In 1919 a wedding in Ufton aroused considerable interest when the daughter of the local farmer married a Squadron Leader. A large white sheet was placed on the ground to guide his aeroplane in to land, carrying the groom and his brother who was also a pilot. The happy couple left by plane, being waved off by the whole village. This was the first time many people had seen a plane on the ground.'

'Weddings at Willoughby were very much family affairs, with sometimes a dance in the evening for local people to attend. The couple did not usually go on honeymoon as money was very short and getting things for a home and a wedding breakfast was all they could afford. Presents they received were on the whole not of great monetary value as most people were in the same circumstances; towels, tea towels, toast racks and china vases were some of the most popular gifts, with the immediate family clubbing together to buy cutlery, dinner and tea services.'

BIRTH AT HOME

'Childbirth in the 1930s when my first baby was born was a very different matter from the sterilised and hospitalised event it is today. Home confinements were the norm and babies were delivered usually in the marital double bed, in my case a feather bed handed down from my mother.

Pre-natal visits were few and the doctor always came to your home and, chaperoned by the midwife, made a few examinations. My midwife was a rawboned Irishwoman who combined her duties as a midwife with district nursing. She was a martinet when her orders were disobeyed but a tower of kindness and strength when the time came. She had a very poor view of men, whom she regarded as the source of all her problems, but was always willing to allow the father to be present at the birth if he kept up a constant supply of hot water and cups of tea.

Two essential requirements for a confinement were plenty of newspapers to spread on the bed under the sheet and a bottle of Dettol. When the baby was coming, she would give you lots of encouragement and although she was a tough old spinster, really loved those newborn babies.

Afterwards she would swill you down with boiled water and Dettol and we were bound round the tummy with a firm bandage. Sanitary towels were quite expensive and we often made do with torn sheets and tablecloths to eke out the supply.

No one under Nurse Buckley's care was allowed off the bed for ten days for any reason whatever. She was even known to inspect the soles of your feet. Bedpans had to be used and a sponge down was all you got. After ten days you were allowed to sit on the side of the bed then gradually progress to a chair. These ten days may seem strange now but it was a real luxury for most women to have such a complete rest and the joy of having meals brought up was something they only experienced when having a baby.

In the winter time we had a coal fire in the bedroom and the thought of all that dust and ash must horrify the modern mother but they didn't seem to have any bad effects. Breastfeeding was a must with Nurse Buckley and she would go to any lengths to encourage you to persevere. After the birth, she made visits for ten days morning and evening and beware if there wasn't a jug of boiled water ready for her.'

'Births were usually attended by a woman in the village who came and delivered the baby and looked to the mother. The family rallied round and looked after any children and did the washing, cooking etc. There were no such things as sanitary pads, these were just old sheets or towels torn up for the purpose. Babies were bound round with a binder (as was the mother) for the first week or so. They then had a vest, a long flannelette petticoat, a long cotton petticoat and a gown and jacket, and for carrying a shawl, cape and hood. At night the day gown was taken off and a night gown put on.'

'My Grannie Juggins would often act as the midwife at Ansley Common, organising good nourishing meals for the family while the mother was in bed for two weeks. Gran was also called upon to attend to the dead. She saw them in and out, as one might say.'

'Women would stay in bed for two or three weeks after a birth. They would have to be "churched" before they could go out again, and would not be admitted to anyone's house until that had been done.'

HOME REMEDIES

'At Christmas the family were all invited to dinner with our grandparents. There was a huge goose with all the trimmings. When we went home Gran always gave me a jar full of goose grease, saying, "There you are. That will take care of your weak chest for the rest of this winter." I always had a troublesome cough throughout the winter months if I did not "take care". To "take care" meant having Gran's goose grease rubbed on to my chest and back and then being covered with brown paper before I put on my nightie to go to bed.'

'A poultice of soaked bread would draw out an infection. Iodine was rubbed on cuts and grazes – how it would sting! Beecham's Powders were bought individually wrapped in paper and given to lower a slight temperature. For coughs, a butter and sugar mixture was good.'

'I came home from school one day and my mother found a nit in my hair! She promptly drenched my hair in Jeyes fluid, stuck a bathing cap on my head and sent me off to bed. I felt I had the plague. When I got up next morning I had no skin whatsoever on my ears!'

'A folk remedy for warts was to rub the affected part with a banana skin and don't tell anyone where you buried it!'

'When I was ill I was enclosed in a Thermogene vest – it certainly was an incentive to get better.'

93

'Every winter we children were dosed with Virol, cod liver oil and malt, Parrishes Food, iron jelloids and, if a cold threatened, vile tasting cinnamon and quinine. In the spring a course of sulphur tablets was given for an internal springclean.'

'Rub chilblains with an onion. Brimstone and treacle was administered each morning in the springtime to "clear the blood". Mr Wilkins, who kept the garage/hardware shop at Brinklow, bottled his own "Celebrated Embrocation", which was much in demand locally.'

'In winter to ward off coughs and colds Mother cut out a sort of tabard of brown paper and liberally smeared it with goose grease, saved from the Christmas goose, and I had to wear it next to my skin under a woollen vest, liberty bodice, cotton petticoat and knickers and dress.
Camphorated oil was also used to rub on chest and back, and sometimes a large piece of Thermogene, a pinky orange cotton wool impregnated with some sort of chemical to produce warmth.
For sore throats one gargled with thymol, or salt water. Any sort of ache or swelling was covered with a hot linseed poultice, bandaged on. Zinc ointment was used for cuts and sores. Chapped hands were smeared with Melrose, a little waxy, yellow tablet like soap with its own very distinctive perfume.
For constipation a dose of syrup of figs or if the complaint was severe cascara, or as a last resort castor oil.
Head lice were very common, occasioning in schools regular visits by a nurse from the clinic, who could order special treatment for very persistent offenders. When I went to school at the age of five, never having had an infestation of lice in my long dark hair, my mother was very upset to find them there. Every night under the glow of the gas light, she examined and combed my tresses with a fine toothed comb and every week my hair was washed in a solution of quassia chips – little shavings of quassia wood, which was strongly aromatic and bitter to the taste. My head was then wrapped in a towel for an hour or two, rinsed and dried. My fingers were crossed for the elimination of the wee beasties, for I hated the whole operation.'

ILLNESSES

'When I was about eight years old there was an epidemic of smallpox in Hartshill and the surrounding district. The schools were closed and there was a great panic to vaccinate all the children as quickly as possible. Mother took my brother and I to the doctor in

Atherstone. She told him she did not want me to have a scar on my arm as it would look unsightly when I wore sleeveless dresses. So he decided to vaccinate me on my left leg instead. Neither Mother nor the doctor realised that one day I would be displaying my legs when I wore a swimsuit or took off my black stockings for PT. My brother and I came out of the surgery wearing red ribbons. His was on his left arm and mine was on my left leg. What a tale there was to tell as we met our friends and relatives displaying their red ribbons. Thank goodness we heard no more about smallpox, but I still have this unsightly group of four circular scars on my left leg.'

'I contracted diphtheria at the age of about eight. My sister was then about two. When the "Sanitary Inspector", as he was then called, came to check our home conditions it was decided unnecessary for me to be sent to the isolation hospital at Catherine-de-Barnes, as my mother could cope. It turned out to be a bad choice for her, as the infection lasted with me for 13 weeks, and during that time I never went out of the bedroom. Every day of that time she apparently had to hang up a sheet, which had been soaked in disinfectant, outside the bedroom door. I can remember that one of the highlights of my day was watching for the man with a long pole to come round and light the street gas lamp which stood on the opposite side of the road.

During the thirteenth week it was decided I might need special injections to kill the germ. Our doctor had been coming in weekly and taking a throat swab, which was sent away for testing. However, as the injections would have been very expensive, they decided first of all to try some "fresh air treatment", so my mother then took me daily up the vicarage drive and into the fields, and sure enough by the fifteenth week I was cured!

There were two doctors in Coleshill, and ours lived next door but one to my home. The surgery door was open all day, and one could sit and wait for the doctor, who might be out on a call, or call in to pick up a bottle of medicine which might have been requested. Behind a partition were shelves full of bottles of various ingredients, powders and potions, a veritable Aladdin's cave for drug addicts, but of course in those days no one would have dreamed of helping themselves.'

'When I was five we had a serious epidemic of scarlet fever in Radford Semele. Nearly all the children went down with it and we had to go to the Fever Hospital. Our parents weren't allowed to see us, but when we were getting better we were allowed to see them through a glass door. Some of us were there quite a long time.'

'I remember I was eight years old, standing at my mother's knee among several other mothers and children in the dark green painted waiting room in Coventry and Warwickshire Hospital.

It was a cold, dull November Thursday afternoon and we, the children, were there to have our tonsils taken out. A nurse called us one at a time. My turn came. I was ushered into the theatre. I had a note from our family doctor stating that I was to be given anaesthetic (a real concession in those days). I was laid on a table, a cold, hard metal object was pushed between my teeth, a mask placed over my nose 'and mouth – I can still smell and taste the chloroform.

I came round cold and shivering lying on a red rubber sheet on a metal bed (no mattress or pillow) with a kidney bowl near my head. A nurse stood over me, "Wake up Mary, your mother's ready to take you home." My mother stood in the doorway holding my coat.

I was still shaking as we left the hospital. I felt sick and faint, my mouth full of blood which I could not swallow or spit out as my throat hurt so. We reached the bus stop after a ten minute walk. The bus was full and we had to stand. I clung to my mother for fear of passing out. Once home I gratefully lay down on the sofa and slept.

Monday morning, my throat still sore, it was back to school.'

'My mother was a sort of unofficial midwife/nurse in our community, probably because of her experience and commonsense, and was usually sent for when a new arrival was making its way into the world, or an elderly inhabitant preparing to leave it. It seemed to me that there was nothing she couldn't deal with, and this was almost so. However, when I was eight years old my brother, who was two years older, became ill one weekend with pains and vomiting. There was no telephone, the doctor had to be fetched, by which time appendicitis had turned to peritonitis. There were no antibiotics in those days, nothing could save him and he died two days later.'

THE PROFESSIONALS

'The nearest hospital to Ilmington was in Shipston, about four miles away. There was no local doctor in the 1920s, but a village nurse cum midwife cum layer-out. Families paid into a medical club, seven shillings and sixpence a quarter for a family.

Mrs Dumbleton had been a nurse at Shipston hospital until her marriage, when she took over the role of village nurse/social worker and was famous then, and now, for her loving care of the village's sick and dying. So familiar was the knock on the door, day or night, that called Mrs Dumbleton from her family to care for someone in need that the children took it in their stride, wondering only who it was that was likely to be born or to die at that time. She would collect a white overall from a cupboard at the end of the corridor before hurrying out on her calls; in fact on one occasion she had to return for a fresh white overall because on her way home from one laying-out she met another villager about to call on her for the same service for his family. No money ever changed hands for her work, though sometimes there would be a china ornament as a thank-you gift. There was no district nurse and Mrs Dumbleton would cycle as far as Wimpstone about her work.

Long term care was shouldered cheerfully; a diabetic received night and morning injections for years, and those suffering from a stroke might need daily attendance similarly for years. White rags were collected and kept in a cupboard so that those who had no sheets could be made comfortable. The village regarded their nurse as something close to a saint.'

'The Manchester Order of Oddfellows and the Nottingham Order of Foresters were Friendly Societies in Long Itchington in the 1920s. The meetings of the Oddfellows were held at The Buck and Bell. It was an insurance against illness, as money was paid out on producing a doctor's certificate – although if you were seen out after a certain time in the evening you could be reported and money would not be paid. Doctor's bills were paid by the society. My mother paid three shillings and sixpence a quarter to the doctor and twopence a month to the Nursing Association, which covered you for care during childbirth and any other illness.'

'I recall visiting Rugby Hospital in 1930 for an x-ray. Bags of shot were placed on my hands and legs to hold my limbs still.'

'In the 1930s I had the misfortune to spend a long period in the local cottage hospital, but the care and attention received was superb. Matron was even aroused one night and came down to my bedside in her dressing gown when my condition gave rise for concern.

Visiting was limited to three afternoons per week so as not to tax the patients. The side door was used by visitors, who were met by Lizzy the maid in her black dress, white lace cap and apron, who accompanied them to the patient's bedside. The front entrance was strictly for doctors and VIPs. My doctor would visit me daily, driven by his chauffeuresse smartly dressed in her cream and brown uniform. All this for the princely sum of one penny per week paid into the Hospital Maintenance Fund.

Contracting scarlet fever two years later was a different experience. The patient was placed in the ambulance along with their bedding, then had to wait while the bedroom was fumigated and sealed to remain so for several days until the bedding was returned and the room opened up again. Visiting at the isolation hospital took place at a closed window, not easy for holding a conversation, for six long weeks!'

THE LAST JOURNEY

'A death meant all the curtains in the house were drawn and were not opened again until the coffin had left the house. The family all obtained black clothes and these were worn for about a year – even children were put in dark grey or navy. The announcement of the death was on notepaper and envelopes with a black band round the edge. At the funeral the immediate family and friends met at the house and walked to the church, the bell tolling from when the coffin left the house. Afterwards the same people plus the vicar and coffin bearers went back to the house for tea and sandwiches and cake. Some people could not afford this but did so if they could as it was considered a mark of respect for the dead to give them a good send off.'

'Only men attended funerals, all wearing black. All the houses passed by the hearse had their curtains closed.'

'When people died they were kept at home in their own bed and the undertaker would come daily to attend the body and bring the coffin. Friends and neighbours would call to pay their last respects and say farewell. Few villages had a hearse. The coffin was placed on the bier and wheeled from the house to the church followed by the mourners, most of whom wore black clothes and black armbands.'

CHILDHOOD & SCHOOLDAYS

CHILDHOOD DAYS

Whether we grew up in town or country, we were never far from the fields and woods that beckoned so enticingly as a playground, and most children between the wars had an intimate knowledge of flowers and animals. We also had a freedom that today's children will never know. Despite hard times for many families – and despite the clothes we had to wear! – perhaps we were the lucky ones.

WE ROAMED THE FIELDS

'From the day of my birth in October 1912, I must have been destined to be a fruit picker and jam maker. Mother was carrying an apron full of apples from our large walled garden, when I decided to arrive and she dropped the apples. When quite young my sister and I spent hours picking fruit; it always seemed very hot, and we used to take our frocks off to avoid raspberry juice stains. We also had blackcurrants, redcurrants and gooseberries, and in the autumn plums, pears and apples, which mostly grew on the walls.

Our farmhouse was very old and draughty, just oil lamps, candles and coal fires. It took Mother an hour each winter morning to trim the wicks, clean glasses and refill with paraffin, as there were lanterns for the cowshed and stables. Washing was always done on Monday, and hung out in the orchard. One day Dad turned some young calves out and they chewed the clothes. Butter was made on Thursdays, and once the shepherd dog sneaked into the dairy and just managed to reach and eat the ends of 16 half pound packs. Mother cut the chewed ends off and had to repat it, and was two and a half pounds short. Friday Dad went to Hinckley by pony and trap to sell the butter and eggs, mostly to private customers, and some to a shop. We children went in holiday time, tied onto the seat behind the driver, as we sat back to back. Our pony was rather skittish and liable to shy.

As children we roamed the fields and neighbouring farms looking for birds' nests, watercress, mushrooms, blackberries and nuts, fishing in the brook for tiddlers, collecting frogspawn and catching butterflies.

A molecatcher, whose fee was one penny per acre, came occasionally on a bicycle, and he always took the skins and left the carcases hanging on the barbed wire fences. We were always keen to find how many he had caught.

School days were happy. In winter we stood all round the old "tortoise" stove for reading lessons. Singing we enjoyed; one song I remember well, and the tune: – "Grow, grow, grow little mushroom grow, somebody wants you so. I will call again tomorrow morn, you'll see, and if you grow bigger you will just suit me. So grow, grow, grow little mushroom grow."

Shrove Tuesday we had half a day's holiday, and girls took battledores and shuttlecocks, and boys their whips and tops to the village square.

Summer treats were held at Leicester Grange, about a mile and a half out of Wolvey. Tables were laden with sandwiches and cakes, usually slab cake, and one year there was a plague of wasps and half onions were placed at intervals in case of stings. We all had a present, mine was a Jack-in-the-box. On one occasion, a boat capsized on the lake, and much to the hilarity of we youngsters quite a number of grown ups got very wet, as long skirts and blouses were the fashion of the day. Mrs Hawley, our hostess, fixed them up with some of her clothes.

Sewing and knitting lessons were big tasks for small girls, making flannel shirts and re-footing stockings for the teacher's father, who weighed about 20 stones.

When our parents went to whist drives and dances, we had a child minder named Grace, who we loved very much. She worked in a hosiery factory in Hinckley, and always brought us a "Tuppenny Variety", a whipped cream walnut or Fry's cream bar. On Saturdays we were given a penny to buy sweets at the village shop.

Dad used to tell us tales of his young days. Several friends used to go sparrow catching at night with a large net on poles, and one night they opened a cottage door and let several sparrows in. The sparrows went for the lamp and the cats went for the sparrows, but they beat a hasty retreat so never knew how it ended.'

WE WERE THE LUCKY ONES

'I was born in 1924, third in a family of four girls. A lovely lady, who we always called Aunt Min, lived a quarter of a mile away. She was to come and attend to Mother at the birth. The message was sent via the paper man that her services were needed. Having checked that the date was 1st April, she didn't want to be an April fool so didn't put in an appearance. But horror of horrors she saw Mother struggling down to fetch her. Needless to say, I was the one who was the April fool.

My father worked on the farm so, in spite of hard times, we always had a roof over our heads and a can of milk. We had a big cottage garden so there were always fresh vegetables, yellow plums, gooseberries and blackcurrants in season. Dad kept bees – honey has never tasted the same since. There were hens at the top of the garden. If there were surplus eggs they were put down in "waterglass" for the winter.

Haymaking and harvest time were great treats for us children, though hard work and very long hours for the workers. We loved to take the sandwiches, usually jam, and cans of hot tea to the fields or rickyards, but none of us liked carrying the tea cans because they were hot against our bare legs.

We used to spin our tops and bowl our hoops the mile to school and never see a car to move us from the middle of the road. We had fields and woods to roam in with never any fear. It was a wonderful life, even though there was never any money to spare. Luckily Mother was a clever needlewoman and hand-me-downs were the order of the day. We did not feel the least bit deprived; we thought everyone lived as we did. We were the lucky ones during the depression, having the cottage, work and always food. No television or radio of course, so we took the time from the trains. You could literally set your watch by them in those days. If we were catching the train and still running along the road as it was coming to the station, the engine driver would wait for us!

We had no hot water bottles to take to bed. Instead we had solid iron shelves out of the oven wrapped in newspaper to warm the bed before we got in, but with three of us in the bed we soon got warm!

We did have a newspaper delivery and if we wanted a letter posted we propped it up in the front window and the postman would get off his bike and come and fetch it. We really had got it made.

We had few toys. We drove Mother mad by bouncing balls against the wall. Hopscotch was not very popular with her because it wore the toes of our shoes out too quickly. We learnt very early to play simple card games, which took care of many a long winter evening. We were taught to knit at an early age and how we did all that embroidery by lamp light I will never know.

Every summer we had straw hats with fruit or flowers made of wax – so pretty they were. I rather suspect they were presents from a grandmother. New brown sandals were another treat, but they were never really comfortable until they had got all scruffy.

I remember with great joy all the butterflies – you only had to set foot amongst the lucerne and clouds of blue ones rose up. We collected caterpillars and kept them until they turned into gorgeous

A little girl and her cade (tame) lamb at Church Lawford in 1947. An interest in animals, birds and flowers was a natural part of life for children brought up in Warwickshire's beautiful countryside.

butterflies or rather drab moths. The nightingales sang all night and the dawn chorus was enough to deafen you.

What memories we all have stored away.'

ON THE ESTATE

'My childhood was spent on a country estate four miles from Stratford on Avon and my earliest memories are of practically living in the stable yard helping the grooms look after the hunters, the smell of the saddle soap, hearing the horses rustling about their stalls, feeding them and mucking out and occasionally riding them – when the "Captain" at the house was away! Being allowed into the tack room and to help polish the saddles and reins and going into the "holiest of holies" – the grooms' rest room. Always full of smoke from their cigarettes but all round the room were glass cases full of sets of cigarette cards. I often wonder what became of them

103

all. War came – the horses went to war and in came the Army so the stable yard was placed out of bounds for us youngsters.

We later moved into a tiny hamlet on the same estate where my mother was school caretaker. My sister and I had to get up early each morning to light the awful tortoise stoves in the classrooms, before walking (sometimes running) a mile up the lane to catch the bus to school at Stratford. Before that it was my job to get up the street and fetch the milk from the farm, in the milk can. Many times in the winter months I'd get nearly home with the milk only to fall down on the icy street and tear a hole in my lisle stockings, receiving a clip on the ear from my mother and being sent back up to the farm with a penny ha'penny for another pint. We made peg rugs during the winter months, with a sack for the base and old clothes cut up in strips to peg in.

I remember watching the local blacksmith at work in his forge and being given the honour of holding one of the beautiful shire horses and hunters as they waited their turn for new shoes. As children we would do anything for a few pence. On Fridays we used to meet the market bus and help ladies carry their shopping up the street to their homes; if we were allowed inside the house to make them a cup of tea we had sixpence, otherwise it was a penny. Helping my mother pick loads of blackberries to take down to the "House" for the cook to make jams and preserves. The lovely huge kitchen with all its copper cooking utensils round the walls and always a lovely smell of cooking and baking, but we were never offered anything to eat!'

EGG ON HIS FACE

'My father was always the first to find birds' nests in the hedgerows as we made our way along country lanes for our Sunday afternoon walk. As a boy, he told me, he had a large collection of birds' eggs. On finding a nest, he would take one egg, replacing it with a pebble. The egg was taken home to be blown, resting safely in his flat cap in the loose fold over the peak. The local policeman, who was averse to such activities, if he met the boys, would give a sharp tap on the cap and my father would be left with egg on his face.'

MONDAYS

'Monday morning – I wake in my unheated bedroom, my breath condensing to vapour in the ice-cold air and I snuggle down into the feather mattress, reluctant to put my feet out onto the lino-covered floor. My mother brings hot water up from the kitchen and I wash in the chilly bathroom, which boasts a bath with a gas geyser and a wash bowl but as yet no inside loo and certainly no hot water on tap.

Downstairs for a breakfast of bacon and egg and strong tea and a little relief from the cold as the one fire in the house begins to burn up. Wrapped up warm and well-lined with woolly vest, fleece-lined liberty bodices and long, black stockings held up by rubbber suspenders, we walked to school primly dressed in identical school uniforms, and woe betide us if we took off our hats or forgot our gloves! Every school day began with an assembly and hymn practice and lessons were formal, discipline rigid, but how we learned and how that knowledge has stayed with us – not for us the split infinitive or the mis-placed apostrophe!

Home for a lunch of left-overs from Sunday because it's washday and Mother has been working hard all morning. No tumble dryers, so pray for a fine day, otherwise the house is like a Turkish bath as the washing steams on the large clothes horse round a blazing fire.

A stop at the Co-op on the way home from school in the afternoon for a few groceries. Fascinating to watch the currants and sugar weighed into stiff dark blue bags and deftly folded shut, butter patted into neat rectangles with wooden pats and the chance to choose an assortment of biscuits from a range of glass-topped boxes. I always admired the way in which the assistant parcelled them all up into a neat, brown paper parcel, tied with string, and was intrigued by the fact that no matter what one bought the parcel was always the same size and shape! And then there was the fun of watching the money and the checks (from which the "divi" was calculated) twisted into the tube and dispatched with an almighty "slurp" up a larger tube to some mysterious destination aloft from where it returned in due course with a loud plop and always the right change.

Home now smelled of freshly-ironed, starched washing and it still wasn't possible to see the fire behind the tall clothes horse.

After tea, homework, learning to knit socks on four needles and maybe darning holes in the toes of the black stockings! The highlight of the evening was listening to the radio, maybe a Big Band show, Jack Payne, Geraldo, Joe Loss, Henry Hall, *In Town Tonight* or *Music Hall*, and on Sundays the Ovaltinies on Radio Luxemburg.

And so to bed, back to the icy bedroom and the feather mattress, armed with a cup of cocoa and a hot water bottle. All very spartan, compared with the cushioned life we live today, but we knew no other and were happy with our lot and it certainly prepared us for the privations of the war, which was just around the corner.'

WE HARDLY LEFT THE VILLAGE

'I was born in Warmington in January 1938, my father and mother having moved into the village from neighbouring Shotteswell during the spring of 1937.

Entertainment was always made between my parents and we three children, such as long walks over the fields where my parents would teach us all about the birds and trees, wild flowers etc. Sometimes as a special treat my mother would pack some sandwiches and a big fruit cake plus a very large container of home-made lemonade and we would take this with us and picnic in the woods some way from our village. Sometimes we were allowed to call at The Hare and Hounds where we would all sit out in the garden and my father fetched us pop and crisps while he enjoyed a pint of beer. This was always on a Sunday evening after church. Following our treat we would all return home and my father would fetch in the old tin bath, place it in front of the fire, where we would be bathed in turn and popped straight into bed. My mother would go upstairs with us, tuck us all in, blow out the candle and there would be the end of another happy day.

Our only other entertainment was an old radio which ran off an accumulator. This was not allowed to be used very much because my father always liked to make sure that there would be enough "power" left to hear the football results on Saturday evening. A man from the next village used to call to change the accumulator.

A lot of our time during the summer months was spent helping in the garden or allotment, where my father would grow all the vegetables needed for our family. Buying such produce was unheard of and if you couldn't grow something or do an exchange with a neighbour, then we simply went without. My father would often swap rabbits for cooking apples, plums etc in the autumn.

There was a village shop and post office where you could buy groceries and the butcher would call twice a week, the baker three times a week. Milk was produced in the village and it could either be collected or delivered as you wished. We children would quite often collect ours as we enjoyed helping the farmer press the cardboard tops into the bottles.

I can remember that in the very deep snow of 1947 my father and other men in the village used an old sleigh (kept by a villager) and two big horses to get into Banbury to buy provisions for everyone, as Warmington was completely cut off for some time. My brother and some more boys also walked with sledges to the next village to collect fresh baked bread from the baker and distributed it round the village. During this very deep snow, the men dug one big pathway straight through the middle of the village, with a pathway leading to each house. We children had great fun playing round this maze of pathways, mostly we couldn't even see over the top.

Our lives were almost entirely spent in the village. The school taught children until they were eleven years old, mostly with one teacher and one helper.

There were several highlights to our year, such as the church fete which took place in the summer. My mother would seem to be sewing for months in preparation, aprons, tea towels etc. This was in addition to all the little smocked baby dresses she would make for lots of people to supplement the family income.

Each summer we would have a day trip to the seaside. This was wonderful and probably the one day each year when we could buy an ice cream and one of the very few occasions that we would go out of Warmington.

There was also an annual trip to see the pantomime at Oxford at Christmas-time. We didn't always go to this and I realise now that it was maybe because my parents could not afford it, as by now there were four children in our family. When we did go, I remember it as being sheer magic to see the colours and the lights and to hear the music and to see the dancers. A fantasy world indeed!

Practically, the only other times we would leave the village would include our annual trip to Banbury to get new shoes and, for anyone who hadn't got a hand-me-down coat, the luxury of a new coat or dress or whatever. We would visit our grandparents in Birmingham once a year, going on a train from Banbury and we would sometimes walk to the next village to see my other grandparents.

I can remember very well the time when the first TV set arrived in Warmington. The gentleman who bought it would set up rows of chairs in his room for anyone who wanted to visit him to watch programmes, it was quite amazing. There was also a man who would show cartoon films, Laurel and Hardy, Tarzan etc in his barn each week. Every child in the village would be there, booing and hissing the villain and cheering the hero.'

WAR BABY

'I was born in Coventry in 1939. In 1940 we lost our home in a bombing raid and after a period of staying with relatives we were rehoused in a council house in Bedworth, right on the edge of the town with a farm opposite and wonderful views over open fields; this was where I spent my childhood and teenage years.

My memories of the war are very vague; gas masks, my father's tin hat, the soldiers from an American Forces camp just outside

Bulkington, with endless supplies of chewing gum which they gave to anyone they met. I do remember the street party when peace was declared. Everyone joined in, the tables seemed to stretch along the street for miles. Balloons, streamers and bunting appeared overnight. There were masses and masses of sandwiches and cakes, huge bowls of jelly and blancmange. More teapots than I had ever thought could exist. Gramophones were brought out into the street and the women danced until late evening in the lamplight. Everyone was happy and laughing and I remember being put half asleep into bed with music and laughter still going on.

In the 1940s there was very little traffic on the road and we children played in the streets quite safely. We also roamed the fields as we pleased and our parents seemed to have few worries for our safety. We fished and paddled in what we called "the little brook", a small stream running from Bedworth to Bulkington. We were always welcome on the farm and would help to bring the cows in for milking, lean over the pig sty and scratch the pig's back and in the autumn the farmer's wife would give us threepence if we collected a whole shopping bag full of acorns for the pigs.

Our lives seemed to follow a pattern with one set of games following another. For days we would play "Sheep, sheep come over" across the road from side to side with only the occasional car to disturb us. The milk came on a horse-pulled dray and the bread in a horse-drawn covered two-wheeled cart, where the driver sat up very high. Then one day the road games would be forgotten and all the girls would have their skipping ropes, individual ones or sometimes long ones with a girl at each end, the rest skipping in and out to the words "All in together girls, very fine weather girls, when it's your birthday please drop out, January, February etc".

Then the skipping ropes would vanish and it would be hopscotch, or rubber balls or marbles or bows and arrows or the seasonal things like conkers, daisy chains, blackberrying, winter warmers and if we were lucky and it snowed, snowmen and snowball fights and sliding and skating on the pond.

Every Good Friday we walked to Corley Rocks to pick bluebells. It never seemed to be planned beforehand but on Good Friday morning after church, my sister would make a packet of jam sandwiches and a bottle of cold tea, take me by the hand and we would go. Children from all over Bedworth, it seemed to me, were doing the same. Via Cross Keys and Smorrel Lane we went, past a house with a huge garden and goats where a kind lady always gave us a drink of water, which helped to eke out our cold tea. At Corley Rocks we would run and play among the bluebells, picking huge armfuls and returning home weary with the flowers limp and wilting. It was a very long walk but we did it year after year and I don't remember that it ever rained, but that's memory for you!

On Whit Monday there was the Whit Walk. All the churches, chapels and various organisations took part in this. There were wonderful banners carried by marching men, carnival floats and a variety of bands from all around the area. People in fancy dress collected money for charity in buckets or we threw our pennies on to the float we liked best. As we were Roman Catholics we did not take part in this walk, but watching from a well chosen spot was still a highlight in my year.

We Catholic children had our own May celebration when the statue of the Virgin Mary was carried shoulder high by four big boys from the school to the church, followed by the May Queen, in beautiful clothes with a long, heavy, richly embroidered train, which was supported by about ten small children from the infants class. The rest of the school followed two by two, the girls in white dresses and veils carrying bunches of flowers, the boys dressed in best suits and shiny black shoes. We sang hymns and prayed and then returned to the school for a lovely tea.

The fair came twice a year and brought much excitement. There was usually a circus once a year but I was never very keen on that, I always worried about the animals.

Bedworth had an open air market three times a week; two mornings and all day Saturday. The stalls were set up on the road outside J C Smith's. My father told me that when he was a boy in the early 1900s, a visiting dentist would set up his chair in the Market Place on Saturdays and the brass band would stand round and play to drown the noise from the patients having their teeth extracted.

We shopped at the market on Saturdays. I loved the stalls, especially towards Christmas when we bought nuts, oranges and crisp Cox's apples. Father Christmas would be at J C Smith's and one of my Grandmas, who lived in the lovely old almshouses next to the Market Place, gave me sixpence to go and see him. He gave me a present out of his sack. It was a tiny rubber hot-water bottle for my dolls, perfect in every detail. I loved it.

Christmas was a magical time. Hoping for a good part in the nativity play, making paper chains to decorate the classroom, a wonderful party with games on the last day of term, buying the Christmas tree, decorating the living room at home, buying presents with the money I had saved in my wooden money box. Carol singing and the smell of mince-pies. "What will Father Christmas bring me?" I would start to ask my father weeks beforehand. Always the same answer, "Two black eyes and a broken nose and a pump-a-larum jig." Years later I would hear him give my children the same answer and knew by the look of thrilled horror and their excited shrieks that they loved the joke just as I had.

Midnight Mass and so to bed to be shaken awake by my sister, "He's been, he's been." The scramble down the bed to fumble in the nobbly, lumpy socks and try to guess what the packages were. Then we would lie contentedly sucking a toffee and wait for it to get light. The first banana I ever saw was in my Christmas stocking, also the first Maltesers I ever saw.

In the morning Bedworth Band would march all round Bedworth playing carols and collecting money for charity. "Here come the Waits," my father would say and give us a handful of coppers to drop in the box when they knocked on the door.

My mother was ill for many years when I was a child and spent months at a time in a hospital in Coventry. We would visit her on Sunday afternoons. I loved the ride on the top deck of the Corporation bus, everything looked so different from up there. My father would tell us stories of the trams and point out where the tram lines had been. As we neared Coventry he would always say, "Watch out for the three spires, it is the city of three spires you know," and we would count them as they came into view.

Our summer holidays, because of my mother's illness, were usually spent with relatives in St Albans or Letchworth Garden City. However, there was always a day trip to the seaside, Skegness or Rhyl. Up early, packing sandwiches, towels and knitted bathers which when wet hung down to our knees. I remember the water oozing up through the sand as we built sand-castles and the seaweed and shells and sleeping in the crook of my father's arm on the way home.

So many childhood memories. Ration books and getting our rations at the old-fashioned corner shop with a flagstone floor, a wooden counter with an oilcloth covered top. The shopkeeper wore a long black dress with a high neck, sleeves buttoned at the cuffs and a snowy white apron. It was cool in there and in the summer they made their own ice cream, threepence for a cornet and sixpence for a wafer.

Another old lady with an apple tree made and sold, in the autumn, toffee apples at threepence each. The big saucepan of toffee would be boiling on the gas cooker and the apples already dipped, cooling on a huge enamel tray on the draining board. You knocked on her kitchen door to make your purchase and went away with a sweet treat that would last for hours.

All our treats were simple in those days but looking back, they all seemed to last for ever.'

LIFE IN A CHILDREN'S HOME

'I was born in a small cottage in the hamlet of Cosford, near Rugby in July 1909. Cosford was situated at the end of a narrow country lane and lay near to the villages of Brownsover and Newbold. At that time there was a population of about 30 souls whose livelihoods were based on agriculture. There were four tenant farms, and six cottages occupied by agricultural workers of which my father was one. Cosford was situated amongst the beautiful water meadows of the nearby Avon and Swift rivers. A canal also ran there. Stretches of the river Swift were maintained by a water bailiff, plying the water in his flat-bottomed boat. He lived in Cosford in a cottage which we knew as "The Puddle House".

There were four children in our family of which I was the second eldest, and the only girl. Although we were poor we spent an idyllic early childhood in the nearby lanes and fields with their cowslips, violets, marshmallows, ladies smocks and yellow iris. We played by the ford, ran over the plank bridge to the further fields and earned ourselves the odd copper by opening and closing gates for the farm traffic and the few visitors who made their way to the hamlet.

Then our mother died. Our life changed. I was nearly four. We were not even told that Mother had died but were taken by horsecab to Rugby where we were placed in care in a children's home. We were later to realize that, given the long working day of the agricultural labourer, nearly seven days a week, it was impossible for my father to rear a young family; my youngest brother was only nine months old at the time. I was placed in the "girls" home and my brothers in the "boys". The only time that we saw each other was through a dividing fence. When we did we wept a great deal. As time went by we saw less and less of each other till eventually the two eldest boys were removed to another home in a different part of the town. The youngest, but a baby, was alone, became withdrawn as a child, and, I think, this affected him for the rest of his life.

The regime within the homes was extremely disciplined but, upon reflection, I think that we came to learn self-discipline which has stayed with us, and benefited us throughout our lives. We were cared for by a "mother". Over the years I spent within the home they were several; some kind and compassionate, others indifferent. The "mother" was also the cook and she was assisted by a young girl.

We all had chores to do from an early age. We had to clean all the shoes, emphasis on the back before the front! The older girls washed the younger ones and brushed their hair and teeth. Every Friday

111

evening we all lined up for a dose of liquorice; it was ghastly. There was cake once a week for Sunday tea but if you had misbehaved you went without. All meals had to be eaten up. If you didn't eat up it was given to you again at the next meal. I loathed oatmeal and black treacle.

When the Great War started the children of the home were exempted from queueing. Schoolchildren at that time were excused lateness if they had been queueing for meagre rations. In a sense we, in the home, were fortunate to have enough. When the terrible 'flu epidemic came the small boys in the home next door were removed and replaced by older ones. By then my eldest brother had been sent into the navy, to the training ship *Exmouth* moored at Tilbury. He then went on to the *Ganges* at Chatham. I saw even less of him, in fact, we were never told that he had gone.

Our clothing consisted of "hand down" garments; dresses, petticoats and coats. One assistant "mother" however did provide us with ribbons for our hair. We had to walk in file, two by two, everywhere we went; to school, Sunday school and to church. But, hard as it was, many of our teachers were kindly towards us and took an interest in our progress into adult life.

Our lives were ordered by the Home committee who met once a month to oversee our welfare, and when the time came, decided our future occupations; mainly those of domestic service, farm work, or, for the boys, the armed services. However, it didn't always turn out like that. I made lifelong friends and acquaintances from those days. Amongst their accomplishments have been hospital matron, nursing sister tutor, owner of a salmon canning factory in Alaska, three petty officers in the Royal Navy, newspaper reporter, lay minister in the church, farmer's wife and a county social services adviser. Myself, I became a lady's companion, chauffeuse, and then housewife and mother.

We were there for six years after which, due to an increase in fees to the local authority, my father took the three of us back again to start a new phase in our young lives. He had changed employment and was working as an under-gardener for the local squire. He was given a tithe cottage in which we lived. Subsequently this building has undergone extensive renovation, and is locally quite famous as it is reputedly the birthplace of Lawrence Sheriffe, grocer to Queen Elizabeth I and founder of the great Rugby public school.

Life remained very hard, especially since I had to care for my father and brothers whilst still only a young girl. Money was a great problem and I learnt the lifetime discipline of thrift and "making do". Eventually I left and went to a live-in situation at a local farm. Although I still went to school I earned my keep by doing farm work

112

whenever I could. Although always tired I enjoyed the freedom and variety and the personalities of the farm; one girl remains a friend, even today. Eventually I married one of the boys from the Home whose sister was with me at the time. We celebrated our Golden Wedding in 1988.'

THE CLOTHES WE WORE

'Economy was uppermost when I was a child, and my father repaired all our boots and shoes in the shed "down the garden". He made me a beautiful scooter but the foot that powered it wore out my right shoe so he reinforced the edge of toe and sole with kegs. Consequently, to my horror, the shoe clicked as I walked.

We were never allowed to change into clean underclothes until they had been thoroughly aired in front of the living room fire, and no amount of pleading was of any avail!'

'Was there ever a garment as ugly and as uncomfortable as the liberty bodice? In the 1930s and 1940s little girls everywhere were encased in these horrors and, with suspenders fastened at one end to thick lisle or woollen stockings and at the other to the bodice itself, the effect was more like a straitjacket. Fortunately the liberty bodice was only really suitable for the flat chested figure. How thankful I was when I started to develop a bosom.

On second thoughts things could have been worse. I could have been born a generation earlier when everyone wore lace-up stays.'

'Girls in the 1940s wore navy blue fleecy-lined knickers with a pocket, a woollen vest (with sleeves in winter) sometimes hand-knitted with fine wool, and a liberty bodice with rubber buttons which were used to attach loops sewn on to lisle stockings and hooked on. School cardigans were home knitted (as were socks, gloves etc) and when the elbows wore out the lower part of the sleeve was reknitted on to a line of stitches picked out. Two extra ounces of wool were always purchased to accommodate this need at a later date. All clothes were home-made, either knitted or sewn by treadle sewing machine.

Sunday best clothes were just that – for wearing only on Sundays, high days and holidays. I remember a pleated kilt on a cotton bodice, a shantung blouse and a petticoat made from parachute silk. A woollen coat and a beret or felt hat, together with Start-Rite or Kiltie laced shoes completed the outfit. And of course, a bow in my hair – a special ribbon for Sunday and school ribbons the rest of the week. I had plaits long enought to sit on, and for special occasions my mother would curl up the little bit of hair at the end of the plaits.'

'Boys wore short trousers until about the age of 14, when they wore their first pair of long trousers.'

'In the shadow of the 1930 slump we were very poor and I, being the youngest, was usually to be found wearing my brother's and my cousin's hand-downs. So that the first time I had a really *new* pair of leather shoes I put them at the head of my bed at night and reached down to pick them up and smell the new leather.

When I reached grammar school age, my agony came to an end because I had to be decked out with correct school uniform, which I took a great pride in. The simple pleasures were so important in those days. The thrill of getting three distinctions for drawing or maths in a row, which gave us the privilege of going to our headmistress for a star, signed by her. The thrill of winning the "colours" of the "House" we were in, for prowess in sport, so that if we had a bar on the gymslip and a coloured girdle you were marked as a bit special in the sports line.'

GAMES, TREATS AND CHORES

The roads and lanes were our playgrounds in the days when cars were very few and far between and most of the traffic was horse-drawn and fairly slow moving. Games followed seasons, and had not changed a great deal over the decades since the beginning of the century. Most of us had our chores to do as well, though some, such as helping in the fields at haymaking, were more of a pleasure than a hardship. Spending the Saturday penny at the sweetshop was a treat to be looked forward to at the end of the week.

WE ALWAYS PLAYED IN THE STREET

'We always played in the street – whip and top, battledore and shuttlecock, wooden hoop and stick, marbles in the gutters, hopscotch (and if you could get a bit of slate instead of a stone you were sure to win), snobs.

With a ball, we could play "one-in-the-middle" (which more often than not meant three or four in the middle), pounds, shillings and pence, statues. There was always the cry, "Don't let the ball go in *her* garden . . . she won't let you have it back till tomorrow." Cricket was great until we smashed a window!

Then there were all the "fancy bits" you could do with a skipping rope – and to get a long piece from the broken clothes line so that everybody could skip in the rope that stretched the width of the road was great. The big 'uns always made the little 'uns turn the rope – and it was hard work!

We could tie one end of the rope to the railings and play "High-jump" or we could just race, or play Tig.

If a car came up or down the road, we just stopped playing and stared. Oh! they must have a lot of money to afford a car!

When it was anybody's birthday their mother always gave a good party and we had all the party games . . . Postman's Knock, Charades, Find the Thimble, Consequences, Railway Stations, Poor Mary, The Man in the Moon, Black Magic etc, etc.

We stopped playing to watch the lamplighter put in a new mantle in the gas light. We were ever-so-pleased when he came because we could play a bit longer when there was light outside our houses.

If we were lucky, when our Dads came home we could get a penny and go round the chippy for a penn'orth of chips.

All play had to stop if we heard an aeroplane . . . and we even came out of the house (if we were having a meal) to see such an unusual object.

In winter when it snowed, we trudged through snow, jumped in "virgin" snow and got it all in our wellies. (There was no such thing as salt on the roads.) Our dads hammered some strips of wood together and whoopee . . . we'd got a sledge. (Never went very well mind you.)

In the summer we put old pram-wheels on the sledge and made a trolley – and with this we could take neighbours' luggage to the station when it was holiday time.

Of course, when war was declared we couldn't play in the street when it got dark because of the blackout. We did play with our gas masks hanging on our backs, though we couldn't have a new whip and top, or a new battledore and shuttlecock. We didn't have to stop for a car for there wasn't any petrol for private motorists, but we did see the bus stop at the bottom of the street and our munitions-work neighbours come back in their turbans and overalls. We watched bombers go over and we could see the barrage balloons surrounding Coventry.

In May 1945, two neighbours got a washing-basket and went to every house with a request to "chuck in what you can spare and we'll give the kids a party on Saturday". What a party we had!'

SEASONS FOR GAMES

'There were seasons when different games were played in Ashorne village in the 1930s. It would range from bowling a metal hoop with a stick to whip and top, five stones and hopscotch, the squares for which were marked in the road with a piece of white stone and then we had to hop and kick the piece of stone into each square. There were also ball games against a brick wall, often against somebody's house, until the annoyed occupants could stand the continual bumping no longer and came out and shooed us on.

Then there would be skipping ropes. Of course, one must remember that the lack of traffic allowed all this to take place in the road.

The spring would arrive and it would be the thrill of the first violets and birds' nests and then bluebell time. We would go up to the woods in droves and come home with arms full of bluebells, filling every vase and jam jar around. They don't really last long when picked, but it was the excitement of picking so many that made it all worthwhile. Then the summer would bring wild strawberries; we had a special place for those and we would eat them unwashed.

A large private kitchen garden grew its rhubarb rather close to the chestnut palings that divided it from the field, and we could put our thin arms through and pull a stick of it out, run home and find a blue sugar bag which usually had some sugar stuck to the sides and put some more in and walk about eating the rhubarb. I'm sure our insides must have suffered somewhat, as the rhubarb would hardly be ripe. At gooseberry and blackcurrant time we would raid the allotments when we thought no one was around, or until the irate gardener saw us and frightened us off with threats to tell our parents.

Then would come jumping-brook time, usually when the snow and rain had subsided and the brook was fairly low. Most boys had a "leap-pole". This was a sturdy pole which you pushed well down in the centre of the brook and leapt over to the other side. Then it would be picking moon daisies from the long mowing grass and other grasses, and running through the long grass was great fun as long as the farmer didn't see you. We played amongst the stooks when the corn was cut.

The long summer holiday would come and go and it would be horse chestnut time (conkers). All the children would gather them, but it was mostly the boys who played the conker game. Then the chestnuts would be ripe in the woods and we would go up in a group and pick bags full. The old fashioned black range was ideal for

Picnics and outings to the seaside were great treats. Remember those waterproof bloomers?

roasting them as long as they didn't burst!

On one of the roads out of the village the brook would burst its banks and flood the road with the snow and rain, making it impassable for senior children to get to school on bicycles. We would go down and try and get through but if it was impossible we would stand and watch other people get stuck in the middle. With the winter would come the icy roads, and sliding on ponds was another winter pastime, and sledging. The sledges were very much home-made affairs, but served their purpose just the same.'

PLAYING IN THE LANE

'Living in a quiet lane in Alcester and with some brick walls to play ball against we spent hours taking turn. We would start by just throwing the ball to the wall and catching it; after ten times if you hadn't dropped it, you went on to a more difficult move such as clap hands or roll your hands, catch with right hand then left hand, under one leg then the other. All sorts of variations could be played and each had to be done ten times, starting from scratch every time you dropped the ball or made a mistake.

When we played hopscotch we had a square bed and you started by throwing the "meg" into the first bed, pick the meg up and hop through the six squares, then on to bed two and so on. The next round you had to put the meg into bed two, hop over the first, pick up the meg and hop round, going on to bed three and so on. Again there were many variations to play, starting from scratch if you missed or the meg went on the line.

One of the best games for a number of players was Pudding and Basin. A line was drawn across the lane and all the children but one stood on the line. Two other lines were drawn on either side about ten yards away, one had "pudding" written on it and the other "basin". The caller shouted out a letter and those on the line had to run to where the appropriate letter was. The last one stepped out, but as there was an I and an N in both, the caller had to say "I or N that you put the pudding in". The winner was the caller next time.

Whip and top was possible then, no cars and few windows to damage.'

VILLAGE GAMES

'Childhood games and pastimes at Clifford Chambers included skipping, tops, hopscotch, "fag" cards, five stones or dids, ball games, hoops etc. The boys' hoops were iron with an iron handle hooked on for steering. The girls had wooden hoops with wooden sticks to hit them along.

Boys kept a look out for men smoking cigarettes and would say, "Can I have your fag card please?"; usually they were lucky. The long skipping ropes were lengths of clothes line and several children would play with two turning the rope. Individual ropes were also short lengths of clothes line. A few lucky ones had ropes with wooden handles bought in town. We would play ring games such as Poor Mary Sits A-weeping, Wallflowers, Wallflowers Growing Up on High and Ring a Ring of Roses (for the smaller ones).

There is a recreation ground in the village where we played on the swings, seesaw and parallel bars. There was plenty of space where we played ball games, leap frog, fivestones etc. The seesaw had a very thick plank, difficult to hold on to. I still have a crooked nose from falling off, though I was rushed by car to see a doctor in Stratford who tried to push it back into place.

118

In the wintertime if there was enough snow we had a great time with toboggans, usually home-made, and Martin's Hill was our venue. It had been known for even grown ups to join in the fun, but two ended up in a hedge with broken legs and badly bumped heads. We also played snowballs and built snowmen. Sometimes where the field flooded near the river Stour we were able to slide in frosty weather and older people went skating there.

We really enjoyed stone picking on Saturday mornings from 9 am until 1 pm. We worked in a field belonging to the Manor farm. Each of us had a bucket to fill with stones scattered round the field. These we emptied into a large heap. We had a grand wage of one shilling and sixpence but we all felt really rich. Usually sixpence was spent on a National Savings Stamp from the village post office, often the boys would run all the way to Stratford to visit the "pictures" that cost sixpence too, and the remaining "tanner" would be a week's pocket money.'

WINTER WARMERS

'As a child I remember making Winter Warmers. We took an empty tin, filled it with rags including woollens and tied a string through it. Then we lit the rags, blew it out when the flame had really caught and then twirled the tin round and round.'

RING, TEAM AND SKIPPING GAMES

'At Brailes in the 1930s we played ring games such as "Drop handkerchief", "Sally go round the moon", "Around the mulberry bush", "Here we come gathering nuts in May", and "Stand and face your lover as you have done before". Team games included "Sheep sheep come home", "Blind man's buff" and "Oranges and lemons". Skipping games were "I am a Girl Guide", "Oliver Oliver last in the ring", "Cups and saucers, plates and dishes", "Blue bells and cockle shells". We also played top and whip, five stars and five stones, and bowled wooden hoops using a stick for guidance.'

'When spring came at Tanworth in Arden, out came the wooden hoops and the whips and tops. We played with our spinning tops in the village street, always being warned by Father to watch out for a car coming in case we were knocked down. We had races with our hoops up one side of the street, round the village green with its chestnut tree, and down the other side.

Skipping was a favourite pastime with girls. "Over and under the moon" was one we played. Two girls held the ends of a long rope and turned it laboriously in a great arc, while the rest of us lined up on one side. As the rope swung towards us we ran through it, one at a time – that was "under the moon" and easy. From the other side, "over the moon", it was much more difficult. With the rope still turning you had to jump over it just as it touched the ground and run away quickly or you got entangled in the rope. "Salt and pepper" was another good game. Again two girls turned the rope while the others jumped as it hit the ground, chanting "Salt, pepper, vinegar, mustard", the rope handlers gathering momentum and turning faster and faster until either they or the skippers were exhausted. Anyone who faltered in her jumping, causing the rope to stop, had to take on the job of turning the rope.'

WE MUST HAVE BEEN MAD!

'When we were children the dangers of swimming in the canal were not obvious. We lived by the canal and would swing from ropes in the trees and drop into the water. When barges went by we would hang on to the line pulling the boat and be pulled along. My father was keen on fishing and when the canal was frozen over we would go with a hot flat iron tied onto a piece of string and throw it to break the ice. We must have been mad!

We don't seem to get winters like that any more when the water froze sufficiently deep to slide on, and there were enormous icicles hanging from rooftops, etc.

I remember once riding along the towpath on my bicycle, my brother following me on his. When I looked round he wasn't there. He was in the water with his bike, because he'd ridden off course. I fished him out (and his cycle) and carried on a little way to my friend's house where her mother stripped him and dried his clothes in front of her fire before we dared to go home.

What a horrifying experience it was to have a perm years ago. Hair was curled up and then placed in cylinder things that were connected through thick black wires to a machine. This would then sizzle and steam and it pulled if you'd been "strung up" a bit tight – until the curls were well and truly "fried". Every time, as a young girl, I was convinced that my hair would be burned off in this process. It was days before it could be combed properly because it always went frizzy.'

SWIMMING LESSONS

'Just outside Brinklow, swimming lessons were given in the canal. There were no fancy swimming costumes, improvisation being the

120

order of the day. Girls wore vest and knickers and boys sometimes wore their sister's navy blue knickers with the elastic removed from the legs.'

PICNICS

'It is difficult to believe that almost 50 years have passed since our last picnic beside the river Cole at Coleshill. A sunny morning during the school holidays would find the family packing sandwiches, bread pudding, biscuits and lemonade into our school bags. Friends would join us similarly equipped and we would walk together to wait for the Midland Red bus, clutching a few pennies for the fare in our fists.

An old kitchen towel was an essential item, because without this we could not indulge in the exquisite pastime of exploring the river bed, paddling, building dams and hunting for creatures under the stones.

The outing lasted until all food had been consumed and we began to feel hungry. The toes wrinkled by cold water and scratched by rough twigs and stones would be dried hurriedly and squeezed with difficulty into socks. Soon we were ready for the walk to the bus stop. If we had sufficient money we would join the queue at the fish and chip shop. This stood on the corner and we would wait on the raised steps at its entrance, leaning on the rail and watching the folk walk up and down the hill.

Sleepily we would alight from the bus and return home, grubby and tired, but happy!'

A FEW PENNIES

'Growing up near the entrance to Birmingham City football ground in the early 1950s, every home match meant the chance of earning a little pocket money. Nearly all the supporters seemed to arrive by bicycle and I would stand in the street and ask, "Mind your bike, Mister?" The bike would be wheeled up the entry into our small garden and minded until the end of the match, when a few pennies would be handed over.'

CHORES

'After school when the evenings were light my sister and I had to go round the fields and collect sticks to start the fire. We always had a cooked breakfast – two brothers at work, my dad and sister and myself, it hardly seems possible in these days.

At weekends my sister and I had our jobs. The worst one was cleaning the knives on a board and I detested it so much that I gave the boy next door a halfpenny to help. This was all my pocket money for the week.

A friend from my schooldays was a farmer's daughter, so I spent days with her when I could. We used to cut the chaff for the cattle. The hens used to lay out so we had to go round the fields to find the nests. We churned the cream for butter and my friend's mother made bread which went into the big ovens which were heated up for a long time with long pieces of wood. We used to go round the village with a big bucket of milk and measure it out for the customers, one pint or a half pint. We walked quite a few miles before we were done.

In the summer we loved hay time. We took the tea to the men and for this we had rides in the cart when they were empty, and we loved threshing time. I remember Mr King who drove the machine used to wear a peaked cap. The kids thought it was a great time and we used to watch for the rats to come out as the ricks got lower. Of course, the dogs were ready to kill them.

Another time when harvest came round we would play hide and seek in the stooks. We had to be careful that we didn't knock them over or we would be in trouble with the farmer. We would go blackberrying around the fields. I have known us gather 24 pounds between one or two of us so our mothers were busy with jam making.'

THE SATURDAY HALFPENNY

'In the mid 1930s buying a thin bar of Cadbury's milk chocolate with your Saturday halfpenny was encouraged, but it didn't last long enough, and there were much more tempting things to choose from.

Raspberry drops and pear drops and other types of boiled sweet were stored in large glass jars, needing a good rattle and shake to loosen the contents which became stuck together as the jar emptied. Sweets sold by weight were put into a deep brass pan balanced against a small brass weight, and a pointer in the centre of the scale indicated fair measure. The contents were then transferred to a small, triangular-shaped paper bag.

A gobstopper was a good buy; it lasted a long time and changed colour as you sucked. It required frequent examination, in case you missed one of the colours.

Orchard fruits were small blocks of fruit-flavoured sweets, and of exceptional value because you got two for a halfpenny. Five chocolate-covered Blue Bird toffees could be had for that small sum, or a quantity of lurid-coloured kali which stained finger and mouth. A roll of liquorice with a sweet in the middle made a change; and sometimes we would gamble on a Lucky Bag which usually contained the scrapings out of the sweet jars.

Beechnut chewing gum was allowed, but was not as satisfying as the forbidden bubble gum, with which large pink bubbles could be blown. But best value of all was the sherbet dab, a triangular-shaped bag containing white kali, a tube of liquorice and a lollipop. You began by sucking up the kali through the tube, and when that got clogged up, you dipped in the lollipop, and finally you opened up the bag and licked up the remaining powder.'

'The first ice cream cart that I can remember was a kind of box on wheels, with a tub packed round the sides with ice cubes – and the ice cream resembled cold custard! A cornet cost a halfpenny. My pocket money when I was a child was a penny from my father and a halfpenny from my mother. If I managed to save anything my father would double it for me to take to the Savings Bank (the school accepted it on Monday morning).'

GOING TO SCHOOL BEFORE 1920

Walking miles to school over rough ground before the days of waterproof clothing and wellington boots, open fires in the classroom or a tortoise stove to huddle round in the winter, the three Rs and very little else – memories of schooldays before and just after the First World War.

STARTING SCHOOL IN 1913

'Starting at the age of five and leaving at age 14, children from the village of Lowsonford had to walk two and a half miles up hill and across fields to Rowington school, and two and a half miles back every day rain, snow or shine. Others from outlying areas, Shrewley, Kingswood, and Mousley End, also had long walks.

Neither mackintosh coats or wellington boots were affordable then. Black leather boots and black stockings were usual – and if we got wet, the clothes were dried round the coke stove which warmed the pipes for heating. Everyone took sandwiches; jam, home-cured lard with a whiff of pepper on, honey, egg and cress – anything available.

The first bell rang at quarter to nine to remind us that we could not dawdle – the second at nine o'clock when we were expected to line up in single file in the playground and walk to our places in school. The school being C of E, a hymn and a prayer began the day and we learned most hymns by heart.

We had a wonderful headmaster, Mr Herbert McWilliams, who lived near to the school and was also choirmaster at the nearby church, and three women teachers. Infants began with learning letters and making them with noughts and pot-hooks, coupling them together in different ways. By age seven we could read and write up to five-letter words and compose sentences in a proper manner.

From then on we studied the history of the world and geography of the world beginning with our own country; arithmetic; nature study with rambles; sewing and knitting; cookery for the older girls in a room at the Men's Clubhouse, the older boys learning woodwork in a room above. We had to wear a white apron and long white sleeves. We had physical exercise every morning in the playground.

During the First World War we collected blackberries to make jam for the soldiers, knitted scarves and collected horse chestnuts to be sent to make explosives.

In the winter when long tongues of water froze in the furrows in the fields, we enjoyed sliding on the way from school, especially if we wore clogs which were provided by a charity to those who wanted, with steel on the soles and heels. Another charity provided £1 to children leaving school when they got their first job and another £1 if they stayed in it for twelve months. Most of the girls went into service and some of the boys started on the farms.

In our leisure time we went "sticking" to gather wood for the fire and also fetched water from the parish pump opposite the post office to fill up the drinking water buckets. Rainwater was caught in wooden tubs for washing and cleaning.

We were allowed to play in any of the local fields and as the traffic through the village was only horse vehicles and bicycles we were able to play on the road.

The only reasons for absence from school were illness and flooding – when all roads out of the village became impassable.'

RED AND BLUE CLOAKS

'At Lapworth school before the days of the First World War the girls wore red cloaks and the boys navy blue, although with the war these were temporarily changed to navy blue for all, with red collars. They were given to the children by a village benefactor, Mr A D Melson, one of the school governors. He also gave the land for the Melson Memorial Ground, to be used for cricket and hockey – stipulating that it must not be used for football.

The schoolchildren all wore black stockings and black lace-up boots, and they walked to school whatever the distance, although one family who lived three or four miles away used to come in a donkey cart, leaving it parked in the lane at the back of the school until it was time to go home.'

START WITH A PRAYER

'Born in 1905 in the village of Stoney Stanton, I went to the infant school and came to Stretton-on-Dunsmore when I was ten years old. I started school and was told to sit in a seat with another girl. Her father was the village farrier. We would run home from school at lunchtime, always calling in the farrier's to see if a horse was having new shoes.

School day started with a prayer and afterwards we learned writing, reading, drawing and poetry. At about eleven o'clock we went into the playground and played hopscotch and skipping. Then home at noon for our dinner. The examinations were taken by the headmaster – we went up to his desk one at a time. The first paper had six sums; I remember having five wrong and one correct. The master said, "I do not know how you got that one right". I knew – I had copied it from my friend.

We used to do concerts and I remember on one occasion we were a garden; we had to lie down on the platform as if we were asleep. Then I had to get up and say, "I am a daffodil – an early flower of Spring." The other children were flowers of different names.

Every Sunday morning the vicar would call at the school where we would be in line in the playground ready to march behind him to church. Our summer outings were a visit to Stoneleigh.

After school was over we would play on the village green. One of our favourite pastimes was making paper boats and then floating them on the brook that runs through the centre of the village, and following them to see how far they would go; this meant scrambling under the bridges that span the brook and so to the meadows beyond. In those days the water level was much higher than it is

125

today and many a child got a good soaking and probably a good smacking as well.'

A LITTLE RC SCHOOL

'I started school in the little RC school in the Priory Road, Alcester, in 1919, when I was ten years old. As I came from Birmingham, where I had attended a private convent school, this was a strange experience for me.

The building consisted of one large room, divided into two by a wood and glass screen with a connecting door, and which could be folded back if necessary. One side was for the infants and the other for children from seven to 14 years.

There were two porches, one for girls and one for boys, with racks of hooks for outdoor clothes, and in the corner of each was a brown stone washbasin (no hot water of course), each provided with a cake of pink carbolic soap, and on the door was a huckaback roller towel which was changed twice a week by the caretaker. Outside the porches were the toilets, four for the girls and infants, and two and a urinal for the boys. These were flushed automatically every so often, and the toilet bowls were like large round pipes with an unvarnished seat on top.

Each classroom had a fireplace, the only method of heating, and the caretaker would arrive very early to light the fires and always had a lovely one going by the time we got to school. There was a large fireguard round each grate, and any wet coats were hung over them to dry.

School was from nine till half past twelve with a half-hour break. We all went home to dinner and came back at two until four.

There were two teachers in my time, one for the infants whom we called "Teacher", and one for the juniors and seniors we addressed as "Governess". They were sisters, both unmarried, but could they keep discipline! The Governess had a small wooden clicker to call us to order, but her desk held a cane which she did not hesitate to use if necessary. The morning began by the communicating door being opened and we would all sing "Good morning Governess", "Good morning Teacher", accompanied by a curtsey from the girls and a salute from the boys.

Then followed morning prayers and a hymn. The register was taken and the number of scholars was written on a small blackboard and put up on the mantlepiece, usually about 63 altogether.

Some of the desks held two pupils and some four. Each had inkwells and every morning the ink monitor would go round with a large can of ink and fill up each well. Pellets of blotting paper soaked in ink were favourite missiles for the boys to flick with their rulers at the girls.

All through the day, the fire monitors had to keep the fires going and often had to fill up the big coal scuttles from the mound of coal out in the playground.

Lessons were taught mainly by rote or by copying off the blackboard. Tables were chanted every day from twice times to twelve times, old fashioned you may say but I've never forgotten. Slates were used at first for arithmetic and when the sums were marked correct, were copied into our best books, using our pens with Waverley nibs. We had a lot of dictation and spelling and of course Religious Instruction.

A small building across the Birmingham Road opposite the school was used by the boys for woodwork, and by the girls for cookery. This was done on a large range, no gas fires, but I remember the tasty dishes we made there.

The playground was divided into two as the boys were segregated from the girls. We used to play hopscotch, skipping and ball games, and round singing games like "The farmer's in his den", "Old Roger is dead", "Nuts in May", "Oranges and lemons" or "I sent a letter to my love", and "Giant strides". We had physical training in the playground too when the weather was dry, and also a form of basketball.

We also learnt plain sewing and knitting. I well remember having a severe reprimand for holding up admiringly a pair of knickers I had just made, because there were boys in the classroom.

One day in the summer term we had our school outing. After a tea of paste sandwiches, buns and mugs of tea in the classrooms, we were taken by charabanc, a rare treat as none of our parents had motorcars, to a field about a mile out of Alcester. Swings had been put up on some large trees and we had egg and spoon races, sack races, skipping races, and the winners received packets of sweets as a reward.

We always had a concert at Christmas, usually a pantomime performed on two nights. The first performance was for the school governors, the parish priest, the teacher's mother and any local dignitaries. After this show a large hamper was unpacked containing a present for each pupil. They were given by a wealthy local family and consisted of boots and stockings for the boys and underclothing for the girls. My share one Christmas was a pair of navy serge knickers! On the second night, the parents were invited; how we prayed that it wouldn't snow and keep people away.

The health of the children was looked after by the "nit-nurse" as we called her, who regularly inspected us for head lice, and a dentist who made periodic visits and actually extracted teeth on the premises. A big iron kettle was put on the fire to provide boiling water for him.

In spite of all the shortcomings we had very happy schooldays and when I was twelve I was quite sorry to leave the little school, but as I failed to pass the exam to go to the local grammar school my parents took me away and I returned to a private school in Birmingham.'

SCHOOL IN STRATFORD

'My school days in Stratford pre-1920 were at a private school, run by two old ladies who were very particular. You had to wear galoshes – rubber overboots – if it was wet. I remember that when we started writing we commenced with what they called pot-hooks and eventually we had copy books of bold handwriting, which we had to copy. I didn't stay at this school very long and I went to another one nearer to home, and also run by two elderly single ladies. One was very strict and the other very soft. They gave us a good grounding. We all learnt reading by reading a passage out of the Bible every morning. We had slates and slate pencils instead of exercise books and a wet sponge to erase our efforts so that they could be used again. Every afternoon we had to go to the older pupils to be tested in our spellings and tables. A lot of this was by rote which has impressed it upon our minds throughout our life. We learnt the rivers of Britain by rote too! London on the Thames, Cardiff on the Taff, Liverpool on the Mersey, etc. In History we learnt the stories of the Kings, like Alfred burning the cakes and Canute trying to stop the tide, the Princes in the Tower, Henry VIII and his wives and the dates 1066 and all that. We also did music and religion. When we were nine we went to the council school so that we would be able to pass the examination for the secondary schools.

There were no biros in those days, you had to have a pen with a nib in it and put it in an inkpot which was fixed in the desk. The ink was made from a powder and water, and the inkwell had to be filled frequently because they dried up, especially in the summer. There were many types of nibs: Relief, Jay, Waverley, Hughes Mercantile (which was made in Birmingham and down Newtown Row, I think). You would pick the nib that you liked best. Some had fine points and others rather thick, like the Relief, some nibs were scratchy and others ran very smoothly. Then you had to have blotting paper to dry the ink as you wrote, otherwise you could smudge it or make a big blot when you refilled your pen from the inkpot. This was a

128

mark against you if your work was not neat and tidy, and if you got ink on your clothes it was difficult to get out.

You mostly left school at 14 if you went to the council school and 16 if you had been able to pass the examination to get into a secondary school. You had longer holidays at the secondary school – six weeks in the summer whilst you only had a month at the council school. Often you were able to get a weekend job of delivering goods from the shops to the homes of the purchasers, who usually gave you a tip of a penny or twopence. This was very welcome because you could probably collect more in tips than the shopkeeper paid you. The wage was usually five shillings.'

SCHOOLDAYS BETWEEN THE WARS

For the next generation very little had changed. Most still received their education in a small village school coping with all ages from three to 14, with few mod cons and very little equipment. Discipline was strict, and outings few. Yet many look back with gratitude to those hard working teachers who gave us a grounding in education in a hard world.

HANDKERCHIEFS AND NO NOISE

'We did handkerchief drill to make sure we were quite clear of snuffly noses, the actions demonstrated by the teacher. Girls were supposed to keep their handkerchiefs tucked in their knicker legs.

At about eight years of age we learned to do "real" or cursive writing, with a straight pen dipped in an inkwell. Blots and crossed nibs!

In the classroom children were mostly confined to their desks, which were in straight rows. Leaving one's seat was not encouraged, and neither was noise of any sort. If you finished your work, you were told to sit up with arms folded in front of you.'

NITS AND GOOSEBERRY BUSHES

'Head lice were rife in schools. Even children from good homes were often unfortunate. The worst cases were excluded from school until given the all clear by the "nit nurse", as we so rudely called her. The treatment was frequent washing with hard, vile smelling soap, and combing with a sharp tooth comb to remove live lice.

I expect we were very naive, but at the age of ten I didn't know my mother was pregnant until she had gone into hospital where my youngest brother was born. The popular story was that babies were found under a gooseberry bush. Sex was never mentioned before the children.

Teachers were spinster ladies – marriage marked the end of their career.'

GETTING THERE

'The school-age children of Ashow all had to attend Stoneleigh school and we had to walk there, a matter of about three or four miles in all kinds of weather. We seemed to get much more severe winters than we do now. The schoolroom had one of the old pot-bellied stoves in it and in the winter there was always a kettle boiling on it. When it was very cold the teacher, who was a kind soul, used to make all the children who had had to walk so far a hot drink of Horlicks or cocoa and she paid for it herself. We had to take sandwiches for our lunch and she made us another hot drink then, because the village men were only farm workers and could not afford to pay for luxuries like hot drinks at school. The teacher also used to dry our wet clothes round the stove ready for the long walk back to the village. It wasn't until the late 1920s that the parents in the village managed to get a bus to take the children to school.'

'Our school was nearly two miles away, as were the church and the nearest shops. We walked of course. The lanes were rough and muddy, but on the whole we enjoyed it. Often we got wet through and had to have our clothes dried by the classroom fire. We went in a group, playing games on the way, from simple tag to whip and top or bowling a hoop. We knew the names of the wild flowers, birds and animals, and delighted in picking mushrooms, or watercress, catkins, pussy-willow and wild flowers to take home to Mother. We knew where the violets grew, and where to find the best hazelnuts, walnuts and conkers. We were a healthy, happy bunch and we were never bored. Of necessity we took sandwiches for school lunch – there was no such thing as school dinner, and the only concession we had was that we were allowed to make a hot drink, this duty being left to the older girls. As was usual in those days it was an all-age school and pupils attended from as young as three up to 14 years

130

old. It worked very well as the older ones helped to look after the younger.

People often wonder how large families like ours were raised in such a small cottage, but they forget that the difference in age between the eldest and the youngest was about 20 years. As the girls left school they went into service where they received bed and board and some very meagre wages in return for domestic chores. My sisters were nice looking and intelligent, and it must have been hard for them to work for what were often their intellectual inferiors who happened to be better off. However, they all learned cookery and housekeeping skills, and to some extent social graces from a somewhat grander lifestyle than they were used to.

The boys lived at home until they married, and in my family they worked for my father who had a small building business. There was not a great diversity of jobs to be had by either males or females, and the opportunity for further education was practically non-existent. In any case it was essential for offspring to earn as soon as possible. I and other younger members of the family were fortunate in having the opportunity to receive a better education as scholarships were introduced, but there was never any question of going on to college or university for which today we would almost certainly have qualified.'

ONE SCHOOL FOR THREE VILLAGES

'There was one school for three villages, including us at Little Wolford, and children walked up to two miles there in all weathers, some across fields. When feet were wet, Teacher supplied slippers from a cupboard she kept for the purpose. There were two rooms, one had a fire and the other an old stove and we were always cold in winter. We rarely heard the teachers called by their real names, they were always known as Teacher and Governess. Books were in very short supply as was everything else – one history book and one geography book and a few well worn readers.

We had a Christmas party with a very large tree, tea and games. The teacher dressed a doll for the tree and it was given to one of the older girls whose name was picked out of a hat. There were races in summer, with small prizes and tea. Very occasionally we were allowed a half day holiday. Governess always threatened to wash out our mouths with carbolic soap if she heard anyone swearing.'

INFANTS SCHOOL, RUGBY

'I was born in Rugby on the 8th December 1922, the youngest of three children. My school life began in September 1926. It still remains one of my most vivid memories. Being the first day back after the summer holidays, my mother put me in the push chair and we took my brother aged five and my sister aged six to school. As it was Monday, market day, Wood Street was alive with cows being driven to the cattle market, trucks full of sheep, and ponies and traps, most of which carried hens, ducks, rabbits, etc. It was quite difficult to arrive at school with clean shoes. As my mother was making sure my siblings were in pristine condition I ran into the school. When she came to take me home I made such a fuss that the headmistress came to see what was wrong. She talked to my mum, asked me some questions – the one I remember was, "Can you go to the toilet by yourself?" I must have given the right reply – because I was taken by the hand and led to the intake class. Thus began my love affair with school.

Wood Street Infants is my special memory. The building, not large as schools go today, was and is quite plain, you could say ugly. Red brick, square, two storeys only. Downstairs was "Infants" and upstairs "Senior Girls" (as juniors we went elsewhere). The playground was a sort of tarmac and on the lower side was a netball court for the senior girls. Up the slope to the left were the lavatories. Our school consisted of three classrooms all interconnected by huge sliding glass-panelled doors. This made life very difficult for the teachers as they were not soundproof and we could see what was going on next door. Every girl had her handkerchief pinned to the front of whatever she wore. This was later changed to a pocket sewn to one's knickers. Girls wore a pinafore that went over the head and tied at the back.

School days were very simple. Doors were opened and each child stood quietly as the teachers came in – "Good morning children," said Miss Midgely, the headmistress. "Good morning Miss Midgely," we said in unison. We then sang a hymn, the words on a blackboard (if you could read), then a short prayer after which the doors closed. Our own teacher then greeted us – we replied – the register was marked and the day began. I was seated in the front row under the teacher's nose. Slates were given out and pieces of chalk. Letters and numbers were put on the board for us to copy. Lots of rubbing out went on with pieces of rag. No wonder we wore pinafores – chalk is very messy. Teacher read to us and we repeated lines of simple poems and songs, played with bricks, jigsaws, dolls' houses and in the sand table. Every afternoon we had to rest. Our tables were turned upside down, canvas hammocks slotted over the legs and we had a small pillow and blanket. Whilst we rested the teacher read to us. Sometimes some of us dropped off.

Much was made of "Special" days throughout those early years. Harvest Festival came first. Produce from the allotments was brought and later taken to the workhouse in Lower Hillmorton Road and to one of the orphanages. Class work was geared for several weeks to this event, as it was for all the other special days. We loved making the pictures, learning the hymns and songs. Halloween caused much excitement – we made witches' hats, cut out cats, spiders, cauldrons, brooms etc. Guy Fawkes again created much noisy excitement. I remember that first year, the teacher brought sparklers and we each held one. The boys got naughty and tried to frighten us girls by waving the sparklers close to our hair. What wonderful bonfire parties we had!

Preparations for Christmas started then, to make gifts for Mum and Dad. The ones I remember making were of wallpaper. For Mum a needlecase, two pieces of flannel stitched to the crease, knitting wool made into plaits and glued either side of the opening, a needle, a pin and a safety pin stuck into the flannel. A masterpiece! My mother used it for years. Dad's was also useful. A pad of tissue papers stuck to wallpaper with a loop of wool to hang it up. This was to wipe his razor whilst shaving. Paper chains were made by the yard, also stiff paper lanterns. The latter we coloured in patterns, then cut and glued, they looked wonderful. A card was also a must. Nativity plays were rehearsed, carols and poems learnt. Then a tea party and Santa Claus rounded off the winter term.

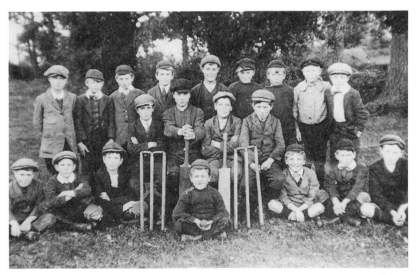

School cricketers at Bourton c1920. A cap was essential wear for every small boy!

133

Valentine's Day was remembered, and Pancake Day, when we tried to outdo each other by bragging how many we had eaten. On St George's Day, 23rd April, we went next door to St Philip's church for a service, paraded the flags in the school yard, sang patriotic songs then had the rest of the day off. May Day was celebrated by crowning the May Queen with her escort of attendants. Here we put our country dancing to the test. As we had no school hall, practice was very limited. May 24th was Empire Day. For this we rehearsed a play and tableaux and for weeks our parents concocted outfits to represent the countries of the Empire. I loved dressing up. My Dad was very good making the outfits etc. We danced round the maypole, wore daisy chains and we went to school in our Sunday clothes, white socks and best shoes. I'm sure the sun always shone on this particular day. In the last few weeks of the school year we had "tests" and took the report home to let our parents know of our progress. A signature was required by the teacher next day to prove we had given up the report.

One particular day out of routine comes to mind. In the middle of class we were told to put down our pencils (I was in a higher class then) and to file in an orderly fashion into the yard. What was wrong? Nothing! The airship R101 was passing over the school. It was so low we could see the men waving to us. I thought it was the most fantastic sight I had ever seen and I still think so today more than 60 years on.'

STUDLEY SCHOOL

'We attended the Catholic school in New Road, Studley. The headmistress was a nun, Sister Joseph-Marie, and an older nun took the six and seven year olds. The other teachers were all single women (a rule in those days – married women left teaching).

Discipline was strict, but on Friday afternoons the "Baby" (Reception) class had a tea party. New starters came to this. One day when I was four, Granny took me round, just for tea. Great trays of home-made jam on buttered crusty bread were followed by hunky pieces of plain fruit cake. The 13 year old Top Class girls helped prepare and serve the meal. I loved it, except for the tea which was handed round in chipped enamel mugs. The year was 1929, I was too young to understand the hardship many families endured. My own mother was not the only one to die and leave a young family; three other girls in my class were orphans too. Three children died of TB before leaving school, and one of diphtheria.

The school had over 100 pupils, divided into six classes, each having upper and lower halves. The playground was divided into two parts, boys and girls. Children under seven went out to play at different times from the seniors. The toilets consisted of small cubicles in a row. Through them passed a large round sewer pipe of fast flowing water – no need to flush. In each cubicle was a ceramic seat, graded from tiny to adult sizes, perched on an opening into the sewer pipe. Anything which went into these openings was swiftly washed away, so you may imagine the smaller children were scared at first to use these toilets. A few years after I started school new toilets were built, and the old ones disappeared.

Older children were taken to play in the village "Rec" or playing field. The girls had hockey or rounders and the boys cricket and football, bravely taken by a lady teacher.

The senior boys learnt gardening, in a part of the church grounds, while the girls learnt sewing, plain machine, and embroidery. When war came we were glad of these useful arts – if one can do embroidery, one can mend most things.

On Derby Day all the older children were crowded into the top classroom to listen to the race on the radio. I couldn't understand the enthusiasm and the holiday atmosphere among the teachers, and I'm afraid it meant very little to me. However, I very much enjoyed the radio lessons for schools and the BBC booklets we were given to go with the broadcasts.

In the 1950s my own children attended the same school. Married women were by now acceptable as teachers and there was a more modern cheerful feel to the place. School dinners were served – so different from the hot chocolate-flavoured Horlicks and home-made sandwiches of my days there. Soon after the school had its 100th anniversary the nuns departed to a large new school in Birmingham. The old school is used for industry now. The little convent is offices, and the garden where the nuns prayed aloud as they worked is a car park.'

SCHOOL TERRORS

'I was the only girl to pass the eleven plus in my year. I started grammar school petrified. I had to go on a train, which was new to me. I had come from a village school of 50 to 60 pupils to a school of hundreds!

We were told to take our books home and cover them with brown paper. This was an unheard of luxury to me, we re-used paper from the few parcels we received and we didn't know where to buy brown paper from. Already I was the odd one out. I also had a hand-knitted cardigan, very different to the shop bought ones – and the wrong shade of green! And they had leather satchels and I didn't.

135

Pupils at Hill Girls School, Sutton Coldfield (then part of Warwickshire) in 1924. School life did not change a great deal until the coming of the 1950s.

Sports were terrible, wearing school knickers and tee shirts. We just weren't brought up to show our underwear, let alone in the playground! And communal showers were the most horrendous hell on earth – I'd never seen them before or other girls naked. Oh, what a shy, terrified eleven year old I was.'

SCHOOL OUTINGS

'There were several cinemas in Nuneaton, two miles away, and if any historical or literary films were showing, arrangements were made for our school to go from Stockingford. We had to pay for ourselves. We also had to walk in twos with a teacher in charge, and we had to behave. There was also an annual swimming gala in which all Nuneaton schools took part, and once again we walked the two miles there.

When we reached top class there was the annual outing. It was London my year, and not many of us had been that far on a train, let alone going on the Underground. I can still remember everything that happened that day.'

'An early school outing is remembered at Radford Semele to Henley in Arden, when the children went in two horse-drawn carriages. Later a trip to Edge Hill was undertaken in a charabanc, when all the pupils had to alight to help push the vehicle up the hill.'

STRICT DISCIPLINE

'At school at Dosthill discipline was strict, but was never any apparent problem. The headmaster was often asked by parents to punish their child if he had been caught in some serious misdemeanour. Offenders were caned in front of the assembled school.'

'Radford Semele school was considered to be a good school with strict but fair discipline. One recollection is of a teacher who kept discipline in her class by rapping the children over the head with her thimble or poking them with a knitting needle – the method depending on what she was doing at the time.'

'At Tanworth in Arden schoolboys were expected to touch their caps when meeting adults. Punishment consisted of the cane – a thick one was known as the "swearing cane" and was used if any bad language was used. A thinner cane was used for other punishment.'

'Discipline at our school was strict. The headmistress had a cane to punish really naughty children and a Black Book in which to enter their names and why they were caned. The Black Book scared me more than the cane because it would be a permanent record. I never did get the cane, although I received several "smackings" on my forearm for minor misdemeanours.'

'My younger brother and I had only one term at the village school, as we joined a number of other children over eleven years of age to walk to school in Stratford. The village headmistress was very unpopular because of her severe discipline. She was so unkind, particularly to the slower scholars. I remember her hitting one boy continually, he was sobbing and gasping for breath. He did not return to school again, he was too ill. Sometimes in sewing lessons this teacher would hit you with the thimble on her finger. Of course talking in class was not allowed so it was a great joy in the needlework lesson to call out quite loudly "40 cotton please" when a new needleful of thread was required. The standard of needlework was very good, as threads had to be counted to get an even row of stitching, and making buttonholes was a real work of art.'

137

SCHOOL DENTAL SERVICE

'After the war I was working in Local Government when in 1947 the first Principal School Dental Officer was appointed to organise a school dental service for the county. I used to go with a dentist to the school, where every child had a dental inspection and if necessary was offered treatment. The treatment was carried out in the school, either in a cloakroom, the head teacher's room or behind a screen in the classroom. We had a wooden folding chair, a spirit steriliser, and a foot engine or drill which operated rather like a treadle sewing machine. The instruments were kept in a small wooden cabinet with drawers in.

We used to enjoy going to the small schools in the Edge Hill area. One school in the morning and moving on to another in the afternoon. When children needed a number of extractions, another dentist and nurse came along with a portable anaesthetic machine. The children had a general anaesthetic and the teeth whipped out and after a short recovery went back to class. We often saw and treated 20 children at an anaesthetic session, all in the school. But by the 1950s mobile dental caravans were used at the rural schools and fixed clinics opened in most towns.'

INTO THE 1950s

'The years immediately following the end of the war differed little from the war years except that "aircraft warning" drills etc had been cancelled.

Life in the classroom remained one of frugal supplies and the eternal "utility", on almost every item used. Exercise books had dull covers and rough creamy paper inside, but they were as precious as diamonds. Each child had two exercise books per term – one for maths and one for English. It was part of the teacher's job to make sure that the books did last a term. Strict rules were enforced to ensure that every square inch of paper was used and I well remember telling pupils to "go back and fill in all the spaces". Paper was so scarce that the pupils brought used newspapers to school. The margins and spaces were used for spellings, mental arithmetic answers and "table practice". That done we even used the papers themselves in certain aspects of art lessons. Newspapers – a dingy off-white colour – readily absorbed water paint and were ideal for practising "patternwork", some of which was quite effective.

There were certain "Golden Rules". If you broke a ruler, or pen or pencil, you replaced it. A broken or unusable nib could be exchanged. And those pencils! You could actually get HB and H but

138

nothing else. Coloured pencils were unobtainable at the time, though some appeared in shops as early as 1948. Outwardly they all appeared the same, the same semi-polished wood making every type of pencil seem identical. At the end of each afternoon if pencils had been given out, they were collected in, each one carefully checked. Teacher sharpened them to prevent wastage. The same utilitarian approach embraced every aspect. All exercise books were covered with brown paper brought from home, as were the limited text books available. These were few. But there was a sufficiency of class reading books.

The classes themselves were, in today's terms, overcrowded. The school was an all-ages boys school and during my first four years there I never taught a class of less than 50 pupils – mixed ability. Each day certain tasks had to be accomplished. A table learned, spellings to be memorised or a piece of verse to learn by heart. Inattentive or lazy pupils soon found out that when the weekly mental arithmetic and spelling tests came along, failure to reach a certain standard meant an encounter with the Head. Not an experience to enjoy. But on the whole most pupils had absorbed the habit of hard work and took pride in their achievements. Any teacher who earned the pupils' respect had no trouble coping with large class numbers. Beyond the classroom, school rules were simple but strictly applied. The school was a "workshop" and as such was respected. There was no running inside the building, no loud conversation when moving through the assembly hall. There was no "slovenliness" in dress by either pupils or teachers. Teachers wore suits and collar and tie with appropriate footwear. Teaching PT both pupils and teachers removed coats and changed footwear. We all wore "pumps" and after PT changed back, donned coats and on with the next lesson. There were no showers, nor even moments for a rub down with a towel.

Despite what seemed a very rigid discipline and routine, the school was a happy school. It was very well run and there were very few upsets. The poorer children were cared for with free clothing, free shoes and, of course, free dinners, but they were never subject to snide remarks from other people. There was always that feeling – "There but for the Grace of God". Yet, when East Coast towns suffered severe flooding these same children brought contributions of clothing in response to a national appeal.

On occasions a school trip was arranged. In 1951, for example, we all went to the Festival of Britain. The organisation preceding the journey was very thorough and practical. I remember returning to the school a few months after promotion and remarking to the Head,

"This school runs itself." To which he replied, "Shouldn't every school?"

Parents, though having no direct respresentation in the school, were always interested and helful and one of the few innovations introduced into the school in those days, was asking parents to come and talk about their jobs or interests. One such was the then Secretary of the Warwickshire Beekeepers Association, another a local farmer and another a local shopkeeper. It is difficult for us today to remember food rationing and ration cards, but these people in particular spoke of the effect on their businesses. The beekeeper had a special sugar ration, the farmer had to account for every animal and every pound of produce. He had a special petrol ration to run his tractors. The shopkeepers and ration cards! Remember how carefully they cut out the appropriate coupons?

Finally – courtesy. It is a somewhat old-fashioned word today, but not then. Pupils were brought up to respect institutions and the people running them. There were no direct lessons in citizenship as occurred later. It was understood that all teachers were "Sir" or "Miss", and outside school pupils would touch their caps when they met a member of staff. They used phrases like, "Excuse me", "I beg your pardon". They never interrupted if two adults were talking. They always stood when addressed and I recall an occasion when a 14 year old, six-footer was being punished for some misdemeanour, when the punishment concluded responded with, "Thank you, Sir". That was, in today's parlance, a "one-off" occasion, but it is true. Teachers, too, were expected to be courteous both to pupils and one another.

Altogether, though we lived through a time of "Utility", and Sir Stafford "Austerity" Cripps, both pupils and staff were proud of their school and tried hard to live up to its high ideals.'

THE WORLD OF WORK

ON THE LAND

Farming has always been the most important of Warwickshire's traditions, providing generations with a way of life hardly changed until after the Second World War. Horses were the power on the farms until then, and nothing has quite replaced the sight of those wonderful beasts at work on the ploughing or the harvesting. The latter, together with the days when the threshing machine came to the farm, was one of the highlights of the year and is remembered with nostalgia for a time now gone for ever.

MY FATHER'S FARM

'My father lived in Warwickshire for over 80 years and throughout that time he had agricultural connections. The farm he bought consisted of a red brick farmhouse with a range of excellent buildings on three sides and a house separated by a small yard on the fourth. On top of the barn was a weathervane with an ear of barley showing the date 1846. Three small cottages were also part of the purchase.

The land was divided by a road uniting two villages and the old LMS railway line formed a boundary on the northern side. In very dry summers, sparks from the engines would sometimes set fire to the banks and in turn the flames would creep to adjacent corn crops, doing damage to crops and fences. After battle, compensation was usually paid.

Fields have changed in appearance since those days. Hedges have been removed to save land wastage and time as cultivation became more mechanised and shire teams disappeared. The colourful oilseed rape crop has grown in popularity since the 1950s and fields no longer have "lands and furrows", even ground being more suitable for heavy tractor-drawn machinery.

Cows provided our main source of income then as now, but the herds are very different. Dairy shorthorns formed the basis of our herd then and of course we always owned our own bulls. I especially remember a docile white one called Basil. The cows were hand-milked with the milkers sitting on three-legged stools.

I recall the time when a neighbouring farmer had foot and mouth disease amongst his cattle. My father was away from home spending the day viewing cattle at Bingley Hall. Many of our young heifers were in a field a mile away from the farmhouse so my brother decided to risk the move and bring them nearer before a general standstill order forbidding all movement of cattle was issued by the police. The general outbreak of foot and mouth in the early 1960s also affected Warwickshire.

Our present farm is approached through a gated road and the church stands next to the farmhouse. With the dreaded outbreak being fairly near, callers were discouraged from visiting the farm. Our understanding rector closed the church for several weeks and held the services in the reading room. Farm newspapers and letters were delivered to our house which is away from the farm and visitors going into the farmyard were asked to douse their footwear in disinfectant. The bulk tanker too had its wheels sprayed on approaching and departing. Each Saturday morning the vet arrived to inspect the herd to see if early signs of the disease were visible. Fortunately there were none.

In the 1920s all sheep and cattle were driven to Nuneaton market, held every other Tuesday. On special days, such as the annual autumn sheep sale, many farmers' sons helped with the driving and school absenteeism was rife among older boys on such occasions. This greatly displeased the headmaster and next day he made each one confess as to why he had been away from school on the previous day. His reply to each was the same, "Pity they didn't sell you!"

Market days were important to farmers, Father attended whenever possible. It was here they met neighbours and friends, paid bills or received cash due to them, bought spare parts for machinery and replenished stores of bolts, nails and such like. Orders were placed for cattle and pig food and fertilisers and it provided opportunities to keep in touch with trends, prices and general farming business.

Our daily supply of milk was collected by pony and float and delivered to houses on the outskirts of Coventry. The same man collected it for 20 years and I never remember him having a day off. He always wore jacket, shirt and tie, breeches and leggings of black leather, with boots to match.

The Milk Marketing Board came into existence in 1933 bringing with it many changes. It operated manufacturing depots for processing surplus milk, so guaranteeing a market. It promoted cattle breeding by artificial insemination and farm bulls were gradually phased out. It was an important change as it gave farmers a wider choice of bulls.

Each season brought its own work load. Threshing was a winter occupation and very labour intensive too. The steam engine and threshing box would arrive in the afternoon before work was due to begin. Seven or eight men would be needed for a successful operation but casual labour was usually easy to find. I can also remember "borrowing" a man from the farm opposite, an experienced man being considered a more useful member of the team. At a later date we would loan a man in return. Word soon spread that threshing was in progress and towards the late afternoon men with sturdy sticks and terrier dogs would come on the scene hoping to kill rats as they bolted from the rick bottom. I remember when a local character with a bald head discovered a nest of young rats. He placed these squirming creatures under his cap, telling us that he would "doff his cap" to the young ladies when he walked into The Lion later that evening.

Threshing may have been picturesque to the bystander but it was hard, filthy, endless work as the steam engine drove on relentlessly making sure no one slacked! The best of the wheat would be sold, the oats retained for winter feed and the "tail" corn or small wheat would be used for the hens. Today, the one man-operated combine harvester is in stark contrast with those labour intensive days.

Haymaking, though a very busy time, had its joys too. I can remember how my father in a June heatwave would commence mowing the grass at 4 am. This was so that his beloved horses did not have to work in the hottest part of the day. For the same reason, considering his animals, no field work was done on Sundays. He would say "The horses need a day of rest, even if the men don't." But this all changed with the war and in August 1941, his diary for the 31st says "Finished cutting wheat in footpath field. Two soldiers did the stooking until dinner time. This was the first time we had ever cut on a Sunday." The last sentence was underlined. But the war brought many farm changes, particularly on the labour front.

In June 1940, three boys from Coventry who were awaiting call up after finishing at university arrived to help with haymaking. They slept in tents but ate with us. One only stayed two days as his papers arrived quickly. Number two lasted a week and the third, a week or so longer. Sadly, only two ever came home. Children helped pick potatoes in their October holiday. Pre-war my father would not have used children for this work. The War Agriculture Committee came into being and told farmers what crops must be grown. This often meant turf had to be ploughed. Food was in short supply for people and animals too.

Soldiers too came to help; we had two land girls, both living in at times, and towards the end of the war, German prisoners were allowed on farms. They were brought and collected by lorry and we were warned not to fraternise in any way. They were not particularly interested in us and spoke little English. I remember one unsolved incident that happened during their period of work. Father and Fritz had been gardening and when Father left to do the milking, he

144

forgot that he had left his jacket hanging on his spade. He went to collect it after tea only to find it had been burnt!

Later we had a couple from Coventry whose home was demolished ask for accommodation. They had a baby about eight months old and lived in one of our bedrooms until they found another home. We also provided a base for three middle aged adults who were too scared to remain in Coventry overnight. They regularly cycled out in order to feel safer and one continued to come for years because she grew to enjoy life in the country.

We too enjoyed and appreciated our environment. Father was our instructor in things natural. It was he who found us skylarks' nests and peewits too, showed us hares at play, taught us how to recognise different clouds and the kind of weather to expect. We helped in all ways we could and I remember still harvesting one night when the church clock struck 11 pm. This was during the war when double summer time was in force. We helped with the loading and often led the horses from the field to home, pulling the loaded waggons with oats, wheat or hay.

In those days oats were supposed to stand in the field in their stooks until the church bells had rung over them three times. Wheat was less fussed over. People with hens would ask if they might go gleaning after the sheaves had been removed. It was we girls who often carried the harvest teas down to the field, sometimes having ours there too if Father was present.

Mother was not actively involved with the farm but remained an excellent back-up partner to my father. She measured and recorded the daily milk supply, attended to the wages and insurance stamps and most farm correspondence.

The station axed by Dr Beeching was used frequently by farmers. We bought our coal by the truck load, fetching it from the station by horse and cart. Corn was sold and delivered via the station. Empty hessian sacks were returned by train too. There was a milk train every morning and this was the only way to reach Rugby unless one cycled as few had cars.

An entry in the diary for 21st November 1942 shows that it was the day our first tractor was bought. I'm sure this was a sad day for father although his horses remained. Bonny was a special favourite and when her yearly foal was due she would spend the night in a pen near the house. During the night Father would go to his bedroom window and call the horse by name and she would come and hang her head over the pen door. This assured him that she was well and saved him dressing and going out to see her.'

HARVESTING AND THRESHING

'My parents came to live at Monwode Lea Farm, Over Whitacre, in the spring of 1919 when I was 18 months old. Monwode Lea Farm was part of the Ansley Hall Estate which was owned by William Garside Phillips, the manager of the Ansley Hall Coal and Iron Company. The farm comprised 125 acres and we had 20 dairy shorthorn cows, the popular breed of the time. We employed a cowman, a waggoner, and casual labourers.

At harvest time the corn was cut with a binder pulled by three horses driven by the waggoner. My father and the men had to go and set up the stooks to dry the corn. Oat sheaves were left out in the field until they had heard the church bells three times, ie they were in the field for three weeks before they were loaded onto a horse-drawn dray or waggonette. The stooks were loaded and unloaded with "pykles" (pitchforks) into the Dutch barn where they were stored until they were thrashed (threshed).

Between September and June, Bill Wright, who drove the thrashing engine, would be asked to come to the farm to thrash the corn. If he was working at the neighbouring farm, he would call and enquire when he was needed. If they had finished at the previous farm, they would pack up and go to the next farm, travelling along the road at night with only a small oil lantern to guide them. This would be the equivalent of a ten watt bulb. The steam engine would pull up alongside the Dutch barn, approximately two feet from the side of the bay. In order to get the steam up the thrashing team, comprising of the driver and his mate, would arrive at the farm at six o'clock in the morning. Firstly they cleaned out the flues which were at the front of the engine. Then they fetched coal from the coal house, which my father had previously collected from Ansley Hall Colliery with the horse and cart. The coal was put in the tender in readiness for stoking as required.

The men would come into the house for breakfast. This would consist of a big plate of porridge with treacle on it, followed by thick, fat, home-cured bacon served with eggs and fried bread and a pint mug of tea. I always remember that when they sat at the table there would be two black marks on the tablecloth, where they had been sitting. For the next meal my mother would turn the tablecloth over so that the marks did not show! At ten o'clock we would take them a huge basket of bread and home-made cheese and a can of tea. This was locally called "snap" but my mother called it "baggin". The engine was closed down during the tea break as all the members of the team were required to man the thrashing machine. This would give them time to go to the "W", the privy in the back garden. The

146

next meal was dinner at twelve o'clock. This was a hot meal cooked in black cast-iron saucepans on an open fire on the range; hot boiled meat served with white sauce, swedes, cabbage and pepper and salt. Afterwards, they would eat boiled pudding made with suet known as "sueey pudding". Only water was given to drink. They had another white enamel mug of tea at three o'clock. They went home at five o'clock having cooled the engine down by damping it with a wet sack and a plate of metal over the chimney. The driver and his mate along with the followers cycled home, dirty, tired and hungry.'

'Threshing was a major activity calling for co-operation between all the farmers, as to get the drum up Ilmington Hill all the horses that could be provided were needed. Eleven horses, five teams of two and a "filler" in the shafts, got the heavy equipment up the hill – no farmer was keen that his horses should be in front because of the additional burden, so the honour usually went to the least likely pair. The farms were threshed in turn, up one side of the hill and down the other.'

THE FARM WORKERS

'As most farm workers at Great Alne lived rent-free in tied cottages, they were "on call" for work at any time of day or night and even the wives had to work long hours. They were called on for potato picking, stone picking, sprout picking, beet thinning, and helping at harvest time. One lady recalled a villager having the job of turkey plucking before Christmas – as her cottage was so small, she had to do the plucking in the living room with the family and their food all around her.

The farmers always gave harvest suppers for their workers. With farm wages being very low, these dinners were a great highlight of the year. As well as good food and drink there were games with prizes, one lady still has the knitting bag she won for "Kim's Game". At Christmas, the farmer gave each worker a large piece of beef and a plum pudding, on condition the basin was returned for next year! One 80 year old lady who had been married to a farm worker told me that her husband always cut the children's hair and mended their shoes. Clothing was expensive so vests etc were washed in the evening, put on the oven to dry overnight and then put back on in the morning.

Until about 1920, a local farmer's wife made cheese regularly for market. This particular farmer had an interesting idiosyncracy. Anyone who came to the door was offered a drink. He would go down to the cellar, draw a large mug of cider and then, standing at

147

the head of the stairs, would say "Good Health", take a drink from the mug himself, and then pass it to the visitor.

The bridge over the river Alne was built by subscription from the local farmers. The stipulation on size was that it must be wide enough to take a waggon load of hay without pulling any off the sides. Prior to the bridge being built, there was a ford.'

BUYING AND SELLING

'Cattle and sheep for Little Wolford were bought and sold at Shipston, Banbury and Stratford markets, horses at Stow Fair. Some farmers went to Scotland or to the Welsh borders to buy sheep and cattle, and these would be brought back to Shipston or Moreton stations and driven from the stations on the hoof.'

SHEPHERDING

'My husband Robert, born at Old Milverton, near Leamington Spa, started working with his father at Park Farm in the village when he was 13 years old. Ten shillings a week was his wage, rising to 29 shillings when he became 21.

He always said that being a shepherd was not a job but a calling. You had to know your sheep and how to treat their various ailments. At lambing time he was often out all night and at the end of the season received extra payment for each surviving lamb. When the lambs were a fortnight old their tails were removed and he would always bring them home for me to make lambs tail pudding. It tasted delicious.

For his work on the farm Robert wore thick breeches and leggings. He couldn't afford an overcoat so he put a sack around his shoulders to keep out the cold. A good sheepdog was worth a man's wages and he cherished the shepherd's crook which had belonged to his father.

A couple of weeks before shearing time all the sheep were taken down to the river Avon and washed. The fleece had to be loose and fuzzed-up before it could be removed. In those days it took 15 minutes to hand shear a sheep and the shepherd was paid sixpence per animal. They were normally dipped a month after shearing.

Crops to feed the sheep included vetch, a type of pea grown for forage which acted as a medicine. They were also fed swedes and mangolds. Each field where they grazed was wired off into strips so that the sheep could be moved regularly to fresh feeding grounds.

Back in the 1920s and 1930s every man who lived in old Milverton worked for the Guys Cliffe estate or on farms in the village.'

148

'A farm process we loved to watch when I was a child at the turn of the century was sheep washing. The brook was dammed up and let out by a sluice gate into a square brick bath into which the protesting sheep were thrown by two men using a stick under the sheep's belly. The shepherd stood on a plank across the sluice gate like some priest at a religious ceremony, with a long-handled tool with which he pulled the sheep by the neck under the rushing water. When released they went baaing and dripping up a ramp to their pen. Not only was this done to our own sheep, but from other farms at Sutton under Brailes came flocks – payment and accounts of this were kept by the shepherd who could neither read nor write. He had a system of his own of notches on a stick to keep accounts and my father said he was sure he never cheated anyone of a penny. He, like so many of the real countrymen, was a fine character.'

WE HAD 40 ACRES

'I was born in 1932 and I lived with my parents at Malt House Farm, Meer End near Kenilworth. I left school just before my 14th birthday and started work on my father's farm.

We had 40 acres, with eleven milking cows, calves and heifers, which were two years old. I was up every morning at six, Sunday included, with one half day off per week which was Saturday

Freda started work on her father's 40 acre farm at Meer End before her 14th birthday. Horses like Starlight and Dick were still widely used on the land in the 1940s.

149

afternoon. I helped milk cows by hand and feed all the animals including pigs and the two carthorses – Starlight and Dick. Then we went for breakfast, which would be perhaps bacon from our own pigs, eggs, fried bread and toast – that would keep me going until one o'clock when we had a cooked dinner. I could plough with two horses, cut the grass for hay for winter feed, and cut and lay hedges, which was a winter job.

My mother looked after the 600 laying hens. We hatched our own chickens; the eggs were put into an incubator which would hold about 100 eggs, heated by paraffin. The eggs were turned twice a day to stop the yolk sticking to the shell; we put a mark on the egg then we knew if we had turned them over. Any surplus chickens were boxed up and sent either to Hampton in Arden market or to Knowle and sold as hatched. When we had electricity and mains water put on about 1948/49 it did make things easier especially for my mother.

It was a hard life but I enjoyed it. It was healthy and I was happy, I would do it all over again if I had the chance.'

FARMING IN THE 1950s

'In 1951 when we started farming at the Leasowes neither of us had a farming background, our sum total of experience was two years, plus one year each at Agricultural College. Talk of fools rushing in!

The Leasowes (about 250 acres) happened to fall vacant in March 1951, as the elderly tenant had decided to retire. We were due to marry on 21st April. I was 21, Fred nearly 23. For a month we hurried between the farm and my home in Nottingham, milking the cows, feeding the calves, and preparing for the wedding. A young man from Yardley would cycle out each day to do some of the work and one of the other tenant farmers kept an avuncular eye on us. He was quite certain we would get in a terrible mess and give up after a couple of years! Our wedding happened, we had a brief honeymoon, then back to work with a vengeance, up at 6 am to milk the cows. It was noses to the grindstone from the outset.

However, it was quite a good time to start farming. We were young, enthusiastic, hardworking, we had family capital behind us and there was a postwar food shortage which meant that unlike today, everything we produced had a ready market. The farmer was a "hero"! Subsidies were paid to encourage maximum food production and to keep the price down for the consumer. Advice from the Ministry of Agriculture was free and easily obtainable.

We took over a herd of diseased TB-ridden cows, some skinny potbellied calves, a tractor stuck up to its axle in mud and another which would not start. There were no stockproof fences and the

150

stock roamed at will, most of the ditches were blocked and the fields deeply rutted and waterlogged. Mud came right up to the front door, the drive was a mile long and full of ruts and potholes.

The house had hardly been touched since Victorian days; no water, no inside loo, no bathroom, dark brown paint and gloomy floral wallpaper, and sadly – no kitchen range and no inglenooks but rather nasty 1930 tiled fireplaces.

Slowly we dragged the farm together, built farm workers' cottages, employed two cowmen, a tractor driver and a general worker, improved the herd and planted corn. Wages were about £5 a week and went up to £7 or £8 by the 1960s (we now farm 1,350 acres with 5 men!). Our children, four of them, arrived as a sort of by-product!

We had a 1937 Wolseley which we bought just before we married, it was in excellent condition and cost us £500. What that would be in today's prices I dread to think. It lasted us until 1957.

In those days we had little to do with the village, we were too busy, but we went to church and we bought our meat at the butcher's and groceries at the local shop, Taylor's.

I caused a minor sensation the first time I went in. I was wearing a pair of green trousers (I had lived in trousers since I left school) and one by one the staff came out from the back and peered surreptitiously over the counter. Mrs Muntz in trousers! What *was* the world coming to? I heard a customer ask who I was, and when told gave an aghast "Is it?" I did *not* fit in with the image of the squire's wife!

I did not drive in those days and the only way I could go shopping, apart from the groceries, was to take a train from Danzey to Stratford. This meant either a walk across the fields to the station or a bicycle ride by the road. Once or twice I pushed a pram two and a half miles to the station, put it on the train, pushed it around Stratford and then home again, and in those days a pram was a coach-built vehicle.

When we had been married for about a year we had our first pig. The local butcher came to kill, cut it up and salt it and the sister of our friendly neighbouring farmer came to show us how to make faggots and pork pies. I was not allowed to touch the salting pork as I was pregnant, it was said that the bacon would go "reesty" if I did! In fact, women were not supposed to touch it at all. The only way we were permitted to kill a pig was by surrendering one bacon ration for a year. In those days our grocery bill came to under £2 a week and that was when we had children.

On the farm we had a milking machine and in our first summer we bought a bailer for the hay. But the harvesting was done by a

151

binder and the sheaves were stooked, loaded and stacked by hand (a lot of it mine).

In 1957 we bought a combine harvester. It was my job to tie the bags as they were filled and to chuck them off the back. At times like this the children would be sat in the corner of the field on a rug, under the shade of a tree, where I could keep an eye on them. How they survived I shall never know.

Although we had few friends and my family lived a long way off, I do not ever remember being lonely and certainly never bored – we were farming, that was all that mattered.'

IN SERVICE

The local big house, large farmhouses, the vicarage and even fairly modest middle class homes, all provided work "in service" – particularly for young girls, whose employment prospects were limited. If you were lucky enough to work for a good family it could be a good life, and one which might provide you with a lifetime's work.

SOME OF THE HAPPIEST DAYS OF MY LIFE

'It was through my older sister Lilian that I went into service. I was the seventh of nine children, four boys and five girls and apart from a bit of childminding there was not much work in our town for 14 year old girls.

Lilian had been working as a parlourmaid for the Leveson-Gower family in Surrey when she heard of vacancies for two housemaids at the Victorian mansion home of the Wrigley family (of chewing gum fame) at Wendover, Buckinghamshire. Lilian's next post was as lady's maid to Mrs Katharine Heber-Percy at her London home in Thurloe Square, near the Victoria and Albert Museum. It was 1923 and her elder daughter, Mary, was to be presented at court which meant that there was all the excitement of coming-out parties.

When the social season ended Lilian persuaded me to leave my job as between-maid to a Member of Parliament to work for the Heber-Percy family at Guys Cliffe House, Warwick.

They were some of the happiest days of my life. I was one of four housemaids. The indoor staff also included a butler, housekeeper, governess, nanny, footman, parlourmaid, cook, kitchen and scullery maids. There was a chauffeur, several gardeners, a boots and an "odd man" whose job was to look after the acetylene and gas lamps downstairs and the candles in the bedrooms.

We housemaids had to be up before six o'clock to clean out the fireplaces, relay and light the fires. I worked mainly in the nursery wing and schoolroom and after taking Nanny King her early morning tea I would wake the Heber-Percy children.

Our next job was cleaning the bedrooms and polishing the stairs and landings before going down to the servants' hall for lunch. The food at Guys Cliffe was good and wholesome and there was always plenty of it. Not like some big houses where the family lived off the fat of the land while those below stairs were underfed.

When lunch was cleared away we would exchange our practical blue morning frocks and pinafores for more formal black dresses, white caps and starched aprons.

When the family went up to dress for dinner we filled their baths to just the right temperature or took polished brass cans of hot water to their rooms.

Evenings in the servants' hall were great fun even though we were officially on duty until the family retired for the night. A game of cards or our knitting kept us occupied and, of course, we kept our ears open for the latest household gossip.

On Sundays everyone walked across the fields to morning service at St James's church, Old Milverton. Evening service was held in the chapel at Guys Cliffe House. Attendance was obligatory, even if you were on half day off, and woe betide any servant who did not wear a black hat.

We worked six and a half days a week. Our big treat on our day off was to walk into Leamington to the Cadena Cafe on the Parade. A lovely smell of coffee greeted you as you walked through the door and a trio of lady musicians played light classics and tunes from operettas to add to the Palm Court atmosphere. Afterwards we used to go round the shops, only to look, of course, as we didn't have much to spend. But even just looking helped to give us ideas for home dressmaking and knitting.

"In by 9 pm" was the rule for domestic staff at Guys Cliffe House. Being late meant a sharp telling off from the housekeeper, Mrs Denney, and having to go to bed without your supper. Our main enjoyment away from the big house was dancing. If we wanted to go to the "penny hops" at Old Milverton or Leek Wootton we had to ask permission from the housekeeper. Oh, the fun of those village dances. We all dressed up in our best frocks, dabbed 4711 perfume behind our ears, and hoped that we would get plenty of partners.

153

No alcohol was allowed, but it didn't matter at all. We were just as jolly and happy on cups of tea, cakes and sandwiches.

Courting was not as simple as it is today when you were a live-in servant. You were not really supposed to have "followers"! I had seen this young man eyeing me on several Sundays as we walked to church and I thought he looked quite nice.

One day, after the morning service at Old Milverton, he came running down the hill, red faced and out of breath. He caught up with me at the bridge over the river and I realised that he sang in the church choir. I felt flattered that he should pay me attention but that soon evaporated when I discovered that he had been dared by the other choirboys to ask me for a date.

Robert worked at Park Farm, Old Milverton and we became friends. After walking out for three years we were married in 1929 at Old Milverton church. Married women were not allowed to be in service and, sadly, I had to leave Guys Cliffe House.'

PLAYING THE PIANO

'In 1902 my mother started work as a housemaid at the age of twelve at a private girls school in Warwick. She had just started to learn to play the piano and when she asked the headmistress if she could practise, she was told she could but only before she did her work – which commenced at six in the morning.'

IN THE STATELY HOME

'Talking to an under-butler who worked in a stately home in the early part of the century, I learned he worked from 6 am to 11 pm, or later if the dinner guests didn't want to go home or, if staying, wouldn't go to bed.

The Hall was so large and the corridors so long that at mealtimes most of the house staff stood in strategic positions along the corridors and had a signalling system to allow the under-butler to ring the gong on time. I was also told that although one saw the master of the house two or three times every day, one had to make an appointment through the head butler or housekeeper (the most important member of the female staff) to speak to him.'

CLOAKS AND COATS

'Burrells Hall, the local big house, employed a lot of people. Every Christmas the daughters of the employees would be given a red hooded cloak, and the sons a blue coat.'

154

THE LADY OF THE MANOR

'Most of the cottages in Clifford Chambers in the 1920s were owned by the lady of the manor and many of the occupants were employed as farm hands, gardeners and domestic help, so it was necessary to watch your Ps and Qs or you could lose your job and your home. Many of the villagers were close relations and it puzzled me as to how the postman knew where to deliver letters etc. When I was older and a member of the village Women's Institute, I suggested that the houses, now no more, should be numbered. Happily the lady of the manor agreed and duly went round delivering the numbers for each house, except those privately owned or named.

The manor had quite a large staff – scullery maid, cook, housemaids, footman, butler, lady's maid, all having to show great respect for their employers. In fact the lady's name was rarely used, she was always "Madam". Outside staff consisted of three gardeners, a groom and assistant, a carpenter who came from Stratford every day, and the chauffeur who also had charge of the turbine engine under the old mill. This was for making electricity for the manor. Later an engine room was built and large batteries installed to supply electricity for the use of the chauffeur, head gardener, rectory and church. The Electricity Board installed electricity for the whole village in 1933. There was a special "switching on" ceremony by, of course, Madam.'

SERVICE IN THE 1930s

'In 1935 I was working in domestic service near Ufton, having to cycle three miles each day and starting work promptly at seven o'clock. My day finished at six o'clock, seven days a week, with half a day each week when I finished at three o'clock. I was paid three shillings a week.'

'I was born on a farm over 60 years ago. My mother had a nurse living with us for a month, a fortnight before my birth and a fortnight after. She also had a live-in maid until the beginning of the war. In the afternoons the maid would change into a black dress with a white lace apron and a little white cap on her head. If we had visitors for afternoon tea, my mother would summon the maid from the kitchen with a small brass hand bell. Later this same bell was used to call the members to order at WI meetings when Mother was President.'

'When I left school in 1938 at the age of 14, the two options open to

155

children whose parents could not afford college fees, were either a job in a factory or private domestic service. The latter was to be my lot. This displeased my headmaster. He protested to my parents that I was worthy of something better; after all, I had reached the dizzy heights of "head girl". However, I took up my post as daily domestic for twelve months at five shillings weekly. I then lived in for twelve months and my wages rose to eight shillings and fourpence. The household also employed a lady two days a week to help with the washing and heavy work. She was very kind to me and always gave me two helpings of pudding. When she came, she and I used to share a big table and the family used the dining room. At other times the family used the big table and I ate at a small table on my own by the sink. I never sat with the family. The man of the house was always referred to as "the master"and the son as "Master Herbert". I have never regretted the two years spent there. I learned a lot which has stood me in good stead throughout my married life and although it was hard work and a long day, it did me no harm.'

THE UNDER-GARDENER

'Tom has been gardening all his life, both as a profession and a hobby. He left school at 14 in 1935 to work on a local farm, but only a year later was taken on at a much higher wage by the Hodgkins family who lived at Crab Mill (and still do) as an under-gardener.

Gardening and husbandry played a vital part in Ilmington village life at that time. Much of the village was made over to allotments, known as "cally" locally, and even on a Sunday evening after church whole families would walk together to "see cally". The soil was very clayey and three-tined forks were used to break up the "clats", clods of earth. Tom recalls that the Saturday work on the allotment was enlivened by the weekly game of women's hockey which took place on an adjoining field. Even the schoolchildren had plots of ground allocated to them, two children to a plot. The older ones did the digging, and sometimes an axe had to be used to chop the frosty soil.

Professor Hodgkins for whom Tom worked was a retired don of Queens College Oxford and so had two homes. Vegetables from his Ilmington home were taken down by wheelbarrow to the Longdon Street station in crates to be delivered to the Oxford (Queens College) location. Tom earned £1 a week (a good wage) and started at 8 am (one hour later than his farm-worker friends). Tom particularly remembers the feeling of "belonging" to the family; once a worker was taken on to the estate they were "really looked after" and felt an intense loyalty to the family.

From his wages, Tom would give his mother 90% and keep the

rest, sometimes earning a little extra from overtime to buy an oval tin of 30 cigarettes.

On the death of his employer, the house was rented out ("set") for some years. The proximity of Stratford on Avon led to the use of the house by some notable stage people, including Ralph Richardson, whose reference Tom still has. (The Hodgkins family is once again in residence at Crab Mill, Professor Dorothy Hodgkins being the famous Nobel Prize winner of whom the village is very proud.)

After the war Tom continued to garden for a local family who had made their money in brewing, so Tom received not only his wage but a pint of beer each day. He recalls the gardens being turned over to vegetables during the war, even the vines were cut down. The allotments were even more important and many grew corn on them to feed the family pig. One family even had their pig sties in front of the house.

Gardening techniques have altered only in as much as the arrival of compost and fertilisers have made it no longer necessary to collect the rotted beech leaves from the woods to enrich the soil for the growing of tomatoes. A lawnmower (a JP Super) was the only machine to be used, scythes still being favoured for work in the orchard, the hay being much prized. The big house made its own electricity with a diesel generator and used it to pump water from the well.

The rest of the domestic staff comprised a living-in maid, two sisters who did domestic chores, a cook, a chauffeur/handyman and his wife who assisted the cook.'

VILLAGE CRAFTS AND TRADES

In the days when villages were almost self sufficient, the blacksmith, the dairyman who also ran the general store, the saddler and the cobbler – to name only a few – were a familiar part of working life, hard working and often proud of their work and their status in the village.

THE MARKET GARDENING VILLAGE

'Welford on Avon lies in a great loop of the river Avon, once a more compact village than it is today. Standing on Cress Hill and looking eastwards over the village at blossom time, one might think that the whole parish was one vast orchard; cherry, plum and damson trees in abundance with some apples as well. One of the most evocative sounds of childhood was the rattle of pebbles in cocoa tins, strung in amongst the cherry trees as the fruit was coming to ripeness. These tins, each connected to its neighbour by string, were the means of keeping birds from pillaging the ripening fruit. As soon as it started to become light, the din began as growers pulled on the strings to scare the birds off the crop that meant so much to the economy of the village.

For Welford in the 1930s was a market-gardening village, with land cultivated in amongst the orchards, and even between the rows of trees. It was all hand work with spade, fork, dibber and hoe. The nearest thing to mechanisation was a wheeled push hoe, or the hand drills with delicately made wheels, adjustable on their axles to allow for varying row width, according to the crop. The seed box would be of wood, a metal plate with holes of varying sizes to accommodate different seeds and sowing rates, and a brush in the bottom of the box to feed the seed down into the single coulter. Seedbed preparation was sometimes by means of a single section of a light seed harrow, pulled with a rope over the shoulder. Light, wide rollers were fashioned from a tree trunk, iron-bound at the ends and set in an iron frame.

Asparagus and strawberries were two special crops in Welford. In due season, the women of the village turned out to cut and pick when the "grass" was fit and the strawberries ripe. Produce was left to be collected by carrier on the grass verges, boxes of this, punnets of that and hampers (or "pots") of fruit. Some produce was taken by horse and dray to Binton station for despatch to the Birmingham or Evesham markets.

In contrast to today, while many went to work further afield, even more were employed on the land, on local market gardens or on neighbouring farms.

There were three public houses in the village. The public bars were known as "the spit and sawdust", where the men played darts and dominoes and no ladies were allowed. On warm summer nights, outside The Shakespeare, pea pickers, all the worse for drink, would race their horses up and down Chapel Street, keeping folks awake well into the night.

The river played a big part in the life of the village. Around 20 punts and one or two rowing boats were for hire for about sixpence per hour and to be had either from The Four Alls or from "Old Man Johnson" who operated from a stretch of the river between Welford and Weston. At weekends in the summer it seemed that the whole village was on the river with their picnics. The riverside properties, of which there were many, of course had their own boats – all adding up to a busy river but, with slow moving punts instead of motor cruisers, a tranquil one. Also, walking along the river banks was popular, especially on Sundays when, for some, it was the only acceptable pastime on the Sabbath.

Welford mill was working in the 1930s, indeed well into the 1950s. The miller, covered in flour and looking like a ghost could be seen cycling through the village. The clanking of the mill machinery was a familiar sound, the bulky sacks of grain a familiar sight as were the hens picking up what was spilt. The mill wheels also drove a cider mill, and a saw mill and drilling bench. Children paddled in the shallow water of the mill race, splashed by the spray of the turning wheels, and catching minnows as and when they could. Many learnt to swim in the river and the eel trap was a favourite place to watch the water tumbling over the weir.'

THE BLACKSMITH

'The blacksmith came to Leamington Hastings once a week, on a Wednesday. He cycled from Marton, a village about two and a half miles away.

The blacksmith's shop was built on to the end of a cottage, where he had a big brick open fireplace, burning coal and coke. Close beside the fire was a huge pair of bellows, which we children loved to pump up and down to keep the fire glowing. There was a big anvil, long bars of iron, and an assortment of iron hammers and boxes of nails. The iron bars were heated to red hot and then skilfully shaped into horseshoes.

Opposite was an open brick building where the horses were tied up to have new shoes fitted. The blacksmith always wore a big leather apron. With his back to the horse's head he picked up the foot and placed it between his knees. He then proceeded to prise off the old shoes, then pared and shaped the hoof to be fitted with the new shoe. This was nailed on while still red hot, giving off a very pungent odour.

Special nails were used in frosty weather to stop the horse slipping. The charge was seven shillings and sixpence.'

'The blacksmith's shop at Coleshill stood on a large area of ground in the High Street. The local farmers used to bring their horses to be shod and their waggon and cart wheels to be tyred. I spent hours watching Jack Smitton and Sid Cooper, wearing big leather aprons and armed with hammers, blowing up the forge fire and making lots of sparks as they heated the iron and beat it into horseshoes. When a shoe was finished it was plunged into a tank of water, making a loud "cushshsh" and clouds of steam. The iron tyres were heated to a glowing red in a fire in the yard and then placed on the wheel. Water was then poured all round the rim to cool the tyre and shrink it on before it set the wooden wheel on fire – then a large jug of something was consumed by the workers to replace the liquid lost in sweat.'

'Regular visits to Jack Merralls' forge in Castle Lane, Warwick were a highlight of my childhood. I used to go with my father when his chestnut horse, Sarsaparilla, needed new shoes. I can still conjure up the sights, sounds and smells of the workshop – the clatter of hooves on the shiny, well worn cobbles and the pungent smell of horseshoes, fresh off the anvil, as they made sizzling contact with the horse's feet.

Jack, in his long leather apron and with a mass of shiny black curly hair, had the gentlest way with horses. He could calm the most nervous and fractious of animals with a few quiet words. With his son, Young Jack, he was also official farrier to racecourses all over the country and in his time he plated many famous winners. The forge moved to Friars Street, close to Warwick Racecourse, in 1968 and there is now a third generation in the business, Jack's grandson, Stuart.'

THE DAIRYMAN

'My father was a dairyman. He would get up at about half past five and after bringing my mother and me a cup of tea in bed he would load up his motor bike and truck, which was a wooden box on the side of the motor bike. Into this truck he would put churns and measures, pints and halves, hanging by the side, and buckets with similar measures and he would go to the farm.

The farm was just outside Wellesbourne. When he got to the farm milking would be in progress; electric milking had just come to the farm and the milk was tipped from the container into what was known as a cooler. The cooler was like a large tank at the top with a corrugated piece extending below like a channel and an outlet. The water would be running within the corrugated part to cool the milk. The milk was put into the tank at the top and passed over the corrugated part into the channel, then into the buckets and the churn. When my father had sufficient milk in the churn and the buckets he would procede to call at the houses which he called his particular milk round.

He would return about ten o'clock. In the meantime, at home, my mother would have had the copper on. This water would be used to wash out the churns, the buckets and the measures and all would be put in a glass conservatory which joined our house, awaiting his afternoon delivery. At about quarter to three my father began another journey to the farm, another milk round around the villages and the boy came out of school and joined my father on the round. About half past five my father returned and the boiler having been on, the water was boiling and the buckets, churns and measures were washed again and put into the glass conservatory ready to be loaded up on the truck the next morning.

There was quite a lot of competition for customers in the village. There was a similar dairyman in the village getting his milk from another farm, and there was a smallholder who had a few cows and he did a milk round using an ordinary bicycle and buckets on his bicycle. When someone new was coming into the village, dairymen would be very anxious to see who could be the first to call. My father had a printed card which he would give and it was considered a great achievement if you got in first to be the milkman calling at that house.

My parents then opened a shop. They bought a house which had a large room which had been used as a milliner's by the former occupier. To begin with, my parents bought £22 of groceries; very simple things which they knew people would need – tea, sugar, butter and margarine, and they hoped by selling milk, eggs and cream to have enough money at the end of the week to buy another similar amount. This way of doing business proved successful and people came and asked for other items, so that when the wholesaler came, who was someone from Coventry, they were able to ask for other items. Eventually most things were sold; black lead, foodstuffs, shoe polishes, vinegar, lard, all the cereals, cigarettes. The fact that there was a shop enticed other commercial travellers to call and if the wares that they offered were not being offered by any other shopkeeper in the district my father would try a small quantity to see if they sold.

People would earn about £2 a week, so that the amount of their grocery bill could not be very high. Often during the week a housewife would send children for half a pound of rice or a pound of sugar or a quarter of tea and that would be booked and a record made and a bill totalled up at the end of the week and then when the housewife came into the shop she would pay her weekly grocery bill. When someone came in for an order it could take anything up to ten minutes to serve them as they asked for the things and held a conversation as the items were weighed up. Many housewives would require the errand boy to call on them for an order, they would have written down things which they wanted to buy. The errand boy would bring the order, my father and mother would put up the orders, weighing out the things, placing them in cardboard boxes with the name of the person on them, then the errand boy would take these boxes in the large basket in the carrier on the front of his bicycle. This would take most of the time from the end of the morning milk round till it was time to start the afternoon one.

Milk was delivered twice a day, morning and afternoon, seven days a week including Sundays, Christmas Day and the bank holidays. In about 1936 there was a change from churns and buckets and measures, when dairies started to use glass bottles for their milk. The bottles which were used were of rock glass and they came from Glovers in Stratford, the agricultural merchants, and the name of my father and the dairyman's address were in paint on the outside of the glass; my father chose purple. The milk was in half pint bottles, pint bottles and quart bottles and at the top of the bottles was a small rim which would receive a cardboard top. This top had "We aim to please, quality our guarantee" and a little cow printed on. There was a small round tab which you used to lift out the top which had sealed the milk. To wash these bottles was a much more difficult task than washing the buckets and churns!'

A FARMING COMMUNITY

'Newbold on Stour was mainly a farming community, with five farms and associated crafts and industries.

Corn was ground at Talton Mill at one end of the village and baked

162

into bread at Newbold Mill at the other end, and then delivered by the baker in pony and trap.

A saddler was established in the village, catering not only for its needs but also those of a wider area. In the 1950s he also had a contract to make martingales to take horse brasses made in Birmingham and sold in the USA. A village street is named after him. His former apprentice now carries on the craft in nearby Shipston on Stour.

The village also had a blacksmith, a shoe repairer and a tailor.'

Mabel Penn, postwoman, was able to take advantage of the new opportunities for women's employment opened up in the villages by the First World War.

'The cobbler's shop at Tiddington was always visited with pleasure whenever a pair of shoes needed "mending". Mr Robbins lost both legs in the Great War and was taught the craft on discharge. The workshop was attached to his home and had a cosy stove to warm it in the winter. He would sit astride a bench behind his last and select a suitable sheet of leather from which the soles would be cut, he would then hammer away or else make holes in the new sole using an awl and hand-stitch this to the shoe using two lengths of waxed thread which were worked through the holes in both directions.

Many were the interesting tales he would tell us – a man full of fun who enjoyed life. He always acted as doorman at all the local dances and the highlight of the evening was when he took the floor with his daughter for the last waltz – this was truly amazing to see.

The undertaker would have a busy three days, often working through the night as well, when someone died, as coffins were made by hand, each one made to measure. A saw cut was made at the shoulders and the sides bent over steam to get the correct shape, each one a masterpiece – there was no mass production then.

The bier had to be collected from the church and the coffin was then pushed by four bearers followed by the mourners, the undertaker walking at the head setting the pace.

My father in law had his own business and many tales he could tell, some amusing, some sad. One gentleman had already selected the timber for his coffin and from time to time would say, "George, it's time to turn that oak to keep it in good shape for when I need it." It was the custom to be paid "while the tears were in their eyes" and on one occasion he was asked to accept a grandfather clock as payment, as they had no money saved to meet the funeral expenses.'

'I have lived in Barford all my life, as did my parents, grandparents and great-grandparents. My father was a lorry driver, delivering agricultural implements to local farmers, but before that he worked for his father and his grandfather, who founded W J Inson & Son, haulage contractors. They started the business using horses and carts for transporting items, then moved on to steam engines, and finally lorries. They also had some land off Wasperton Lane which they farmed, and my father used to tell how he would be haymaking at midnight on hot summer nights. This was during the war when we had double summer time.

My grandfather on my mother's side was a farmer, and also kept the butcher's shop. One of my earliest recollections is being taken up the lane by my grandfather with my cousin John, both of us riding in the butcher's basket on the front of Grandad's bike. We used to have family picnics on the farm, Granny providing the food and cold tea in bottles. Everyone who was able bodied was expected to work on the land at busy times like harvest, haymaking and potato picking.

My uncle Bob was a painter and decorator. He was very fond of brown and cream and would paint every room in these colours if you were undecided about what you wanted. He also did a bit of undertaking in his spare time and I can remember the bier being kept in his garage.'

'The stonemasons at Ilmington were skilled and knowledgeable. They were responsible not only for dry stonewalling, an art now almost lost, and stone building, but for some of the restoration at Ettington Park. They also made gravestones, and some in the churchyard show particularly good lettering. The traditional skills of stone building are happily still present in the village.

At the turn of the century or thereabouts gangs of mowers from the village used to travel south for the earlier hay crops of Middlesex and work their way north even as far as Cheshire. Great was the surprise of one when he was charged in the south one shilling for a hair cut, which in his own village would have cost him twopence.

Soon after 1920 tree fellers also worked away from the village, taking with them on bicycles their tools and food for the week, including apple dumplings. They would return on Saturday, work in their allotments, play in the football team and leave again on Sunday evening.'

'At one time there were two carpenters and wheelwrights in Clifford Chambers. The carpenter or cabinet maker would also organise bearers and funeral arrangements at the church with the rector, for burial in the local churchyard. Sometimes you would hear the carpenter tapping away and you'd say, "I wonder who the coffin is for," if you'd not heard the news.

There were two shoe repairers both very good at their trade and people from other villages would bring their boots and shoes for repair. One of them strongly objected to being called a "snob", which was the name often used for shoe repairers.

There was a market gardener who also had a delivery round in Stratford. He was very popular because the greengrocery was always fresh and of good quality. He would not sell you anything on Sundays. His other trade was as the village carrier. If you wanted something taken to Baileys Saleyard or delivered elsewhere he would take it in his carrier cart, horse-drawn of course in those days

165

and in fact right on and during the Second World war.

Many of the men were employed in farming, ploughing with horses to draw the plough, shepherds who, as today, had a busy time when lambing, and the Manor farm had a prize herd of Freisian cattle which produced a plenteous supply of milk, which was sent off in churns. Other people were mostly employed in Stratford as shop assistants.

"Botton" mill was the mill by the bridge over the river Stour on the road to Stratford. It was a flour mill and also a bakery. People from the village would sometimes take ingredients for lardy cakes and dough cakes which were baked in the oven after the loaves were removed with a long "peel". The ovens were heated with wood. When the milling ceased, the mill was taken over as a weaving mill which employed a number of men and women. Lovely woollen cloth was woven, some for furnishing ships, curtains and upholstery. Remnants were sold at a special sale in Stratford and were in great demand as the cloth was so hardwearing and colourful.'

'There were mills sited all down the river Alne from Henley as far as Tewkesbury and their history goes back as far as Saxon times. The Domesday Book mentions Alne and its mill.

Originally, the mill at Great Alne was water-powered and then, as it became more commercial, by a diesel engine, and provided much of the work for the men of the village. Three engineers looked after the big engine and they worked on a shift system – three shifts a day, six days a week. Every third week it was de-coked. A horse and cart used to transport the flour and pick up grain as far afield as the docks on the South coast; latterly a lorry did the job.

The mill owner provided accommodation for the workers. Some cottages were rent free but half a crown was the rent during the 1930s. The daughter of one of the engineers recalled that when her father got the job, there was no cottage available, so for six months he cycled every day to and from his home in Worcester, some 17 miles away. He then acquired a council house near the mill, and in the 1940s earned £2 10s 0d a week and had to pay seven shillings rent.

A rather unhealthy job for the women was having to mend the dusty old flour sacks.

The lane from the village to the mill was owned by the railway as the track passed over this lane at one crossing point. Every Good Friday the railway company closed the lane to signify to all that it was a private road. However, the mill owner made a point of walking up the lane and cutting through the barrier to show that he had the right to walk on the footpath.'

166

DRIVING THE BREAD VAN

'Before the First World War, George, the eldest son of a growing family established for 30 years at Kineton, started work with the bread vans of Fancott's of Kenilworth. The routine was loading at the rear, collecting basketfuls to carry to customers, and walking back and alongside the horse to the next delivery point. At some houses, he greeted servants – especially a dairymaid at the home of an owner of a Birmingham factory.

George spent the war in France preparing bread in field ovens and he returned to Warwickshire strained to near breaking point. In searching for work and accommodation, he was helped by uncles and ended with job and house from H. Faulconbridge of Bedworth. Now George was able to marry the dairymaid seen seven years earlier. He also began 300 days per year of early rising to bake bread, to harness the horse to the van and to make a day's delivery to the houses of miners and factory workers.

Each afternoon his day ended late. He led the horse back to the stable for rubbing down and food. A walk to the field or bedding down with straw followed. Each autumn, bedding and manure were pitchforked from the manure heap onto a coal cart or lorry. Often the driver delivered to George's home garden or to his distant allotment. In one or other place two or more hours of digging by George, his wife and two or three children followed the work of most days. Some years both potatoes and mushrooms grew on the patches cultivated.

Warwickshire winters are variable. The winter of 1941 brought weeks of trouble. Dolly, the mare, hated snow and the fall of melting snow from roofs. A boy was asked to stand beside the horse's head throughout the delivery round. He persuaded the mare to remain still and not walk off with the van towards her stable. The boy chilled slowly from his extremities inward. My typing this with supple fingers shows how excellent the genes for circulation are in George's descendants. Together with his wife, he gave them other qualities – perseverence, energy and commonsense.

Though the 1914 to 1921 years were times of much stress for him, in the following decades George and his wife achieved much in family and work. In 1944, the firm of Faulconbridge accepted him as a partner; the bread van became the equipment of younger men on their discharge from the army in the following years.'

OTHER WAYS WE MADE A LIVING

From hurdlemaking to needlemaking, telephonists to nurses, there were so many other ways we made a living that this can only be a glimpse at past occupations and professions.

NEEDLEMAKING

'The needle industry has been documented at Studley since the 1760s and carried on under various names and at many locations. However, in 1930 these came together as ENTACO (English Needle and Fishing Tackle Co Ltd), subsequently renamed Needle Industries.

The industry has always played an important part in life in the village, industrially, socially and educationally. Workers started as apprentices and frequently spent all their working lives in the industry. Special coaches were laid on to bring in workers from outlying areas. A large range of needles was produced, including gramophone needles. On the demise of the old gramophones, the process was used to make points for darts – diversification is not new.'

'I was born in a country cottage at Washford in 1919. My grandmother was a very religious and superstitious woman. Her name was Shrimpton, one of the Shrimptons that came with the needlemakers to Studley from Long Crendon, and the cottage she lived in was a smallholding with a needle shop on the side. My grandfather, who was a needle straightener, used to bring work home and straighten in the workshop.

As a boy I would watch the workmen scouring needles. They used to put the needles in a long cloth parcel, and roll them up and tie the two ends. The parcel would be filled with emery dust and soft soap, and be put under the scouring runners which went up and down in the mill for an hour or two until the needles were polished. I well remember riding on these runners with my friend whose father was the foreman. We were always being chased out of the mill because we were putting ourselves in danger really, but of course being children we didn't think anything of it.'

WALNUTS AND HURDLES

'My father was hurdle maker at Brailes in the 1920s. I often went with him on Saturday mornings. As he stripped all the bark off the willow poles he had cut down earlier in the season, it was my job to collect all this bark in hessian sacks to be taken home and to be put out to dry. Later it was used to keep the fire in underneath the copper which my mother used for heating water on washdays.

My father charged ten shillings and sixpence for twelve hurdles and he often had to wait till the farmer had his haymaking season before being paid.

My father also used to "buy" walnut trees in late September and early October. These he harvested by climbing the trees with a hessian sack tied with bagstring slung across his shoulders and a long prop. He picked all he could reach and then beat the tree. My job was to pick up those that fell. Wooden boxes and sacks were filled, and most nuts had the hoods still on them. After getting them home by hand truck, they were laid out to dry. Then the hoods were removed by cutting with a knife. Walnuts were then put into 14 lb wooden boxes. These were collected and taken to market at Stratford on Avon where local greengrocers came to buy them for resale in their shops. My father was paid threepence per pound for the single nuts and fivepence for the double ones. How little was earned for so much hard work.'

TAKING IN WASHING

'My family moved to Radford Semele in 1905. My father was a dairyman with a round in Leamington. After the First World War, when money was very short, we took in laundry from the hotels in Leamington. This was collected on the milk float's return journey to the village on a Monday, with a second journey to collect the rest in wicker hampers. It was returned on Thursday and Friday. Tablecloths were starched and ironed until they shone!'

NURSING IN THE 1940s

'On 4th January 1944 I began my nursing career, which was to last 40 years. During those years changes were beginning to take place in the nursing profession.

Introduction to basic nursing began on my first day when I was sent with five new students to a Preliminary Training School which was in another town. The PTS course lasted six weeks. We were taught nursing ethics and etiquette, anatomy and physiology and hygiene. We also had cleaning jobs each morning (eg dusting, cleaning carpets, cleaning washbasins and toilets) which was inspected by a tutor. If not up to standard we had to do the job again. We had to be ready, looking neat and tidy, for 9 am to start our lectures in the lecture room.

We all wore the same style of uniform, loose, white dresses (which fitted both fat and thin), a starched white belt and a starched butterfly cap, black shoes and black stockings. On duty we were not allowed to wear makeup or nail polish and had to wear neat hair styles. Rings and watches could not be worn – watches had to be "fob" type. When Britain began to receive help from America, we were sent some very attractive white nurses' dresses. These were made of a very soft material with pleats and zip fastener. If we were issued with one to be worn on the day (Saturday) we spent in our own hospital we felt very grand.

At the end of six weeks we sat a written examination as well as a suitability and oral appraisal. If successful we returned to our own training school to start three years of general training after signing a contract with the hospital authority. If the contract was broken we were expected to pay £20.

The working day commenced at 7.30 am and finished at 8.30 pm with a three hour break during the day, either morning, afternoon or evening. One day off a week was allowed, and all lectures were taken in "off duty" time. Night duty hours were from 8 pm to 8 am with four nights off per month (two nights off together). Night duty period covered three months per year.

Meals were taken in the dining room. First year students sat at certain tables and as they progressed in seniority moved on each year until they reached Staff Nurse status. Promotion to the rank of Sister meant they shared Matron's table. No one was allowed to leave the dining room until Matron made the first move, we then all stood until she left the room.

After three years we took a Final examination (General Nursing Council) and if successful became a State Registered Nurse. This was the opening to many nursing opportunities.'

BOOKBINDING

'As a school leaver in 1945, work was quite plentiful and a wide variety of occupations was available to me. My choice was to learn bookbinding and print finishing in Birmingham.

Print finishing entails several operations, such as perforating, collating, numbering, stitching etc, and in those days most jobs were done by hand or with "pedal power", and of course the old glue pot

170

was always on the boil for binding.

Being the youngest employee I was sent out on errands, one of which was to take printed menus daily to several hotels and restaurants in Birmingham city centre. This task I must confess took longer than need be on most days because there was an old battleaxe in charge of my department who didn't allow conversation among employees and so we worked in comparative silence from eight o'clock to six o'clock, making some days seem very long.'

TELEPHONIST

'I started work at the Alcester telephone exchange in September 1940, joining two experienced operators.

The war had been going on for a year and the pace of life was increasing. Even then there were fewer than 200 subscribers on the Alcester exchange. You were either in business or somewhat high up the social ladder before you aspired to a telephone, many of which were still the old candlestick design.

No one dialled anyone else. You just picked up the receiver and hoped for a speedy response from the operator asking "Number please?" There were no little flashing lights on the switchboard. It was all "eye lid" shutters; an open eye when the line was not in use and a closed eye when you picked up the telephone. If you became impatient and jiggered the telephone rest up and down, the eye lid clattered away like a pan lid on boiling cabbage.

Now Great Alne was slightly different. They had eye lids for calling the Alcester exchange for outside calls but for local Great Alne calls they dialled among themselves.

We soon knew all the local numbers; no need for Directory Enquiries. The police, doctors and fire station were, of course, priority numbers and marked with an orange label.

For the first year or so of the war the air raid messages were received in the exchange and we had to sound the siren. Yellow message – be prepared. Red warning – for the siren, which was operated by a switch on the wall. Timing on and off was important to get the familiar waving tone. Great relief when the Green message arrived for the "All Clear". Later it was all dealt with from the police station.

Everything was done manually. You were literally plugged in with twin plugs from one number to another; the switch pulled back and you hoped the bell was ringing at the other end. No automatic ringing tones in those days. Every call was recorded on a ticket. Local calls could go on virtually for ever. Timed calls were interrupted every three minutes to announce how much time had

171

elapsed, and start and finish times were recorded. The tickets were sorted the next day and sent off to Head Office in Birmingham for processing.

There were many so-called standard expressions. When three minutes had elapsed on a timed call from a call box, you said, "Your time is up, will you have further time?" The various coins – penny, sixpence or a shilling – dropping into the coin box made different noises so we knew exactly what was being inserted. Those were the days of Buttons A and B. Of course people often forgot to press Button B to get their money back on a failed call, so it was always worth popping into a box and pressing Button B just in case there were pickings to be had. That was thought very daring in those days!

Most subscribers were a joy to deal with, some always impatient and some very apologetic for even picking up the telephone. Pleasantries were often exchanged which always helped customer and staff relations. We worked shifts covering 8 am to 8 pm when the night duty officer took over. In the evening it was obviously not busy, so after 6 pm we were allowed to knit or read. Food and drink on duty were strictly forbidden.

When I left in 1949 the system was still much the same. Many more people were wanting to "go on the telephone" which, due to lack of equipment and resources, gave rise to the "shared line" whereby two subscribers with different numbers shared the same line, so they obviously couldn't both use the telephone at the same time. Rather inconvenient and not very private it may have been, but better than nothing.

All this is a far cry from the telephone system these days, when almost every house has at least one telephone and it is regarded as one of the absolute necessities of life. The personal aspect has gone which, in some ways, is a pity. It was a very pleasant way to earn a living and we look back with a sigh and say "Ah! Those were the days." '

MINING

'People at Kingsbury worked hard and earned their living in agriculture, mining or at the local brickworks. Lady Middleton "took the turf off" (a term for starting a deep pit) for Kingsbury Colliery at nearby Piccadilly – which got its name from the London club of the Chairman of the Board of Directors of the colliery. Pit number one was christened "Dry Bread" and number two, "Cold Water". The mine was completed in 1896. In the 1930s Hams Hall electricity generating station provided work for many and was further extended in the 1940s.'

'Life in mining communities in the 1940s was very hard, not only for the men working in seams of coal 2000 ft down – in tunnels only 3 ft high, they picked and shovelled coal into tubs (wheeled containers), very often kneeling in wet and hot conditions, air thick with dust and hard to breathe – but also think of the good wife and mother. It was her job before the provision of pit-head baths (1950 in this area) to fill the copper with water, light a fire underneath to heat it for bathing in the tin bath in the kitchen, scrub her man's back, then clean and dry his damp pit clothes over the fireguard ready for the next shift at work. Some ladies had a husband and also sons at the pit – sometimes on different shifts – so days of making fires and heating water several times a day, all had to be fitted in with the housework and cooking for her family!'

'Work prospects and aims were not high at Warton in earlier decades. Boys went into agriculture or mining. There was no coal mine at Warton, but if you stood in Church Road and listened carefully, miners from nearby Pooley Hall could be heard burrowing away underground.'

'In the 1926 miners' strike some of the worst off children in Stockingford were given breakfast at school, and the chapels in the district set up soup kitchens which had queues outside.'

WOODCUTTER AND CARRIER

'Joseph Bolton was the Shilton village carrier at the beginning of the century, as well as being a woodcutter. In Kelly's Directory of 1908 he is recorded as "going into Coventry on Monday, Wednesday, Friday and Saturday".

Carriers went into Coventry from the surrounding villages. They all had their own route. Joseph's went through Ansty, Sowe (now known as Walsgrave on Sowe), Wyken and into Coventry past Gosford Green. In those days the carrier's cart was one of the few ways that the ordinary people could travel. A few people had their own pony and trap but the majority of people had to walk. Of course, the railway was available to go to Rugby or Nuneaton, and it was possible to get on a train at Shilton station and go direct to Liverpool or London. However, if you wanted to get to Coventry, it had to be the carrier's cart or walk.

Joseph's cart was a covered waggon like those used in the wild west. When he had passengers, he would put wooden benches in for them to sit on. People would know the approximate time that he would be passing through their village and waited at the side of the road to be collected. A small fare was paid and they would either travel all the way into Coventry or be dropped off at places on the route to be collected on the return journey later in the day.

Joseph carried goods as well as people. He took the work from the ribbon weavers in the surrounding villages and brought them back their orders for the following week. Some of the cottages had "top shops" built above their living accommodation, making them into three storied buildings. These were rooms which accommodated looms and the women were able to do their work not far from their family and domestic duties. Some of the cottagers had a loom in a spare room in the cottage to enable the women to be able to work to earn money to supplement the family income.

As well as the work from the ribbon weavers, Joseph collected grocery orders and anything else that had been ordered from the shops in Coventry. Atkins and Turton was a very high class grocery shop in the city and Joseph would call at Shilton House, Ansty Hall, and other large houses for their orders on his way into Coventry, take the order into Atkins and Turton and deliver the goods on the way home.

He also collected the beer for the local public houses from the brewery of Phillips and Marriott Limited in Much Park Street,

Joseph Bolton carried on a 300 year old family tradition as woodcutter in the Brinklow area. He is pictured here at High Wood, Brinklow in 1925 with his horse Prince.

174

Coventry. The Old Plough at Shilton and The Red Lion at Barnacle were two of the Phillips and Marriott tied public houses. The barrels would be slung at the side of and beneath the waggon to allow room for the passengers and other goods to go inside.

It was said that Joseph did not have to do much driving because his horses knew his route and the way into Coventry and back home again, as well as he did.

As well as being a carrier Joseph was a woodcutter as his forebears had been. In Brinklow churchyard is a very unusual gravestone memorial to Thomas Bolton the woodcutter. This stone is so unique it is a "listed building". The gravestone reads:

"This man (his character to sum)
From infancy was deaf and dumb.
His understanding yet was clear,
His heart upright and sincere.
He chiefly got his livelihood
By faggotry and felling wood.
Till death, the Conqueror of All
Gave the feller himself a fall."

The top of the stone is decorated with the tools of Thomas's trade, an axe, a billhook, a glove and a faggot of wood. Thomas was christened at Brinklow church on the 14th February 1719 and died on the 11th August 1779.

Times change and the last time that we know that Joseph coppiced a wood was in 1925 when he worked at High Wood, Brinklow. Coppicing is one of the oldest of woodland crafts. The easiest way to describe it is to say that the wood is "farmed". The trees are cut down a little way above the ground and the wood used. Then, as years go by, new growths spring from the stumps and these, in turn, can be harvested. The wood would be left for a few years and then worked again. Sometimes it would be up to ten years before it was worked again, it depended on the type of trees growing there.

Different trees and parts of trees each had their own use. Bark from the oak tree was especially prized for tanning leather. Willow would be used for making baskets and hurdles. Hazel was used for making pegs for thatching and for making besoms or brooms. Larger growths would be used for fencing posts and for logs, and brushwood would be used for pea and bean sticks. These were very important in the days when families relied on their garden, and maybe an allotment as well, to provide them with food. Nothing was wasted from the wood, everything had a use.

As the years went by Joseph's way of life changed. He was no longer needed as the carrier and motor vehicles became more

175

common and buses started to serve the village. He became a coal merchant and haulier, first with his horses and then with lorries. As his health declined he was helped by his son in law Robert Thom, who had married Joseph's eldest daughter, Florence.

Robert and Florence had married in Canada. Robert had emigrated with his family from Scotland in the 1920s and Florence had gone to Canada as a girl of 17 for Courtaulds of Coventry. The firm wanted to set up a silk mill in Cornwall, Ontario, and Florence, together with many girls from the surrounding villages, went out to teach the Canadian girls how to spin the silk. Robert and Florence met at Courtaulds and they returned to Shilton in 1935.

Joseph Bolton died in September 1953, the last in the line of the Bolton family in the area who were first recorded in Brinklow in 1604 and the last of the woodcutters who reach back at least 300 years.'

GLOVEMAKING

'Dunchurch WI was formed in 1918, when 36 women met in the old girls school building in the churchyard of St Peter's church. By the end of 1919 membership had increased to 160. Glovemaking was started by members and it proved so popular and profitable that a cottage industry was formed and put on a financial basis with members holding shares. Each week the members met to bring finished gloves for sale and to take materials home to be made. By July 1920 nearly 500 pairs of gloves had been made and sold. Eighty one pairs were sold at the London Exhibition and four prizes were awarded to the exhibitors.

The Queen of Spain purchased twelve pairs of long white chamois leather gloves and the Prince of Wales was another customer. A set of Elizabethan gloves were made for use in productions at the Old Vic theatre and an acknowledgement ("Made by the Dunchurch and Thurlaston WI") appeared in the programme. Gloves were sent to Canada, the United Sates of America and to South Africa. The expert glovemakers gave demonstrations and lessons to other institutes. Moccasin-type slippers were made with the remnants of the skins and window cleaners and pen wipers with the final remains. The WI started a shop in the village in 1921 where goods such as Barbola work and lace mats, made by members and those in other neighbouring institutes, were sold. Classes in skin curing, slipper making and knitting were also initiated about this time.'

BUILDER

'The old established firm in Penn Lane, Tanworth in Arden,

Cottage industries such as glovemaking or, as here at Stoneleigh, basketmaking gave many village women a glimpse of new horizons.

originally James Woodcock & Son and latterly George Woodcock & Son, had been a family business since 1857. At that time, in addition to the building trade, the adjoining fields were used to keep a few cows, for haymaking and hens, and of course for a pig in a sty. Transport was by horse and cart and there was no railway then.

As the firm grew work became more varied and included church restoration, sale of building materials and undertaking. All the woodwork, including coffins, was made on the premises. In the pre-war years the firm was employed to build the village hall and the Muntz Memorial Hall.

Materials after the war were very scarce and licences were required for certain repairs and also for new houses – the ratio then being one private house to eight council houses.

Houses were in very short supply and Albert and I were very fortunate to rent a semi-detached cottage at Tom Hill. George and Albert Woodcock were characters from an early age and both were very involved in church affairs. George for a time rang the Curfew

Bell, and was also clerk and bellringer, while Albert was churchwarden for a time.'

IN THE SHOE SHOP

'In 1944, when I was 14, I went to work at the shoe shop in Shipston, Spencers, and stayed there for eight years until my marriage. I cycled there every day from Ilmington and started work at nine o'clock. I would have to stay until the last customer had left, and sometimes, particularly on a Saturday, this would not be until nine at night. I was often alone in the shop, particularly during the war. As well as serving I gradually took over the duties of ordering the stock and doing the books. In 1952 I was earning £3 10s a week.

The shoes I sold included wooden-soled clogs made of rough leather, often blue and red, black boots with hobnails, and a variety of styles for women. It was customary in those days for every single pair in the customer's size to be brought out for their inspection, and this often involved climbing up steps to get the boxes down.'

PAY AND HARD TIMES

'My father spent most of his working life as a grinder at a factory in Holbrooks, White & Poppes. It meant a walk from Lower Stoke and back every day, leaving home at half past six and arriving back home twelve or 13 hours later. I remember Dad coming home highly delighted once and showing my mother a pay slip. He had been awarded a halfpenny an hour extra, so on a 60 hour week that meant the princely sum of two shillings and sixpence rise.

As a family we did experience hard times, when Dad nearly severed his hand in a machine and was off work for a long period without any pay. He was able to collect ten shillings a week from a "sick and divi" club, but to qualify for that he always had to be indoors by seven in the evening in case "the man" made a snap visit.'

WAR & PEACE

THE GREAT WAR 1914-18

The fighting took place far from Warwickshire, though the first hints of the terrors of modern warfare came with the sighting of Zeppelins in the county's skies, and life seemed to go on at much its usual slow pace. Yet in every town and village, women and children did their best to help the war effort and waited with dread for news of their husbands and fathers at the Front. When peace at last came it was indeed a great cause for celebration, and for sadness.

OUR WAR EFFORT

'I was born at Weston under Wetherley, and I was five and a half years old when war was declared in August 1914. I remember the sadness of the children whose fathers had been called into the services. Later my elder brother joined the Royal Flying Corps as it was then called. Our war efforts were knitting for the troops; the young ones knitted scarves (quite fancy, with dropped stitches etc!), the older children worked on balaclavas and gloves. These were presented to one of the governors of the school who arrived in her carriage and pair, driven by her coachman. She packed the woollies in a trunk to be sent off. Another effort was sending eggs when they could be spared, with our names written on them. Some pupils received thank-you letters and would feel very proud.

We started our National Savings at school, and also we had large stamps to buy, with photographs of war heroes who died in action, Lord Kitchener, Lord Roberts, Jack Cornwall and heroine Nurse Cavell. The cash from these also went towards the war effort. The large houses were taken over for Red Cross hospitals, and it was a great treat for us to be taken to perform our school concerts for the wounded soldiers, and we felt it was a great honour to be asked to hand round cigarettes and sweets to them.

One night the elders of my family heard a heavy drone and from their bedroom window, watched a Zeppelin passing over. Luckily no damage was done. I remember them being very anxious at breakfast next morning. We used to go with Mother to queue for certain foods in exchange for the ration coupons which were issued. We were quite fortunate in having large gardens and farm produce etc. The ladies met for jam making sessions and were very busy trying out and exchanging economical recipes. Many women had gone to work in the factories, to replace men who had been called up. They were all very industrious with sewing, knitting etc.

There was a great joy when at last the armistice was signed at 11 am on 11th November 1918. At that time there was a serious influenza epidemic and most households were affected. I remember how very cheerful our doctor was when he came in, and now I realise how relieved he must have felt.

We had a great celebration of peace during the next summer, when we wore our best dresses of broderie anglaise. Down came torrential rain and the colours in the red, white and blue ribbon trimming on our hats ran – we looked a very queer sight.'

HORSES AND HORSESHOES

'My great grandfather was a blacksmith and my mother remembered watching horseshoes being made and packed in boxes to be sent for the cavalry horses at the Front.'

'During the war most of the working horses, and especially the best ones, were commandeered from the farms and sent to France. As a young girl at Newbold on Avon, my mother's favourite horse was Dolly and it was heartbreak for her when Dolly was collected and taken away.

Not understanding the volume of horses sent, or the size of that country, she always gave a bag of sugar lumps to each of the visiting soldiers who were returning to France, innocently asking them to be sure to give the sugar to her precious Dolly.'

GROWING UP IN STECHFORD

'Before the First World War, Stechford was a close knit community linked to the outside world by the railway, opposite which was an imposing row of shops.

When the war broke out, my friend Mary and I joined our brothers at the village school. The headmaster, Mr Griffin, was a fine man, firm but fair and respected by all. He and Mary's father were members of the Birmingham Philharmonic Choir and we used to listen to them and other gentlemen practising in Mary's drawing room once a week. They sang together in the choir's first rendering in Birmingham of *The Dream of Gerontius*, conducted, I believe, by Edward Elgar.

A little later Mrs Farmer started a private school in a house in Frederick Road and Mary and Bob were sent there. About the same time a small group of sad little Belgian refugees came to live with nuns at the bottom of Victoria Road and came to our school.

My father joined the forces late in 1915 and my sister was born in 1916 so that my mother was kept very busy. At this time Mary's parents were very good to Joe and to me and we loved them. I remember her father used to read *The Rainbow* to us from cover to cover each week and we accompanied them to Yardley church where her father and Joe sang in the choir.

One house was turned into a military nursing home and Mary and I were sometimes taken over to give the soldiers baked cakes and sit on the men's laps and polish their buttons. I remember one man had a long waxed moustache which I liked to tweek.

About this time Queen Mary and King George V came to Birmingham and Mr Griffin conducted a boys choir, including my brother, from the steps of the council house. Mother took me to see them and I had a wonderful view as someone lifted me onto the top of the GPO letter box.

One night Mother awoke Joe and me and took us into the road where she pointed out a Zeppelin gliding through the sky lit up by the many searchlights on Castle Bromwich aerodrome. She told us to watch carefully as we were watching history in the making.

When I was seven years old, Rachel came with her parents and baby sister to live opposite and we two became lifelong friends. Now my life broadened as we were allowed to wander further afield. There was no danger; when Mr Jones in his horse and cart with glistening milk churn and shining copper measures had passed there was only the occasional bicycle to watch out for and we walked miles to picnic in Chelmsley Woods at bluebell times and Sheldon fields full of wild daffodils, Kent's Moat where we dreamed of finding Roman remains and to paddle in the river in Morden Road.

Once a year a fair came to Washwood Heath and Rachel and I used to walk along the narrow Stechford Lane to enjoy it. It had high banks on each side and the fair people used to park their caravans along the side. Rachel was a wonderful story teller and she used to make my hair stand on end as she wove fanciful tales of their adventures.

Later in the war the house next door was taken over as a police station. They gave my mother a whistle which she could blow if she was in trouble. It was very useful one winter when a pipe burst.

When they knew the war was ending they came and warned mother that they were to fire a rocket at 11 am. Mother placed a chair up against the fence and Joe and I were allowed to look and see the wooden box about 12 inches square standing in the middle of the lawn. Then she climbed onto the chair and clinging onto the fence, kept assuring us that there was nothing to fear and that this was the best day of our lives. When the bang went off she fell off the chair onto the irises and sobbed and sobbed. We thought her very queer. We were then packed off to school and Rachel and I were sent to Bradbury's to fetch the Union Jacks which had been ordered. Each child was given one and we processed around the village, returning to school via Lyttleton Road. As we' passed Mr Cottrell's butcher's shop we were told to walk quietly and not talk as his daughter had died of the dreaded Asian flu that morning.'

MAKEWEIGHT

'Prior to and during the Great War, "Makeweight" bread was bought from the local shops which had a small home bakery attached. Hand-made loaves were of different weights. The total of two or three or four loaves were weighed and any weight shortage was made up with a piece of bread cut off a spare loaf on the counter. As children we always ate "makeweight" before we got home!'

PEACE MEDALLIONS

'In 1919 the school children at Lapworth were presented with a medallion each, to mark the end of the war, donated by a local benefactor.'

THE SECOND WORLD WAR 1939-45

When war came again in 1939, it brought death and destruction to the very heart of the county. Many families watched night after night as German planes flew over on bombing runs to the industrial towns of the Midlands, the red glow of fire in the night sky a terrible reminder of what those who lived there were suffering.

GRANDMA'S SUSPENDERS

'During the war years my grandmother lived with us at Dunchurch. When the siren went off, warning us of an air raid, we would all troop down into the cellar. My grandmother would not be seen anywhere without her corsets, so these were always snatched first if it was during the night. They were usually tucked under her arm with the suspenders all dangling down the back and always gave us a laugh. Clothes to put on top of this monstrosity didn't seem so important to her.'

PRAYING FOR DELIVERANCE

'Wartime brought changes to Ansley Common. One or two Anderson shelters were sunk into the allotments. We had a family shelter and when the sirens sounded we snake-filed up the garden path into the shelter. We sang, and prayed for deliverance from "Jerry". He missed us by only a few feet during the Coventry Blitz when a 500 lb bomb landed in the gardens. My uncle's Austin Seven was buried by rubble, but after a few days of digging, loud cheers went up from all the neighbours when the little car chugged to life again.'

WATCHING THEM GO OVER

'A Coventry firm specialising in making aircraft parts was built in Radford Semele and heavily camouflaged. Workers coming into the area to work were billeted on already overcrowded households. As the neighbouring cities were bombed, evacuees began to arrive and although the cottages were very small, no one was turned away.

Enemy planes flew over the lower part of the village on their way to Coventry and Birmingham. People stood in the streets during the blitz on Coventry watching the raiders and seeing the balloons go up. Twice the village was affected. On one occasion a stray bomb fell a quarter of a mile away by the Southam Road, and on another occasion an enemy plane appeared out of the clouds at midday one Saturday and flew over the church, circled the village and then went on to drop bombs on the Lockheed factory in Leamington Spa.'

'I remember during the war standing on Bidford Bridge listening to the German planes going over to bomb Birmingham. When the searchlights were on, Bidford was lit up like a Christmas tree. Luckily no bombs were dropped on Bidford, although one was dropped at Borton and two at Broome, one hitting the railway line and the other landing in the river. The blast of the bombs dropped locally brought my living room ceiling down. I also remember again standing on the bridge when Coventry was bombed, watching the glow in the sky 25 miles away.'

ALONE IN THE HOUSE

'I was born in 1935 and some of my earliest recollections as a child are of the blitz on Coventry and Birmingham. We lived in Knowle, which was part of Warwickshire then, about ten miles from those cities with the main Paddington-Birkenhead railway line less than a mile away.

One incident, which cannot be directly attributable to the Germans, still remains with me. One Sunday morning in 1945 my parents had gone to church and I was alone in the house when I heard the sound of a plane clearly in some trouble. I ran to the window just in time to see a Mosquito diving straight into the ground. There was a tremendous explosion and a great ball of fire behind the trees on the Warwick Road about a quarter of a mile away. My immediate instinct was to run to the scene of the crash but, perhaps fortunately, my parents returned and restrained me.

Later my father told me that the occupiers of the house nearby had been in the habit of putting their baby in its pram out in the field at the precise spot where the plane came down. On that day the baby had a cold and was left indoors.'

D-DAY

'The day war was declared, Sunday 3rd September 1939, is imprinted on my memory and I'm sure will never fade. I can remember the exact spot where I stood to listen to the news; it was just inside the living room door and I remember fixing my eyes on the light switch. I can also still see the sky on the morning of D-Day. We were all up and hanging out of the bedroom windows at daybreak – about four o'clock. The sky seemed to be full of aircraft. The noise was like thunder. Wave after wave of planes were going east. We didn't really need to put the radio on to know what was happening. It was all very exciting until a few weeks later when one of our neighbours at Nuneaton had a telegram to say their son had been killed on the beaches that first day.'

'BOMBS'

'The Boot public house was the ARP post at Great Alne and during the war a telephone was put in for the ARP wardens. The Home Guard were stationed at one of the farms. On the cricket pitch was a searchlight battery and one night following a raid on Coventry, German planes being chased by the RAF discharged their bombs over Great Alne having been attracted by the large searchlight.

185

Several of these bombs were detonated, but villagers believe there is still at least one unexploded bomb to be found in a nearby wood. There were not many air raid shelters, although the cellar of the pub was used. At school the children had to dive under a desk when the mistress shouted "Bombs!", and they had great fun on the way home from school as the boys would shout "Bombs!" and all the girls would jump in a ditch, only to arrive home soaking wet.

During the war a fund was set up called the "Local Lads Fund", this provided money for any local lad in the forces when he came home from the war.'

THE RAF BOMBING RANGE

'During the period between 1940 to 1943 an area of farming land between Grandborough and Sawbridge, South Warwickshire, was used for target practice by the Royal Air Force. The land was commandeered by the RAF for the purpose of training pilots in bombing enemy targets. The area of land covered approximately 500 acres and formed a large circle, incorporating land belonging to farmers Mr Andrew Baine, Miss Hannah Gilks, Mr Sam Spencer and Mr J R Pickering. The road around the perimeter ran from Grandborough to Sawbridge, down to the Flecknoe Station Cottages, along Dead Man's Lane (so named after a tramp hanged himself in a barn nearby) to Woodbine Farm and back to Grandborough.

The actual target was sited on Grange Farm, Grandborough, owned by Mr J R Pickering. Aircraft, thought to be Wellington and Oxford bombers, practised dropping dummy bombs onto this target; which was constructed of concrete, 18 inches deep, in the shape of an arrow, measuring approximately 40 yards long by two yards wide. It was painted white and pointed due north. According to the locals, the target was seldom hit by a bomb. Bombing continued at night with the target being illuminated by lamps and the use of a diesel generator.

Two quadrants, or observation posts, were situated on the perimeter of the range. The bombs "flashed" on contact with the ground and a message, stating the reference of the bomb, would be sent to an RAF base at Bramcote, near Nuneaton, and then relayed to the pilot flying the bomber. Small red wooden crosses were nailed to field gate posts, and red flags flown to warn folks of the dangers of crossing the range.

Farmers were still allowed to graze the fields, but at their own risk. Mr Baine lost one red heifer, which was struck by a piece of flying shrapnel on the hip and had to be destroyed, and one ram was hit in the neck and died. His duck shed was flattened one night by a dummy bomb, killing all the ducks and nearly injuring Miss Ruth Baine's tethered pet goat.

Flares were parachuted to the ground at night as markers. In the morning, silk parachutes lying in the fields became highly prized by the local women, as dress material was rationed. The ribbons holding the parachutes together made decorative features on garments, whilst the silks were made into petticoats and nightdresses.

One summer evening in 1942, Mr Billy Powell's men were harvesting in the Big Gog at Flecknoe Fields Farm, when a flare was dropped into the field. The men scattered, anticipating a bomb to be released above them. Fortunately it was a false alarm, but sometimes live bombs were dropped in the Back Field of Lower Grandborough Farm, from aircraft returning from missions over France. Having failed to release their bombs during the mission, the planes then released their load on the Back Field. On one such occasion, Mr Andrew Baine was standing on a nearby haystack when an aircraft released its bomb carriage into the field. The bombs exploded on contact with the ground with such force that Mr Baine was blown off the haystack.

Mr and Mrs Fred Quinney had a live bomb drop onto their pantry roof one night. The bomb was made safe by the aircraft crew, and then released above the Flecknoe Station Cottages. The bomb hit the pantry, slid down the roof, knocked the window sill off and buried itself in the blue brick paving. The next day it was removed by the bomb disposal team.

After the war, the land returned to agricultural use. Much debris was left behind, such as nose cones, bomb flights and metal shrapnel. Most of the land drains had been damaged by the impact of the bombs, leaving the fields very wet. All the fences, hedges and trees had been bulldozed to clear the range, so the land was very flat indeed. Debris caused a nuisance for the farmers when ploughing and draining the fields, as it would tangle in the plough shares, and cause great alarm to the tractor drivers when they found dummy bombs. On one occasion, the Army Bomb Disposal team were called out when a bomb was ploughed up and thought to be live.

Today the countryside is more peaceful with cattle and sheep grazing contentedly. Only memories remain for a handful of locals.'

REMEMBERING COVENTRY

Though Coventry is no longer a part of the county of Warwickshire, the terrible destruction suffered by the city is seared into our memories. It would be impossible to recall the war without also recalling the ancient city as it was and the sufferings of those who lived through a blitz which reduced it to rubble.

TAUGHT UNDERGROUND

'I was eleven years old and living in Coventry when the Second World War began and my first memory is of a Civil Defence display being put on to give us an indication of what to expect during a war. There were fire-fighting displays and mock battles and I found it very disturbing. The occasion that really frightened me was when a man came to the door with gasmasks for us to try on. I remember being terrified of this and being of a nervous disposition I ran and shut myself in another room and refused to come out until he had gone. It was weeks before I could be persuaded to try one on but eventually I learned not to be afraid of this strange contraption.

During the height of the Coventry blitz we were summoned every evening at nine o'clock by the sirens wailing and had to make our way down the street to the large underground shelter. One night in particular the bombs were falling before we reached the shelter and I remember throwing myself headlong into our privet hedge as a bomb landed in the next road. Once inside the shelter I felt quite safe. We shared it with three families and had to put up with old grandads snoring and younger children crying, not to mention the planes droning overhead and bombs falling.

The humorous aspects of this period remain in my memory, when for instance if anyone wanted to use the chemical toilet, which was situated at one end of the shelter, everyone was encouraged to sing loudly, for obvious reasons. During the daytime we children gathered shrapnel and proudly compared notes on who had the most fantastic shaped piece of metal or glass.

Most of our lesson time at school was spent underground with the walls all streaming with water, not very nice! In the cookery lesson we had to prepare meals for the Rest Centre and it was always my job to stir the custard in large metal containers. I had to stand on a chair to do this and my hand was always getting scalded by the steam.

On summer evenings later in the war we used to like to watch the barrage balloon unit working and loved to see those large silvery grey elephant-like shapes gleaming in the sunlight. We had RAF personel billeted on us and I used to knit them socks and balaclava helmets, and I remember being very impressed when the officers came once a month to pay my mother for looking after them.'

THE RAIDS

'My husband had volunteered for service with the RAF early in 1940. He said if he waited for his "calling up papers" the war might be over!

My mother resided with us, so when the air raid sirens wailed at tea-time on 14th November 1940, our neighbour collected us to join them in their Anderson shelter that they had built in the garden, and there we remained for twelve hours. The noise of the planes and gunfire was terrific and we could feel the shelter shake and wondered if we would survive. It was a very bright moonlit night and looking out of the shelter we saw parachutes with what we thought of as soldiers being dropped from planes. They were landmines and a whole row of houses just up the hill from us was completely demolished. We had no "all clear" siren and soon discovered we had no water, gas or electricity. As not much could be done except pray and thank God we had survived, I decided to walk into town (about two miles) negotiating huge craters, fire engines and a maze of waterpipes everywhere (I never discovered where they were getting the water from). It was a dangerous mission as it wasn't properly light and when I reached the Alvis Works on the Holyhead Road I was stopped by a policeman and asked, "Where the hell do you think you are going?" I explained that I had the office keys and was concerned to get everything out of the safe. The electrical business I worked for was situated in a close in Bayley Lane near the cathedral, still smouldering while people were kneeling in prayer all round. I joined them and wept, eventually going to my destination only to find nothing – all the businesses were gone and the safe I was so concerned about, a red hot piece of distorted metal. I then went to the police station to see if they could contact my boss (who was a Squadron Leader in the RAF in London) on their emergency telephone, and let him know the news.

The next big raid was in April 1941. My husband had just arrived home on embarkation leave when the sirens went, so he put down his kitbag etc immediately and went outside. The house opposite had a direct hit; it was very sad as the husband had been killed previously whilst on duty as an auxiliary fireman at the hospital and

189

he had four young children. We had a delayed action bomb which came through the coalhouse and pantry roofs, embedding itself under the kitchen floor. Everyone was so busy that my husband (who was covered in dirt and sand) and myself went round telling our neighbours to get out of their homes until the Bomb Disposal Squad had been and we roped off part of the road and put up notices "DA Bomb Keep Out". However, someone thought it was a joke and removed them. Strange to relate, we were told we must not go into the house to remove anything but we had to show many officials the hole where the bomb was! The wonderful Bomb Disposal lads removed it after five days and asked if I would like the pins! My husband had returned to his squad and we weren't reunited until four and a half years later.'

WORKING ON

'I remember Coventry in the 1930s, when life to me as a child seemed very peaceful with long, hot summer days. In Max Road, Coundon, where I lived, we were surrounded by fields filled with buttercups, moon daisies, cow parsley, clover and many more lovely scented wild flowers. My friends and I used to paddle in the tiny brooks with clear running water. In Barkers Butts Lane, nearby, local farmers used to walk their cattle down to the city centre for the cattle market.

I remember the cobbled streets in the city, with some quaint old shops. One in Spon Street had the door opening to the sound of a bell ringing merrily. They sold a large variety of items: children's sweets and treasures and, strung across the ceiling, displays of socks, vests, towels and all kinds of linen items. If one went in after dark it was gas-lit, which seemed quite magical to me.

My most vivid memories of Coventry, however, are from 1939 to 1945, during which years I became a hairdresser.

On the night of the terrible blitz on Coventry in November 1940, the sirens had sounded so we all prepared as usual. My sister, mother and myself sat in a Morrison shelter under the stairs; this was made of solid iron and my parents chose to have this instead of having an Anderson shelter in the garden. We had my grandmother with us at the time, and she sat under the stairs with us on a chair; at 84 years of age she found it difficult to get in our shelter as one could not move about in it.

My father and brother were outside seeing if they could help anyone. Bombs were exploding all around us; housing going down and some people being thrown on to high roofs. At two o'clock in the morning, we were advised to leave the house as an unexploded land mine had landed a few yards away. Having put grandma in a wheelchair, we all dressed up warmly, and when Mother had found her favourite hat we all set off. Coventry was lit up by this time, on fire in the city centre. We walked through about five streets and found a brick shelter where we sat until daylight.

It wasn't safe to go back to the house, although my father risked it to fetch a few personal belongings for us all. Then we travelled to my grandparents' farm at Four Oaks, Berkswell.

What a sight when we came home; part of the roof had blown off and a few windows were broken, but the builders soon laid tarpaulin across the roof until it could be repaired. There was no gas to cook from, but Mother quickly became used to managing on the fire.

The hairdresser's in Coundon where I worked was, thankfully, still standing, but the butcher's shop next door had been blown down. My boss kindly offered the butcher the use of part of his downstairs shop whilst we carried on upstairs.

During this time my boss was in the fire service, and one night there had been a chink of light showing through the blackout curtains, which was a serious offence as it could have been spotted by an enemy aircraft. So the butcher and I had to appear in court. However, the butcher kindly pleaded guilty and paid the fine. The court report in the evening paper read, "The age of chivalry is not yet dead".

In time I was called to war work. The Land Army was my choice, but I could not get my parents' permission to sign the necessary forms. So I became a clippie on the buses. What a different life; up sometimes at four for the early morning shift to take factory workers, then schoolchildren, office people and shop workers and then shoppers.

It was quite hard work running up and down stairs, carrying a heavy bag on one side, filled mostly with large old pennies, and on the other side a steel ticket machine. I made many friends, though, with my passengers who came regularly. Often at the terminus my driver and I were offered a cup of tea, and I felt quite fit with all the fresh air and exercise.

Sadly I lost my first sweetheart during the war: his first mission in the air force was a big raid over Cologne in 1942 and he didn't come back. No one ever knew what happened to him. They were so young, those men who gave their lives for their country; most had not long left school.

The fields where we used to spend so much time were covered with barrage balloons, which were used hopefully to stop enemy aircraft flying too low. These were removed when the war came to an end. Slowly all those fields were filled with new houses, and

Coventry City came alive again.
I consider I am so lucky to remember Coventry before the war. I was born there, in Gulson Road, and most of my ancestors were Coventrians.'

THE GEORGE MEDAL

'After a bomb exploded near my home in Three Spires Avenue, I was taken by bus on a very roundabout route avoiding fires and craters, to receive first aid at Whoberley School. These bus trips were extremely dangerous as there was the ever-present threat of more bombs falling, and the man who drove the bus was eventually awarded the George Cross.'

EVEN THE TRIFLE GOT HIT!

'The war began for us in Coventry on 25th August 1939, with the IRA outrage in Broadgate. I heard the explosion and was very frightened. Five people were arrested, and later we heard that three of them were deported and two were sentenced to death for their part in the plot.

When Mr Chamberlain's announcement came over the radio, my mother was in tears and my father talked of his brother who had died in vain for the utopian ideal of peace in the First World War.

At the time of the November blitz my family were having a party to welcome my father home from hospital. Our living room had two doors at right angles to each other, and the locks were damaged by the vibration of gunfire close by. My brothers took off their ties as a means of tying the door knobs together. There was a trifle waiting in the kitchen – with a long-hoarded tin of cream and decorated with cherries. The ceiling fell on this delectable treat. But we were all unharmed beneath our Morrison shelter.'

YEARS WITHOUT A ROOF

'I lived in the centre of Coventry during the bombing. I remember one particular day going into the cathedral whilst it was still on fire, having spent the night a few yards away. We lived for years without a roof, just a tarpaulin, and with our windows boarded up. A 560 lb bomb landed in our little yard and thankfully didn't explode, just left a huge crater. We survived.'

LIFE GOES ON

Ordinary life still had to go on – families had to be fed and clothed, farmland had to be cultivated for much-needed food crops. Villages changed as new priorities took over the old way of life. But it was not all doom and gloom, there were dances to go to, new people to meet and romance in the air for some.

THE LADS GO AWAY

'In 1939 the vicar presented a prayer book and testament to each lad from Middleton called up for war service. A list was hung in the church with the names added as they went away. The mothers whose sons were away attended church at twelve noon each day to pray with the vicar for their safe return.

The first lad from Middleton to be called up to the militia reported for duty three days before his 21st birthday in July 1939, having been told it was for six months' training. His mother always tied a pair of his shoes to the bottom of the bed when he returned to his regiment after being on leave. The idea was that he would always return home to wear them. This was proved true, and after six and a half years in the army he came home and still lives in the village today.'

FARMING LIFE

'I lived on a farm with my parents and grandfather on the edge of Radford Semele parish on the Fosse Way. My father was in the Home Guard and the local headquarters were at Tudor House on Radford Hill. My mother used to complain that she was left on her own to look after me and my grandfather, who was then in his seventies, and she used to make me sit under the dining room table or under the stairs when there was an air raid. One day a German aeroplane flew very low over the farm and my grandfather who had fought in the First World War was absolutely incensed and his language was foul. He said he wished he could have shot it down with his shotgun. Also a German aeroplane flew very low over a bus by Radford Hall. My mother and I were passengers and we all thought we were being machine gunned. The driver pulled the bus to the side of the road under some trees until the aeroplane flew away.

We had Land Army girls helping on the farm, also German prisoners of war at hay and harvest times, and when the threshing machine came – no combine harvesters then. We had two lovely big carthorses, Bonny and Bess. Bonny was my favourite and I used to lead the horses when they were pulling waggons of hay or stooks of corn.'

'I have very clear memories of not being able to get to bed before midnight during double summer time. The free range poultry naturally would not go to roost till dusk. I had to be there to lock them up or by the morning the fox would have helped himself to some.'

'I was born in 1929, in a 17th century stone thatched farmhouse, under the Edgehills. The area is called the Valley of the Red Horse, because in the olden days a horse was shaped in the red soil of the hill and could be seen from long distances.

My grandparents lived there, and my father was born there too. He had three brothers and three sisters. The brothers all worked on the farm, although one joined the army in the First World War and died in France. I have a photograph of them milking the cows in an open yard, each sat on a three-legged stool. My grandfather bought the first mowing machine in the village and my father said that men came and stoned and broke it, because they came and scythed the grass for farmers in those days and they thought a machine would mean no work for them.

In haymaking times we used to carry cans of tea to the haymakers, hurrying across the fields so that it would remain as hot as possible. There were hundreds of grasshoppers then, and they used to try to commit suicide in Dad's cup of tea – he always called it "Grasshopper Broth". On the way home we would collect wild flowers, and my brother would collect grasses and make lovely windmills with them. We would spend hours looking for birds' nests, and watching the babies grow. My favourite pastime was collecting caterpillars, keeping them in jars to see what butterflies or moths emerged and then to let them fly away.

The war changed the whole way of life for every farm, and the community. The farms were all grassland, the clay soil being thought unsuitable for corn growing, but soon the Ministry of Agriculture visited each farm and the farmers were told how many acres had to grow corn – they had to produce enough to feed the nation, as German submarines were sinking ships bringing supplies from overseas. The whole valley turned from green to patchworks of gold.

The first Fordson tractor was bought, the plough, the binder and

194

winnowing machine and all the essential equipment for corn. My father had grave misgivings as field after field was ploughed up, but the clay soil, not having been worked for years, yielded bountiful crops. Horses still pulled the waggons, now filled with sheaves of corn and not so much hay. Corn ricks were everywhere; these had to be thatched to keep the wet out, and then in the winter months the threshing machine arrived to thresh the corn. Most farms had to have extra help, some had land girls and some prisoners of war, and being near an aerodrome often airmen would help shucking the sheaves and unloading the sheaves onto the ricks.

After the war was over and the celebrations finished, life became very quiet, the cornfields returned to pasture, the binder and plough were put aside.'

THREEPENNY HOPS

'During the war, every Monday evening in the village hall at Ufton there was a Threepenny Hop from eight to ten o'clock. Music was supplied by three villagers, consisting of piano accordion, violin and drums. A whist drive was held every Friday evening at two shillings each, raffle tickets twopence each. The prizes were usually savings stamps.'

BANANA SANDWICHES

'Very little was available for cake-making, but occasionally we made one using liquid paraffin! There were no bananas but I remember "banana sandwiches" made from boiled mashed parsnip with banana flavouring added.'

MAKE DO AND MEND

'I remember renovating my dresses, which were very few, by inserting strips of different coloured material to lengthen them and smarten them up. I once spent hours unpicking a silk parachute to make a lovely long nightdress.'

'With rationing we learned to make do with very little. Mother would darn socks and mend all our clothes. Dad learned to drive carefully in the blackout with very little allowed in the way of headlamps and two-inch wide white painted edges all round cars to make them more easily seen.

Illegal bartering of foodstuffs went on – farmers, for instance, obtaining many a bottle of whisky from the publican in part exchange for a chicken or eggs.'

195

NOT ALL GLOOM AND DOOM

'Through the war years we were living in Stivichall just outside Coventry. We were very aware of the bombing raids on Coventry and after a good many nights spent in the air raid shelter we cycled to Kenilworth and slept at a friend's house for a week or so, during which time the Luftwaffe made their memorable raid on the city. The next morning we returned home to find our house slightly damaged by blast. During this time the Army came nightly down our road and if the wind was in the right direction they lit the smoke-screen stoves which stood on the verges. The evil smelling black smoke poured right through and over our house in order to give cover to the city – what it did to our furnishings and lungs can only be guessed at.

But it was not all gloom and doom. There were RAF dances at Baginton aerodrome for which we girls tried to dress up as much as coupons and make-do-and-mend would allow. Stockings which were made of rayon and not very good colours, were worn inside out, they looked more sheer that way, although the tricky business was to trim away the fuzzy ends round the heels with sharp scissors. Hair grips were in short supply so often hair was worn rolled up and over a tightly tied stocking which was put on the head like a crown and the hair all tucked into it – giving a sort of halo effect.

During the war years, holidays away were not a patriotic thing to do and we were all aware of the slogan "Is your journey really necessary?" So I joined an organisation called "Lend a Hand on the Land". This was the idea of Lady Stapleford and consisted of parties of women volunteers doing useful work on farms etc where there was a lack of male workers. Through this organisation I spent a few weeks in the summer picking plums in a village near Evesham. We lived in bell tents. One member of the group had catering experience and was put in charge of meals. It was hard work but enjoyable. Another time I went to a large house near Welshpool where our job was to go on the mountainside and cut down the bracken to make it easier for the sheep to find the grass.

One embarrassing moment for me was when I had to produce my identity card in Stoneleigh! I had arrived in the village for a friend's wedding, rather too early, so was walking about up and down and trying to pass the time. I suppose I must have looked rather suspicious, particularly as I was a bit dressed up. Anyway, I was challenged!'

GETTING MARRIED

'Just prior to the war, Arthur was conscripted to Hore-Belisha's

Militia along with another public-spirited friend and was called up a few months later when war was declared. He was initially posted to Chilwell, Nottingham but soon became a member of the British Expeditionary Force and was drafted abroad to France. As a member of the Force he was still in Belgium at the time of the Dunkirk evacuation. Ten days after the mass evacuation he was relieved to be given a lift by a small Scottish coal boat and brought back to Margate. Arriving at Monwode Lea at 8.30 am on Tuesday 11th June, Arthur had been granted 48 hours leave. We decided to get married the next day! We went to see the Archdeacon at Castle Bromwich at 11 am to sign an affidavit in order to get a Special Licence. From there we proceeded into Birmingham where we bought a wedding dress for me, which cost £3, and a jacket and trousers for Arthur. Meanwhile my sister Joan and Arthur's sister Hilda were enjoying a hectic day in Coventry buying bridesmaids' dresses. At the end of the day, they had managed to buy two dresses of the same cornflower blue but of different designs, so I had no influence over their choice! As a result of their impulsive buying they had spent all their money and missed the last bus home.

Having returned from Birmingham, Arthur and I realised that in our haste we had forgotten to buy a wedding ring. Johnson's the jewellery shop in Nuneaton, was due to close at 7 pm and the wedding was fixed for the next day. Undeterred, I telephoned to ask the shop to stay open until we arrived. Arthur and I drove into Nuneaton and parked outside the shop. Mrs Johnson served us and we chose a plain band costing £1 10s from a tray she showed us.

Meanwhile my cousin Annie was at Monwode Lea baking cakes for the wedding breakfast. Smith's Departmental Store in Nuneaton were asked to provide a wedding cake and as they did not have time to bake one especially, they gave us one that was intended for another couple later that week. My mother telephoned the guests to invite them to the wedding. The local villagers rallied round and decorated the church and the parish hall with moon daisies from the churchyard. On the morning of the wedding the bridesmaids and my mother were taken to the church by Uncle Sid from Meriden. Unfortunately he forgot to return to Monwode Lea in order to collect my father and me. Having stood on the front door step until eleven o'clock, father decided to get the car out of the garage and drive us to church himself! The bells of the church were rung for the last time until after the war due to the air raid precautions. My mother said, "Married in haste repent at leisure!", but we have now been happily married for over 50 years.

Our honeymoon was spent just over the Leicester border at a relative's farm with Arthur's aunt and uncle. Uncle thought that we might like to go to hear Donald Soper, the President of the Methodist Conference, on our wedding night! However, we said that we preferred our own company! Arthur returned to his regimental unit on the Saturday of that week and I did not see him again until August, and I continued to live at home with my parents as before.'

'When I was married in 1942 I wore a hat and coat and consequently needed gloves. Having no clothing coupons left (gloves were two coupons) I had an old pair of kid gloves cleaned. They came back so stiff I couldn't open them – as my wedding photos show. I was clutching them like a baton!

My wedding cake, which I made myself, was full of prunes, cut up to resemble currants.'

'One man at Little Wolford was taken off to court for wasting petrol after he had taken his daughter to church to be married. He got off because a little petrol was allowed in country areas to attend church, or as it was stated, "divine services". The magistrate decided that marriage was a divine service, but when another daughter got married the family went to church by bus.'

BLACK-OUT

'The gloomy days of war were made even darker by the "black-out". It is impossible for today's generation to imagine how very dark our villages and towns were during the Second World War.

No street lights, no brightly lit shop windows, not even strong torchlight, the few remaining cars on our streets had their headlights covered, with only a downward slanting slit of light being allowed, and all windows were tightly covered with heavy curtains and shutters. A chink of light showing brought an air raid warden quickly to the culprit's door. Offenders could be heavily fined but usually a shouted order, "Put out that light," sufficed to remedy matters. A pinpoint of light could be seen by enemy bombers and helped them to locate towns and villages. This stygian darkness did, however, have its compensations. In winter the sky on clear cold nights was velvety black, star-spangled with a clarity not seen today, with so much street-lighting reflecting into the heavens and diluting its natural brilliance. On the night of the Coventry blitz in November 1940, a great orange arc of glowing light could be seen hanging over the city, even from our village six miles away. It was an awesome sight set against the blackness of the night with vibrations from the exploding bombs being felt even at that distance.

198

An amusing incident occurred in our family due to the blackout. At that time we lived in the village of Wolston which has a brook running through the centre; several small bridges are situated at regular intervals along its length for pedestrians to cross the stream. My youngest brother, who was in the Royal Artillery, was home on a rare spell of leave. He and my father decided to pay a visit to the local Red Lion pub to celebrate. It was a dark, raw winter's evening. Before they left, the landlord handed my uniformed brother a precious half-bottle of whisky, which in wartime was a very scarce and highly prized commodity. Nothing was too good for the local lads in uniform who were home on leave. On leaving the hostelry they stepped out into thick fog and absolute darkness with not a gleam of light anywhere to be seen. At that time we shared a large house at the end of the village with a London evacuee family. It was situated near the local post office and bakery close to where the brook finally disappeared into the Church fields. My father suggested they follow the course of the brook feeling their way, and counting bridges as they came to them. When they reached the last one they could cross and follow the tall brick wall which surrounded the house, and hopefully locate the gate, thus arriving home safely. They were probably in a somewhat inebriated state as they crawled gingerly along with hands outstretched, feeling their way – one bridge, two bridges and at last, the third and final one was reached. They ran their hands along the wall of the bridge and suddenly with a loud splash they found themselves sitting waist deep in freezing water. They had followed outside the bridge instead of the centre! They sat for some moments in a state of shock and then became helpless with laughter. Through all this my father had held the precious bottle of whisky safely aloft in one hand. A very cold, wet, and hilarious pair eventually found their way home, much to my mother's dismay and amusement. The precious whisky was immediately brought into use to warm them up! On another occasion my father walked straight into a neighbour's house by mistake on a particularly dark evening – much to their surprise.

Going to church across fields lit only by the moon and a myriad of stars was an unforgettably beautiful experience. However, these bright moonlit nights which illuminated the countryside with startling clarity were dreaded by many big cities for these "Bombers' Moons" made the location of towns and other targets so much easier for enemy aircraft. How we all came to dread the "vroom vroom" sound of the German planes; they had quite a different sound from British aircraft and could easily be distinguished in the stillness of the night.

One of my greatest joys as a child was carol singing with a couple of friends. We wrapped up warmly and donned our pixie hoods – at that time in fashion and ideal for keeping heads and ears warm. Round the neighbouring houses we trudged clutching a small torch containing a somewhat weak "No 8" battery. These torches had, at all times, to be held downwards, so as not to shine up into the sky; and with this dim illumination we did our rounds, singing the familiar carols in childish voices that became progressively weaker as the evening wore on. Negotiating long dark garden paths was by no means easy and I'm afraid many a flower bed was trampled on. After we had finished singing we knocked on the door and thrust a tin marked SSAF at the householder. These initials stood for Soldiers', Sailors' and Airmen's Fund; all our collection went to this charity, which helped local members of the forces and their families when they were in need. Sometimes the lady of the house gave us sweets or a precious bar of chocolate which was very welcome indeed in those days of sweet rationing. In many ways children were much safer then than now for we could play in the streets or go carol singing unaccompanied by an adult, without any worries on our parents' part.'

WE ALL DID OUR BIT

Soldiers turned up in most unlikely places and we got used to seeing them around. Everyone who was not called up for the Services did something: from the Home Guard to the Women's Land Army, from nursing to making jam, we all did what we could for the war effort.

SOLDIERS ON THE MOVE

'Close to our house in Knightcote there was a small army camp with several wooden huts and on Sunday afternoons all the local children would gather in there to watch films. There was only one telephone in the village, in the farmhouse, so when needed the army officer took the shortest route – through our orchard, past the back door of our house to the farm.'

'Harold and I moved from Hunningham to Budbrooke Farm on 4th

October 1938. War broke out on 3rd September 1939. Our farm was an exercise area for the Royal Warks Regiment and over the war years we had many laughs. One particular occasion happened in 1943.

Soldier swarmed over the farm daily so it took quite a while for us to realise something different was afoot. About noon one day we noticed soldiers arriving very quietly at odd times and hiding themselves in the buildings, until in every corner there were one or two soldiers hidden, even buried in the hay. The day was a very stormy one, rain with very high winds, and this seemed to add to the excitement. At regular intervals during the afternoon I had to answer the ring of the doorbell. Every time I opened the door the soldier would gently push me to one side and shut the door behind him, "Excuse me, we are on a stunt and must not be seen by the 'encircling army'." A tin pushed into my hand, "Will you make us some tea?" and the number given as to how many to brew up for. Living in "civvy street" I'd never seen tinned tea, milk and sugar in one sticky concoction. My first attempt was not a great success but by four o'clock I was almost expert.

We were of course used to daylight attacks but this was something quite different. All was so quiet we felt zero hour must be approaching. Bill and Ralph were busy milking when the "invading army" arrived. Suddenly soldiers swarmed all over the buildings, inside and outside, men and yet more men. One of them asked Bill if he had seen any soldiers about. Bill promptly said he was the first he had seen that day. With the bayonet only inches away from his tummy, Bill felt far from happy and thought of his tea flying away on a cloud of tablecloth.

We never really knew what the exercise was for but most of the men were still there next day having stayed the night in hiding. The next morning there were requests for cooking their breakfasts. I asked for two of the soldiers to gather all their rations, made the fire up, gave pots and frying pan and the two did the cooking. I was by this time miles behind with the dairy work. The sight of soldiers with braces hanging down, shirt necks open, coming with their tin mugs for shaving water from our pressure boiler and squinting into a little square of tin in efforts to get a good shave was very funny indeed.

An officer of the "invading army" had come to the door on arrival at the farm and asked to use our indoor toilet. On being told we had not one indoors, the only one was up the garden and he was welcome to use it like all the other men, he drew himself to his full height and informed me, "Officers do not use the same toilets as the other men!"'

DEVELOPING THE JET ENGINE

'Looking back, I suppose my recollections and experiences during the years of the Second World War must have been second to none. It was early in those war years that my life became totally different – as I started to work in the field of aviation.

It was thrilling to become involved in the early stages of Sir Frank Whittle's great invention of the jet engine – an engine which actually performed without a propellor and developed the speeds which soared above the sound barrier. Whittle was a Leamington man – an old boy of Leamington College for Boys and truly one of the greatest inventors of the 20th century.

It was in conjunction with the old Rover company of Coventry and Solihull that the very first engine was built in a remote factory tucked away in the Yorkshire Moors. I was recruited by the Air Ministry, one of the very few women to be selected, and was soon introduced to the jet engine and to the "bed" where it was tested.

It was exciting to be able to check the assembly of all the parts through the machine shops and the heat treatments until they arrived at the assembly shop where the last touches were put to the engine prior to the final testings and despatch to the RAF.

In fact, the initial flight testing of these first jet engines was made by fixing them in parallel with the ordinary piston Rolls Royce engines on the Wellington bomber so that the safety of the crew and aircraft was maintained during these very experimental flights.

Only a few of us knew exactly how that wonderful new type of engine could perform. We took all the readings as it was strapped down in the engine shed and to us it was almost beyond belief that it could reach speeds of over 600 miles an hour – an absolutely wonderful feat so many years ago. There is no doubt that it helped a great deal in the performance of our wartime planes, and from it came the great jet planes of today.

It was decided by the Ministry of Aircraft Production and the Government to send one of these new jet engines to the United States. I was involved with the testing of that engine and saw it crated up and despatched to Pratt and Whitney in the USA, who now are also large manufacturers of jet engines for civil and military aircraft.

Everytime I fly now I feel a tingle of pride at having been in on the ground work all those years ago.'

EVERYONE HELPED

'A number of men at Clifford Chambers joined the Local Defence

Volunteers. At first there was no uniform but an armband with LDV on it. They were white when issued but the men had to dye them in strong cold tea so that they were less noticeable in the dark. The men slept two to a tent in a field at the foot of Martin's Hill. They were supplied with rifles. After a time they were supplied with khaki uniforms like the army and became known as the Home Guard. Of course in time several of them were "called up" into the Army, Navy or Air Force so only older men or those in reserved occupations remained.

There was a First Aid Post in the Jubilee Hall. We trained and took exams with St John's Ambulance and the Red Cross and did 80 hours' duty in Stratford Hospital. Extensions were built there to take war wounded and those who were injured in the Coventry blitz.

There were air raid wardens in navy blue uniform and tin helmets. Their important duty was during the blackout to see that no chinks of light were showing in the cottage windows. One cottage had wooden shutters which closed at night but elsewhere we had special blackout curtains, black cloth. Those who worked in Stratford had to spend one night a week on duty for firewatching. Each received two shillings for a night's duty and some were billeted in a school with camp beds for sleeping. There was no war damage in the village but one evening a row of incendiary bombs was dropped along the banks of the Stour which runs parallel with the houses on one side of the village.

Evacuees came from a Roman Catholic school in Edgbaston, Birmingham and were taken into the villagers' homes. Their schooling took place in the Jubilee Hall as three teachers came with them. We had three sisters at our house, though we only really wanted one or perhaps two, but they refused to be parted! We had an awful job trying to get their heads clean. We had visits from their mother and grandmother to see that the girls were happy. About Easter 1940 the children left Clifford Chambers.

Although we had no bombs at Clifford, we had very disturbed nights especially when the Germans flew overhead to bomb Coventry and Birmingham, and we could hear the bombing all through the night.

In July 1943 it was decided to set up a Forces Fund and the first committee meeting was held on 28th July in the Jubilee Hall. Funds raised were for men and women who had gone from the parish to serve in the armed forces when war broke out in 1939. We had wonderful support from Mr Radnell and family. They were business people from Birmingham who evacuated to Clifford. They gave a bicycle to raffle and it was displayed in the High Street window of J C Smith's, now Debenhams. The funds were increased by £75 13s as a result and a deposit account was opened at Lloyds Bank. By May 1944 we decided to send postal orders for 10 shillings to forces serving "at home", the cigarettes at this time were not getting through too successfully overseas so we decided to pack parcels of items which might be useful eg shoe polish, toilet and shaving soap and toothpaste. Later we returned to sending cigarettes as some parcels got damaged. We held whist drives, had a cinema show nearly every Saturday evening thanks to Mr Radnell, and all committee members took part in concerts. Cigarettes sent to forces overseas were arranged with a local tobacconist and cost five shillings and sixpence for 200. Troops at home received postal orders for five shillings. As our funds grew we increased this to ten shillings.

On 25th May 1945 a decision was made to close the Forces Fund and as each man or woman was demobbed he/she received a cheque for £3 10s. This fund was registered as a War Charity under the War Charities Act 1940 and all books and accounts were finally audited by a Chartered Accountant from Stratford on Avon.'

'Bert Cranmer was an air raid warden at Lapworth during the war and it was largely through his efforts that a Wardens' Tobacco Fund was set up for the soldiers' parcels which everybody had a hand in filling, with whist drives and concerts held in St Chad's church.

Because there was no village hall in those days, a special building was provided on land next to St Chad's for billeting American soldiers, but when it was discovered – a bit late in the day – that there was no water available the building was abandoned and later pulled down. In another part of the village an Italian prisoner of war camp was set up.'

'My four brothers were conscripted and my husband too. My second oldest brother went missing, believed drowned in 1941 at the evacuation of Greece. We never knew what happened to him. His wife was expecting a baby, so that baby never knew his father. We were all heartbroken. My third brother went out to France on D-Day and my eldest brother was at Nijmegen, but they came back safely.

My mother was caused much anguish but she threw herself into the war effort. She ran a National Savings group, and then the WI were asked to make jams and chutneys for sale in the shops. Oil stoves were bought and the village hall at Long Itchington was a hive of activity. Children gathered blackberries, elderberries, hips for rosehip syrup, and jam jars. We also sold the Woolton pies once a week. The profits from this were used by the WI to buy a canning machine. Several of us went for lessons on how to operate the machine and then we had sessions of peeling apples, gathering any fruit in season, and even buying trays of apricots and peaches, so that everyone had a good stock of tinned fruit. In those days of rationing this was an enormous help.'

'When I was 16 the war came and my life took a completely new turn. Throughout the war years I was employed by Uffields who produced Spitfires and Lancaster Bombers. I remember running down our lane on dark mornings, eating a dried egg sandwich, to catch the 6.20 train to get me in to work for seven o'clock.'

'Young ladies from Middleton had first aid lessons in the front parlour of one of the houses, and they took their exams in Wilnecote. Having been successful, they were called out at each air raid, prepared for any emergency. The air raid wardens met in the next door house, and sandbags were positioned at the front doors of both houses. The Home Guard was stationed at Moxhull Hall.'

ENTERTAINING

'During the war years everyone was expected to "do their bit". My particular contribution from a tender age, was entertaining the troops and factory workers. I belonged to a dancing troupe of young girls whose ages ranged from about nine to 14. Our dancing teacher, Olive Meacham, who had originally worked in West End musicals, set up a small school of dancing locally, and soon, with a talented group of youngsters, ballet and tap-dancing lessons, much practise and diligent rehearsal, we became a proficient and professional "chorus line".

It was decided to form a concert party, and we were joined in this project by an adult conjuror, a duo consisting of a soprano and tenor, a comedian, and John Hanson the singer who was later to become famous in various London musicals. My father acted as compere or link-man as they are now called. For several years during the Second World War we toured factories in the Midlands performing "Workers' Playtime" during lunch hour breaks in the large factory canteens, many of which had excellent stages with lighting and microphones. The workers in their overalls sat eating their lunch at long tables, whilst we performed on the stage. It was considered important to keep workers' morale high in those grim days and they certainly made enthusiastic audiences.

We also put on shows throughout Warwickshire and neighbouring areas in remote army camps and airfields. An evening show livened things up for the men serving in these very cut-off camps, where

205

transport to nearby towns was often non-existent. They made an enormous fuss of us and usually laid on a meal for the cast after the show. Often the camp chef or "cookie" would make special treats for us, wonderful cakes and tiny sandwiches the like of which were never seen by most people until well after the war. Ham appeared as if by magic, tinned salmon, jellies and pineapple, what treats!

On one never to be forgotten occasion a long trestle table had been covered by a spotless white cloth; it was carefully set out with a variety of goodies and, we could scarcely believe our eyes, bowls piled high with sugar were placed at regular intervals along the length of the table. "What was special about that?", the modern generation will say, but when the tiny amount of sugar allowed in our weekly ration could be measured in spoonfuls it was treasure indeed!

Often stages had to be especially constructed for us by the servicemen and many is the time I've danced away on bouncing boards supported by oil drums; they even rigged up curtains made of blankets, and laid on primitive stage lighting.

Of course, in order to perform at lunch-time concerts, we had to obtain permission for time off school. The headmaster of our local school gave grudging consent but he had little choice in the matter, for to refuse would have been "unpatriotic" and he would never have lived down a slur like that!

Special buses were laid on for us as private cars were almost non-existent due to lack of petrol, and together with our various costumes, dance shoes, identity cards and gas masks we set off to entertain. What a panic ensued if we forgot either of those two last items. It was felt by most people that to forget your gas mask would immediately trigger off a gas attack from Herr Hitler. It may sound funny now, but it made you feel very uneasy, though what good mine would have been is hard to say, as it had a small hole in it neatly ringed in indelible ink by the local warden, but no one ever attempted to replace it with a new one.

Our costumes were made from whatever materials we could get hold of. All fabrics except black-out curtaining was on rations, and the coupons did not go far. Also, pretty coloured silks, nets and satins etc suitable for stage costumes were very scarce indeed. Some of our costumes were extremely ingenious – the most memorable one was made entirely of Union Jacks (off ration!) hanging cornerwise from a waist band, whilst the top was a tiny bra made from a triangular section of flag. One wag was heard to remark, "I wonder what happens when they lower the flag?"

These costumes were worn in a grande finale in which we marched and danced in intricate formations to such patriotic tunes as *Land of*

Hope and Glory, There'll Always be an England, Hearts of Oak, British Grenadiers, The Royal Airforce March etc. There wasn't a dry eye in the house after that number which ended in much saluting and flag-waving.
These shows lasted from 1942 to 1945 when peace came to Europe. I was by then twelve years old and a seasoned trouper.'

NURSING

'When the Second World War started, I was in my final year of nursing and took my exam in October 1939. Because so many doctors were called up we could not complete our exams until June 1940. I worked in an emergency hospital for a time where we took in casualties from the blitz. Our operating theatre was very inadequate with everything in short supply as the forces had first call. We were short of instruments, and we made up disinfectants etc on the premises. Of course there was strict blackout enforcement so trying to cycle in for emergency operations was quite hazardous. Meanwhile at home we had two families of evacuees from Coventry, nine people in all, and my aunt had two Irishmen who were working on an Army store. Food was rationed and in the villages there wasn't the opportunity to queue for offal and sausages. What my mother would have done without rabbits and old hens I don't know. They certainly helped with the meat ration but of course you couldn't always rely on getting them.
My boyfriend was called up in 1940 and I didn't see him again until 1946. During that time I was called up and went in QA Army Nursing. I was on a draught for the Far East but as I was engaged to be married my boyfriend asked if I could be taken off as we had lost so much time together as it was. Nearly another year went by before he returned. I didn't know he was coming as they were unable to let anyone know where they were. I was home on leave fortunately and when he looked in the window as we all sat at Sunday dinner you can just imagine the surprise and joy. It was completely unbelievable. I had to go back to the Military Hospital but managed to get an extension of leave. This was September and we were married on 13th October.
Being in the forces I got clothing coupons but the things civilians were able to get was very limited not only because of coupons but also the shortage of goods to buy. But we considered we were well off in comparison with some of the German and Italian troops we had nursed. Their dressing and bandages were like crepe paper.'

THE HOME GUARD

'Dad's Army is a favourite of many watchers of television, young and old, but I sometimes wonder if the young and very young realise this was a real live major defence of this country in the dark days of the 1939-45 war.

Colonel Cash, a local Warwickshire man, was the Zone Commander of the County of Warwick Home Guard. He writes, "It will be a thousand pities if the history of this great citizens' army should go unrecorded. The Home Guard was a thoroughly British affair and it may be doubted whether a force of just this kind could have come into being in any other country. As a nation we have a faculty for improvisation, and it was this faculty, coupled with an unlimited willingness to serve, which resulted in the growth of the Home Guard, in a surprisingly short time, into an important part of the armed forces of the Crown which would, without doubt, have given a good account of itself had it been called upon to do so."

Britain has shown a marked tendency, throughout its eventful history, to meet its international crises in a state of woeful military unpreparedness and to summon hastily contrived civilian lives as one means of plugging a few of the more obvious gaps that have inevitably appeared in the nation's defensive fabric.

There was confident anticipation that any assault upon these islands would be preceded by parachute or airborne landings. Holland, Belgium and France had been overwhelmed and the British Expeditionary Force extricated from Dunkirk with great losses. So the Home Guard (originally called the Local Defence Volunteers) was conjured into existence, this time by the magic of wireless broadcast. The response to Anthony Eden's wireless call was overwhelming; within a few days the million mark had been passed.

The first duty imposed upon the Home Guard was that of observation and report and that primary function was fulfilled night by night in many thousands of scattered observation posts. Throughout the land and from city roof tops and village church towers, from the high ground of hamlet, moor and fell, men (and women) waited and watched, night by night, year by year. Thousands of volunteers spent Christmas night in the chill comfort of observation posts.

We must remember the men and women fulfilling these exacting watches were also the men and women making the guns, the planes and the shells in long days of factory work – or engaged in growing a blockaded nation's food – or reserved in different occupations and professions from the armed forces.

The first personality to emerge from the lists of volunteers in the

Rugby rural area was Captain D C M Beech, MC, ex cavalry officer, rider to hounds, squire and magistrate, whose home was at Brandon Hall. He was appointed to command what was designated as The Rugby Company. This Company was well over 2,000 strong. Their armoury consisted of a motley assortment of "arms" ranging from twelve bore double-barrelled guns and .22 rifles to last war trophies and beer bottles filled with a mixture of pitch and petrol. The Molotov Cocktail, as this mixture was coded, was the Home Guards' main weapon against enemy tanks. Fortunately they were not called upon to put these weapons into action.

Well may the young and very young laugh at "Dad's Army", but for those of us who had fathers, brothers, sons in this truly British force, those critical days of 1939-45 were very real and serious.'

THE WOMEN'S LAND ARMY

'I was 17½ years old when I joined the WLA (Women's Land Army). I joined them because my father was in the RAF, I had a brother in the Navy and another brother was in the Horse Guards and none of them would have me joining the female equivalent.

To join I cycled from Mere Green to Shenston Hall where a Mrs Godfrey lived. She was the person in authority for Sutton Coldfield.

Another girl named Pat and I met on Snow Hill station to go to Hatton Mental Hospital to do a month's training. We were issued with overalls, cow gowns and hobnailed boots and were housed in the nurses' quarters of the hospital.

The farmer taught us to milk cows and we used to pick potatoes with some of the out-patients and the wardens. One day I was running across a ploughed field thinking I would catch a rabbit, and a warden thought he could too when we both collided and I pulled a muscle in my thigh. I was then transported back to the hospital by tractor and put in a room where everyone who entered or left locked the door after them.

On completing our very informative month we were to go to Shipston-on-Stour, in a hostel where we were to join another 28 girls. It was a bit basic but we were well fed and there were plenty of opportunities for keeping clean and believe me, we needed them. If you were allotted to work on a farm more than six miles away you were allowed to go by van, if it was under six miles you were given a very heavy bike which meant a ride there, to work all day in the open and then ride back at night. Being in a hostel we would follow the tractor drum around, so that would mean we would be threshing till all the farms had finished harvesting the crops. Then there would be potato and sugar beet crops to be gathered in, that would be another few weeks. The only time we didn't work was if it was pouring with rain, then we could go into Shipston, where we counted 13 public houses and they had a very good cafe. The baker used to allow us into the bakery to watch him throwing jam into tarts from as far away as three feet!

After about 18 months of this Pat and I decided we would volunteer to be rat catchers. We were billeted out to a lovely cottage and went to Henley in Arden for a fortnight's training. We had a man in charge of us named Mr Pritchett from Shire Hall. If it was raining he would come with Italian prisoners and take us all round the farm baiting for moles and rats. When it was lunch-time the Italian prisoners used to light a fire and make us coffee. It used to taste much better than I have ever tasted since.

On the back of our bikes we had a round tin and a long spoon strapped to a pannier. In the tin we had oats laced with strychnine and Archie Pritchett said we must guard it with our lives as we had enough poison there to kill all of Warwickshire. One day Pat and I cycled to Ilmington where one particular farmer welcomed us with open arms. We baited every rat hole and run we found and bade him goodbye for a couple of days.

When we went back he had the threshing drum there and said we should stop and help, as he still had the rats but we had killed every cat on the farm. Well, we waited until the rick was about four feet off the floor and the farmer put netting all round the rick and everyone armed themselves with big heavy sticks. By the time we got to the bottom of the rick we had killed about twelve rats. I know I must have whacked a few because next day I had a blister all down my first finger.

Being at Shipston we weren't near any American camps so one night we decided to have a Hallowe'en party. We invited the Pioneer Corps. They were all old enough to be our fathers, but they were good fun and joined in the hilarity as well as the games.

Unfortunately Pat became ill and had to leave the Land Army so that meant I had to go back into the hostel.

Of course, the highlight of the week was Saturday. We used to work till twelve o'clock then we would all rush back to the hostel, get washed and changed and then run the length of Shipston to the Oxford Road where at about half past two, two low-loaders known as "Queen Marys" used to come through from Oxford. They would stop and pick up about 20 girls and take them into Birmingham for the weekend.

My luck didn't last very long and having been sent to a farm on my own and worked a track round a field all day in the rain, I fell ill and ended up having to go home. Eventually I went back to Moor

Life in the Women's Land Army could be hard, especially for girls not used to country life, but they coped with good humour and enthusiasm.

Hall where I worked in the greenhouses in the morning and I did reception work in the afternoon until I got married in 1945.

Thinking about getting married – there was a very good scheme which was run by one of the American women's organisations, whereby if you wrote to them enclosing your measurements, shoe size, glove size and any other size, for the price of cleaning which was 15 shillings, they sent everything you would need, including a blue garter, all wrapped up beautifully in a large cardboard box. The only other thing which was required was a photograph of yourself on your wedding day so that they could put it in their album.'

'I joined the Land Army aged 17 and started my training at Leamington at Lady Fielding's farm. There we learnt to hand milk, using a three-legged stool and bucket. They had a herd of shorthorns plus a few Jersey cows and it was one of these that I milked. Her name was Flower and she was a very gentle soul so we got on famously. I used to take the milk up to the house for the Blue Boys (convalescing soldiers). After eight weeks I was moved to another farm where they milked by machine, so I had to learn the procedure all over again. We carried the milk to the dairy and put it onto the tank which held ten gallons. I wasn't allowed to watch when a cow calved.

After 18 months I moved on and was at my next farm for three years. To start with, the Gaffer would not let me be around when the AI (Artificial Insemination) man came, but one time the Gaffer was asleep when he arrived so I nipped out and from then on all was well. One day the Gaffer was going to market but instead asked me if I could manage – from then on it was my job. I really enjoyed it all.'

A CHILD'S WAR

For children, war rapidly became the normal state of affairs, with British and Germans replacing Cowboys and Indians in the ruins of Coventry. School life was disrupted by the arrival in small villages and towns of evacuees, while other Warwickshire children found themselves waving goodbye to their mothers as they themselves were evacuated to safer areas. The celebrations at the end of the war were greeted with delight, not least for the goodies which made their appearance after years of shortages and rationing, but many a child also began to understand the horrors of what had gone before.

MY KIT BAG WENT TO FRANCE

'I was at Guide camp in Criccieth, North Wales when war was declared and we came back to Stratford on the 4th September. The trains and stations were crowded with men in uniforms and chaos reigned. Our kit bags were sent over to France and it was weeks before we had them back!

As a teenager during the war, I used to cycle miles and miles to dances and socials. My sister and I were cycling along a country lane the night of the first blitz on Coventry. It was clear moonlight and every time the bombers came over my sister made me get off my bike and hide in the hedgebottom.'

SENT AWAY

'I remember waving goodbye to my Mum as I left from the station that took my class to stay in Tenbury Wells in September 1939. There was a label tied to my coat and we were all given carrier bags of food.'

SCHOOL LIFE WAS DISRUPTED

'The first thing I remember about the war was that our school, Campion Central for girls at Leamington, shared lesson time with a girls school in Coventry, which I believe was Barr's Hill if I remember correctly. The Campion girls went to school two or three times a week then on to Barr's Hill at other times. My parents were not keen on this idea so I was packed off to a boarding school in Wem, Shropshire.

In the holidays I came home to a house full of evacuees. We lived in a fairly large old farmhouse in the heart of the country and my mother, father and six children lived in one room, a family of four lived in the sitting room and a family of three in the dining room with bedrooms adjoining. Can you imagine the chaos that ensued with only one bathroom?

In the holidays I found that some of the Home Guard used to signal from our house to Napton windmill and I was enlisted to take down messages. Then when that was stopped I used to go up the church tower at Long Itchington and take messages there while the others were signalling. On holiday in the summer I was enlisted to help with the shooting. My father had a large sand pit on the farm, big enough to hold two or three carts and horses. There was a big bank at the back of this which was full of rabbit holes and fox holes. The Home Guard decided they would do some target practice, so they dug a trench for me to get in and had a very large target against the bank. They went three fields away and fired about 15 rounds and then I would get out of the trench and with a pointer show them where they had hit the target. Talk about my life in their hands.'

'Earliest recollections of school during the war years were of being given gas masks, trying them on, and all the children sitting in class with them on. Of course, we all thought it was great fun, but in reality it certainly was not. They were made up of rubber face masks with a celluloid vision panel and filters in the bottom which contained charcoal and blue asbestos, which today is considered highly dangerous especially if inhaled! During mock air raid warnings, we used to sit for half an hour at a time doing lessons whilst wearing our gas masks; they used to mist up inside and in those days most children seemed to have runny noses and it was impossible to wipe one's nose whilst wearing the gas mask. I leave the rest to the reader's imagination.

Occasionally there would be daylight raids, in which case the sirens would give out a dreadful wailing sound and this would strike fear into us all. We were quickly marshalled together by our teachers who would put on their tin helmets and take us to the air raid shelters which were situated underground on the school playing fields. There were several passages with timber-slatted seats each side of the corridors, and we would all sit there clutching our gas masks until the all clear was sounded. We would then make our way back to the classrooms and resume lessons – sometimes this would happen twice a day.

All our food was rationed – sweets and chocolates were non-existent except when the school was allocated jars of sweets from America, and then if we were very good we would be given two boiled sweets on Friday afternoon. We thought it marvellous that we had sweets that had come all the way from America.

In those days teachers were quite strict and the cane was used as punishment for a number of offences – getting wrong answers to arithmetical questions, making blots in our exercise books, talking in class, and being late for school. If we were late, we would go first into the cloakroom and rub soap onto our hands to hopefully soften the blow and sting of the caning, but somehow it never did. Occasionally a child would rebel against the caning and would run out of the class and go home; an irate parent would perhaps come to the school to complain to the head teacher, but it did not make a lot of difference, we still got the cane. Another punishment was having to write 500 times "I must not be late" and this was done during playtime, and playtimes were missed until the said lines were completed.

School dinners were set out on long tables in the assembly hall and usually consisted of some sort of meat in gravy, mashed potatoes and stringy dark green cabbage that no matter how one tried could not possibly be swallowed. Puddings were either semolina or tapioca, and if we were lucky a spoonful of jam on top, which we would stir in making a sickly mess – invariably we left it uneaten. The menu did not vary very much and was considered full of vitamins which we as children needed.

The school was used at weekends by the Home Guard. As we lived by the school we would go and watch the men drilling and would make fun of them, which would usually end up with being "clipped round the ear" as the saying went, but that did not stop us. I think we were secretly proud of "our Dad" in uniform and would help clean his brass buttons on his uniform.

Some schools in the outskirts of Coventry were used by the Women's Royal Voluntary Service as refuges for the people who had had their homes severely damaged by the bombing. After the two big raids on Coventry, people could be seen leaving the city pushing prams or carts piled high with their possessions, including cats and

214

dogs, with the injured following on behind. The German bombers used to raid on bright moonlit nights and so we came to dread what was known as the "Bomber's Moon".

Then came VE Day – Victory in Europe – and everywhere people celebrated by having huge bonfires which were kept going all night. Everyone sang and we all went to bed very tired but happy at last because the war was over. It took many years to rebuild lives, but by that time we were approaching school leaving age and were looking forward to happier times.'

'School life at Ullenhall was totally disrupted by the war. Evacuees flooded in to the village. They were taught in the morning and we had our lessons in the afternoon. Many of them came from London and were very disruptive in school and in the village. Several of them ran away, presumably back to London, but some of the boys remained after the war and eventually married local girls.

We had two bombs dropped very close, one because someone had left a light on and the other because the Germans used to jettison any bombs they hadn't used on their raids over Birmingham. On this particular night I was hurriedly dressed in my liberty bodice (with linen buttons) and taken to the cellars of the village pub where we sat amongst the beer barrels in deck chairs until the all clear went.'

'I attended Ryton on Dunsmore village school and during the war I can remember having regular air raid practices when we had to quickly line up and walk briskly in single file across the playground and down the steps to the air raid shelter.

During the summer months when the weather always seemed so hot, we had lessons outside, and the afternoons when the girls did sewing the headmaster took the boys to the school gardens 15 minutes walk away. We also went rosehip picking from school. The teacher had a walking stick to pull the branches down to our height. The hips were made into rosehip syrup for babies, obtainable from the welfare clinic.'

'During the early years of the war, pupils at our junior school on the outskirts of Birmingham were trying to raise money towards the war effort – together with knitting lots of warm woollies for the armed forces. Food was beginning to get scarce at this time, and fruit in particular was a luxury. So when my grandfather, who was a CSM with the Royal Warwicks, brought home some lemons, I was over the moon to be given one to take to school. I made rather a bad job of explaining to my form mistress that it was not for her but a donation for the school raffle! This was eventually done and we managed to raise the princely sum of £4, which was duly donated to the Red Cross.'

'Starting in 1939, and for the following five years, I attended the school at Alcester which entailed a daily bus journey from Stratford of some 16 miles in total. The opening of school was delayed that first year of the war because the building of the air raid shelters had not been completed. A school uniform was very definitely required, including Vedonis knickers (used for gym) with white linings; black stockings in winter and grey-fawn stockings in summer. Hats had to be worn travelling to and from school and these were black velour in winter and panama straw in summer.

During my first year pupils were allowed to attend school during the holidays but there were no lessons – sports facilities were used but a great deal of time was spent reinforcing the windows with strips of sticky tape as a precaution against bomb blast. As soon as the shelters were completed regular air raid exercises became very much a part of school life: everybody was required to proceed in an orderly manner to those damp, dark, underground places. Gas masks, in purpose-made cardboard containers, had to be carried at all times and regular practises in their use were held in the classroom – these always heralded by a cacophony of tuneless honks.

As the war years went on Stratford changed and the hotels were taken over by mainly RAF recruits doing their initial training. When I was confirmed at Holy Trinity church more than half the candidates for confirmation were young RAF conscripts. Many nights were disturbed by the waves of German planes flying overhead on bombing sorties. It was possible to look into the skies at night and see fires burning over Birmingham or Coventry with the cluster of incendiary bombs lighting up the sky. It was quite easy to see which city was being attacked and remarks were made such as "Poor old 'Brum got it last night".

On leaving school in 1944 I was employed by the Treasury Solicitor, the Treasury having been evacuated from London to the Welcombe Hotel. Apart from four young locals all the staff had come from London and were accommodated in private houses in the town. Consequently they were allowed a period of time, an hour or so, to take a bath and do their personal laundry during office hours. The hotel's cloakrooms were festooned with washing lines and it was on these that we first saw nylon stockings. The existence of these garments was not unconnected with the fact that there was a social club shared by American soldiers living at The White Swan.'

CHEERING UP THE POWs

'We walked to school in Tanworth village from the hamlet of Aspley Heath about three miles away. When the bombing was heavy there were many evacuees – so many that we had to share our school with them, going just mornings one week and afternoons the next. Life was very hectic with little sleep.

We grew all our own vegetables at home and went to the local farms picking potatoes and peas, for which we were paid ninepence a week. There were a lot of prisoners of war working on the farms too, first the Italians and later the Germans.

To the eyes of an eight year old, the Italians seemed very friendly and affectionate and not at all frightening. Some were only 16 or 17 themselves. They missed their families greatly and made a fuss of the English children. They were brought by coach from a large camp in the Redditch area, and some worked on digging out the river Alne. The children brought them sweets to cheer them up. I remember that they could turn a florin into a ring with your initials on it. They also used to weave all sorts of baskets from the willows which they had pollarded. They would sit on the river bank, chatting and weaving. With the money they earned from selling the baskets they would get the children to buy them cigarettes and sweets.'

WAR GAMES

'During the war, Coventry's bombed buildings provided the ideal place for boys to fight the war on Saturday mornings. People who had been bombed out would doubtless be less than entertained by the sight of war games in the ruins of their old home, but none seemed to think it strange. It was always British versus Germans. There was often a preference to be on the "German side" for some unaccountable reason, and the Americans were never in it. The war games duly stopped as soon as the war ended.'

CHOCOLATE SPREAD

'Sweets were in very short supply and my mother would give me a dish or a paper bag with cocoa and sugar mixed and I would eat it with a spoon. Syrup and cocoa was another mixture. Chocolate spread could be made with cocoa and condensed milk. I can taste it now 50 years later!'

EXTRA LONG DAYS

'The double summertime during the war seemed to provide extra long summer evenings on which the children at Warmington played cricket and rounders on the green. The vicar at that time, Rev Simpson, had been a keen boatsman during his college days and had three model sailing boats called Hare, Tortoise and Brittania, and the local young lads were allowed to borrow any one of them to sail on the pond as a rare treat. I can remember the house martins skimming the pond like dive bombers and building their nests all along the eaves of the village shop opposite.

One day I watched hundreds of aeroplanes towing gliders, an exercise in preparation for the second invasion. Another time a regiment of tanks churned up the green during their manoeuvres.

The night Coventry was bombed I watched the enemy aircraft pass overhead in the moonlight, thrilled to be allowed to stay up past my normal bedtime at eight o'clock, but later less thrilled when the shudder of bombs in Coventry rocked the pictures on the walls of our cottage home.'

FRIENDS WITH THE SOLDIERS

'American servicemen built a Bailey bridge over the river Avon at Bidford, this was obviously a training routine as the bridge was dismantled the next day. The whole operation drew an interested crowd of village spectators. British soldiers of the Pioneer Corps dug deep trenches with sand-bagged fortifications overlooking the river. Were the "powers that be" expecting an enemy invasion up the river Avon?

The boys made friends with the soldiers and one Sunday they were smuggled into camp in the back of an army lorry to watch a cricket match, the boys being very keen on sport. This army camp was on Stratford on Avon racecourse. At tea time the boys were delighted to see such an abundance of jam, being used to rationing. They had the option of spreading it on bread in the normal way or eating it with a spoon from a dish as some of the soldiers did.

One day in about 1943 a German plane passed low over the farm and everyone ran for cover in the buildings. This was thought to be the plane which had been firing on Kidderminster market that day. On another occasion an American Flying Fortress passed over losing height rapidly. The crew had all baled out and the plane crashed at the nearby village of Temple Grafton, narrowly missing the village school.'

BORN AND BRED IN STRATFORD

'I was born and bred in Stratford and well remember wartime here, especially as regards school. My friends and I were aged eleven when the war started and attended the newly built high school on Alcester Road. We were very apprehensive starting at such a large school after our little junior schools, but not half so apprehensive as the poor little evacuees coming from the GWR station in long crocodiles, waiting to be billeted all around the town and district. Some of the older ones later attended our school. We all tried to make them welcome but their strong Birmingham accents sometimes had us foxed. I expect our country voices amazed them, too!

When the sirens sounded we walked in orderly fashion to special "points" – underneath the stage in the hall, in the Domestic Science sugar cupboards and book cupboards – never frightened because at that age we really didn't understand the danger.

Most of my close friends were daughters of shopkeepers in the town, and at one point we were allowed to cycle home when the siren sounded – if we were sure we could do it in five minutes!

On the night of the awful Coventry raid, my parents took my brother and I down into the cellars under C A Rookes Wines & Spirits where bunks etc had been installed. I can remember the wonderful smell of gallons of wines and spirits even now – and I remember how cold it was down there!'

A WONDERFUL DAY

'At the end of the war we had big celebrations for VE Day and VJ Day. The first one was a very special occasion. My sister Margaret was chosen to be Queen of Radford Semele at the celebration. I was very annoyed about this. I was chosen to wear a Dutch girl's costume. I was dragged out of the lilac tree where I had gone to sulk about the injustice of it all and taken to the street party, which I was determined not to enjoy. Margaret was driven round the village in a decorated donkey cart and was attended by matrons of honour and she had a wonderful dress. She sat at the top of the table, which was laden with all the things the mothers had managed to produce.

I can remember going into Leamington sometime at the end of the war, in a group, to see the King and Queen who were visiting Leamington and we waited opposite the Pump Rooms to see them.

I can also remember a chap coming home from a Japanese prisoner of war camp to the village. His mum laid on a great celebration with a huge banner across the street saying "Welcome Home Eddie". We children guessed from all the whispering that went on between the

219

grown ups that something horrible had happened to Eddie. We did notice that he was very thin.'

'I shall never forget VE Day in Tanworth. It was wonderful, after all the sadness and worry people had had to go through. The days before were so busy with people making flags and sorting out the ration books for points to buy the ingredients for cakes, trifles and sandwiches. The tables overflowed with all the lovely goodies. All we could do was stare in amazement. The day went on and on, dancing, eating, watching firework displays (Wilders Fireworks were a local business). These were the first lights at night for six years and *McNamara's Band* the first street music for as long.'

FROM FIRST TO LAST

'We had just started back to school after the August holidays when the war started. I was excited to be going back to school as we were to begin swimming lessons that year. There was only an outdoor pool in Nuneaton in those days so we had about two lessons and then the pool was closed for the winter. Shortly afterwards daylight raids began and the pool remained closed for the duration of the war.

They built an underground air raid shelter in the school yard. When the sirens went we would all leave the classrooms and go down to the shelter and continue our lessons as best we could. Then the strafing started. Physical Education classes were transferred across the road to the parish hall and included instructions on how to throw yourself to the ground and roll into a ditch, gutter, or against a wall to escape machine gun fire.

With the commencement of night time raids there began a rest period in the afternoons. We would fold our arms across our desks and put our heads down and go to sleep for half an hour. Another, non-curricular, activity was to go down to the police station every lunch time and read the previous night's death roll. Sometimes there were people on it that you knew.

One night in May 1941 the raid was particularly bad. We lived about a quarter of a mile from the LMS marshalling yard where all the munitions trains from Coventry came to be redistributed to the various docks, military establishments etc. We were in an Anderson shelter with neighbours when the ARP man fetched us out as the *Tribune* offices next door had received a direct hit and we were in some danger, as the whole place had gone up in flames.

We ran down the street to the main shelter in a maelstrom of flying debris, screaming bombs and explosions. My sister received a piece of glass in one eye but fortunately suffered no permanent damage. Not so lucky was our next door neighbour who had elected to go across the road to the shelter in the schoolyard. On the way she was hit by a falling ridge tile from the school roof, and died in hospital the next day.

When we emerged from the shelter the next morning, after the all clear had sounded, it was to find the street in ruins. The men pulled wood from the wreckage and built a big bonfire in the middle of the street, while the women scavenged what food they could from the ruins and cooked it on the bonfire.

We all had a good breakfast amid much laughing and joking. It was all a big adventure to us children, but for the adults, in spite of

I WISH TO MARK, BY THIS PERSONAL MESSAGE, my appreciation of the service you have rendered to your Country in 1939.

In the early days of the War you opened your door to strangers who were in need of shelter, & offered to share your home with them.

I know that to this unselfish task you have sacrificed much of your own comfort, & that it could not have been achieved without the loyal co-operation of all in your household. By your sympathy you have earned the gratitude of those to whom you have shown hospitality, & by your readiness to serve you have helped the State in a work of great value.

Elizabeth R

Many families welcomed evacuees into their homes from the early days of 1939. After the war they received thanks from the Queen for their efforts.

221

all their joking, it must have been quite devastating.

After breakfast Mother sent my sister and I to my aunt and uncle's house at Weddington, while she went to the council house to try and sort something out for us. It was eventually decided that we should stay with them, as they had spare bedroom capacity. The school was transferred to Higham Lane school and life went on through a long hot summer.

In August we obtained a little two-bedroomed house in Bedworth, and I started another new school. It was a dump. The first week I was there I asked my mother to move me to another school, but she either could not or would not.

The building was condemned and due for demolition as soon as a replacement was built. Unfortunately that was postponed until after the end of the war. There was hardly a classroom without a broken window. One year I wore an eye patch all winter, as the draught from a broken window caused my eye to discharge continuously.

The equipment was almost non-existent; one sewing machine for the whole school. You got one go on it for about 15 minutes each. The science equipment consisted of four test tubes and one bunsen burner. Not that it mattered very much as the science and maths teacher was called up a few months after I started. There was no replacement. The surplus children were simply redistributed. There were approximately 45 children in each class. I know because I did the school attendance figures and wrote the weekly report for the school attendance officer for a year.

School secretaries were an unheard of luxury and with teachers so over-stretched many such jobs were undertaken by the older children, who were also called upon to supervise silent reading classes should one of the teachers be off sick.

Shortly after VE day we were all taken in a long crocodile to one of the local cinemas and shown film of the concentration camps.

There were many accounts in the newspapers of the atrocities committed in the camps. My mother would hide the papers from me but I usually found and read them, often fainting with horror, especially at the obscene experiments on women and children. I did a lot of fainting that year.'

HIGHDAYS
& HOLIDAYS

MAKING OUR OWN ENTERTAINMENT

There seemed to be so much to do in days past, when every village had its clubs and societies, dances and whist drives were regular features of local life, sporting teams enjoyed enthusiastic support, and there was always a show to enjoy or the nearest cinema to go to on a Saturday night. Television had not entered our homes so we went out to have fun, although the early radios had their avid listeners!

THE WHOLE VILLAGE WAS THERE

'There were many social events held at Water Orton during the early years of this century, when it seemed that the whole village was there. Our Football Club activities were enjoyed by all who attended them; in 1926 the sixth annual meeting was advertised as "one long revelry" and it certainly lived up to its publicity. The programme consisted of songs, competitions, games and dances, the pianists and singers all coming from the village. Refreshments were plentiful and managed successfully by a willing band of helpers. The proceeds were given to the old and infirm of our village. During the same year a dancing and singing display was held on the vicarage lawn, the entertainment given by a group of young girls led by a local lady who also gave piano and singing lessons. The event was well supported despite the bad weather (October) and the proceeds were given to the Women's Institute.

There were several other groups in Water Orton during those early years who held social events and all gave their profits to deserving causes. A large house in the village called The Woodlands used to open its beautiful gardens and grounds for the use of many local events. There was a wonderful miniature railway that ran around the garden, built by the owner of the house and a local man. There was a mile of track, a steam engine, several trucks, a station, embankments, signals, a bridge and a loco shed. The trucks would carry children and adults on a magical ride and continued to be used long after the owner had passed away, his wife continuing to open the property for local events. The Woodlands was large and roomy and many whist drives were held there.

The village whist drives were always well supported wherever they were held. At a Cricket Club drive and dance in 1926 there were 29 tables (over 116 players). The Savoy Band from London provided the music and there were eight prizes for the lucky whist winners. The Boy Scouts held displays and entertained at the council school; there were many local young artists and the whole school seemed to be involved. Dances were also held in the NUR room (National Union of Railwaymen). At a fancy dress dance held there on Boxing Day 1924, 97 attended and the festivities did not end until 3am!

At the end of the First World War big celebrations were held on the village green. A large bonfire was lit, the material coming from the villagers and a horse and cart was used to collect the rubbish. Fireworks were obtained at short notice and dancing went on all through the night.

In 1935 a pageant was held at Welland House, a large building now used by British Coal as offices. A long meadow adjoining the house was often used by Pat Collins Fair. There were merry-go-rounds, lots of side shows, the house of mirrors . . . what fun, fortune tellers who were right sometimes, a big man and lady and a little child, and tall swingboats . . . they were happy times.

In the 1920s and 1930s outings were spent at Sutton Park, not far away from the village, the transport being a well cleaned out hay cart and coal lorry with sacks to sit upon, though much of the time the children would stand up to see the sights and enjoy the excitement of the journey. In later years a local charabanc would take us to far away places such as country pubs; it cost a shilling for evening trips. A church outing took us to the Tontine Hotel at Stourport in Worcestershire. We had our tea there after returning from a long river trip, which was great fun and everyone enjoyed themselves.'

DANCES AND CLUBS

'The village hall at Middleton was built by the young men of the village in 1926/28. The floorboards and windows came from Drayton Manor when it was sold by Sir Robert Peel. Dances, known as "sixpenny hops", were held in the village school to raise money for the building work.

A Crazy Gang was formed by a group of ten lads and lasses in 1938 and the sketches they put on attracted full houses at every performance. Besides appearing at the village hall they travelled to Wishaw, Kingsbury, Minworth and Duddeston. The proceeds went towards the eradication of death watch beetle from the timbers of the bell tower in the church.'

Wolvey Dance Band c1930. There was a huge pool of talent in local villages, and many a small band played at the Saturday night hop.

'We held dances regularly at Long Itchington. It was the main entertainment and a good way of raising money for worthy causes – and it was only sixpence to go. The hall was so crowded you couldn't dance much, but we all had a good time. The lads who played in the band were from the village and often gave their services for a good cause.'

'Welford boasted a village band which played on many local occasions, such as for the maypole dancing and at the village fete. The Memorial Hall, built in memory of the men from Welford and Weston who served in the Great War, was always in great demand. The chapel pantomime was put on there, and the village Dramatic Society put on two plays a year. The minute kitchen, then complete with copper and black iron fireplace, served as a dressing room. In 1939, with the outbreak of war, twice weekly dances were held with servicemen attending from the neighbouring camps, most of them arriving on bicycles.

Children and teenagers had to find their own amusements and activities in the village itself in those days. The Scouts met in the old school at Weston. The Girl Guides had a room for their use at Manor Farm. There were Cubs and Brownies as well. There was also a Girls Friendly Society, founded in the middle of the 1930s. Members were

226

allowed to play on the Rectory tennis courts and met in the Rectory Lodge. The leader took girls on picnics in the summer, walking to Cress Hill bordering on the river, and on an annual outing to Weston-super-Mare by train for less than five shillings each.

On Easter Monday and August Bank Holiday (then the first Monday in August) a dance in the village hall was arranged, a band from Stratford run by a lady pianist with a drummer and saxophonist having been booked. The young and not so young all came along and enjoyed the dancing and refreshments.

There was also a Rat Club for the older men. Some 20 or so men used to gather on most Sunday mornings with sticks and dogs to help rid farms and smallholdings of this plague.'

'There was a private dance hall at Lapworth known as Concannon's Hall after the owner. A dance was held every Saturday and a whist drive in the week, when people travelled by train, cycle etc from other villages to take part.'

'We used to have marvellous Saturday nights at Chesford Grange, Kenilworth, dancing to Ronnie Hancox and his band and listening to his singer Susan Maughan. We could actually talk and dance at the same time and be heard! The last dance was always *I'll see you in my dreams* – how romantic.'

SPORTS AND LEISURE

'For some years after the war spectator sports enjoyed a boom. Football matches were well attended. Coventry City was not a first division side in those days but still drew reasonable crowds. There was always a full programme of league football at Christmas and Coventry always seemed to be at home on Christmas morning.

County cricket was watched by good crowds, especially on Saturdays and Bank Holidays. Warwickshire improved rapidly after the war, and won the County Championship in 1951. The visit of the Australians in 1948 attracted big crowds wherever they played. Their match at Edgbaston was not blessed with good weather (1948 was a poor summer sandwiched between the two glorious summers of 1947 and 1949) but they defeated Warwickshire, though for Warwickshire Eric Hollies took eight wickets for 107. This earned him a place in the England team for the last Test Match at the Oval, when he bowled Don Bradman (in his last test innings) for nought; the great man required only four to attain an average of 100 in Test Matches – a figure not approached by anyone before or since.

Coventry had a great rugby team at that time, being one of the

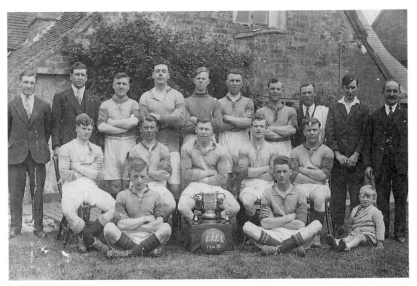

Long Itchington football team in 1930. Sports had a strong local following in the years between the wars.

premier sides in England. Crowds at Coundon Road were modest, however, rugby football did not have the popular appeal that it does now. Relatively few people generally played at school, though Coventry was somewhat of an exception, as there were a number of local schools with a great rugby tradition.

The average person's choice of leisure was rather more restricted than it is now. The freedom to go almost anywhere by motor car was not available to many people. Consequently leisure was taken locally. Cycling was very popular. There were numerous cycling clubs in Coventry, and small groups of cyclists from youth clubs, perhaps were a common sight on Warwickshire roads on Saturday and Sundays.'

'There was, and still is, a very flourishing Working Men's Club at Clifford Chambers. Here men play darts, snooker, whist and practice shooting. The best shots made a team to compete with other clubs in villages around and in Stratford. Whist drives were held there nearly every week and were well attended.

A Girls' Club was held at the rectory with Mrs Meredyth Brookes, the rector's wife, in charge. We did knitting and hand sewing for charities, and there was a lending library for us. I remember reading most of Warwick Deeping's novels borrowed from the rectory.

228

There was a Girl Guide company and a Boy Scout troop. As the girls reached school leaving age (14 years) they started work in service or as shop assistants in town so gave up guiding and the company closed down. The Scouts continued meeting at a large house in the centre of the village known as The Lodge. Miss Weldon was in charge and she was very kind to the boys. In 1933 some of them with Miss Weldon's help, attended the Scout Jamboree in Hungary, spending a month there. This was a wonderful experience for holidays abroad were not so well known then.

There was, and still is, a well supported football team when, no matter how cold the weather, we would cheer on our players. Cricket too was very popular with the "ladies" preparing tea after the match. Sometimes we had mixed cricket matches, ie men and women competing. For a few years there was a very keen ladies hockey team which was disbanded soon after the Second World War broke out.

As the river Stour is easily available, fishing is very popular with young and old alike and we youngsters had fun swimming or splashing about in the river. This wasn't a very safe pastime as there were deep holes in places where we could easily have drowned.

My brother and his pal made a "float", boards on petrol barrels with a pole to work it along. They would often take a wind-up gramophone for entertainment. Later my brother made another boat more like a box in shape but it floated well and friends often joined him – one at a time.'

'At Willoughby we had a cricket team made up from boys from three or four villages nearby; the hockey team was made up in the same way. The boys walked or cycled to fixtures in the early days, even when they were ten to 15 miles away. Later when there were two cars in the village, we all crowded in for a ride.'

'There was a time when the Tanworth in Arden football club was not doing very well and the married men of the village challenged the team to a match – and beat them.'

'The Hockey Club at Lapworth flourished for many years. In the early days the rector was the referee. He also provided transport, in a very large car, for many of the team to away matches. After home games, both teams walked across three fields to the church room, where a roaring fire and an excellent tea awaited them. Home games were played on the Melson Memorial Ground.'

A CONSUMING PASSION

'My father, Ted Mason, didn't become an engine driver when he grew up because he was colour blind, but he developed a consuming passion for making railway engines. These and one or two traction engines, were built to scale and burned coal to make steam to move the pistons. He built his own railway track and ran the engine at summer fetes, pulling open trucks, also made by himself. He had to lay the track each time the engine was in use. During the war, to encourage holidays at home, he ran his engine in the Whitehall Recreation Ground in Rugby – it ran straight up and back where the road leads to the Ken Marriott Sports Centre.'

THE FIRST RADIOS

'My father was a keen amateur radio buff. It must have been in the 1920s when we had our first set. We all sat round with bated breath while he fiddled around with the "cat's whisker" to get the right spot on the crystal. He later, along with two friends, progressed to making sets with valves, which were much more satisfactory. When I think about the results from a set with a little bit of wire and a crystal, though, it seems a very remarkable achievement.'

'In about 1920 we noticed a tall pole being erected in the garden of a house in Frederick Road, Stechford, to which was attached a double wire which ran to the house. We were told it was an aerial and that Mr and Mrs Casey's young sons Pat and Harold were running a radio programme with Percy Edgar who lived in Yardley – 51T Calling the British Isles. They later became Uncle Pat and Uncle Harold and I believe were the originators of Children's Hour. Their programme was taken over by the BBC.

Our brothers soon started making crystal sets and woe betide us if we walked across the "path". Rachel had an early set in her bedroom and we had to climb over the bottom bedpost or we cut ourselves off.'

GOING TO A SHOW

'At Polesworth we had a picture house known as the Palace, which had previously been a steam mill. It was our most regular form of entertainment and a great treat. Programmes were changed twice a week. To begin with it was silent films, starring comedians such as Jackie Coogan, Buster Keaton, Harold Lloyd etc. As soon as the talkies came in we had films such as *Broadway Melody*.

Sometimes there was Billy Holloway's travelling theatre for a week. A marquee would be erected in the Hall Court and *Uncle Tom's Cabin* and *Maria Marten, or the Murder in the Red Barn* would be performed by the Holloway family.'

'Down Bell Lane at Studley was the Imperial Cinema. It is now converted into a spring factory and Liberal Club. The highlight of our Saturday in the 1920s would be going there. Mr Washbourne and his son, who owned it, would start the gas engine to supply the electricity for the lights and projection and when the lights came on a great big cheer went up from the crowd of lads assembled round the doorway, then they would dash to the entrance to purchase the ticket to get in. The heating was a cast iron stove, which got hot at times in winter. In those days they employed a person to keep good order, and to stop the children throwing orange peel around while they watched the picture and the piano playing.
On the corner of Bell Lane was a wooden building known as the Cosy Corner fish and chip shop. The owner and his assistant were Villa supporters and if you pulled their leg on a Saturday night when Villa had lost, you didn't get many chips for your penny.'

'How we looked forward to the theatre at Stratford or Birmingham, or cinema outings to Leamington or Warwick – and did we dress up! We would spend ages dressing and putting on our make up just so – and those awful suspender belts and stockings!'

'To visit the cinema, young people from Lapworth would cycle about three miles on a Saturday morning. Adults would do the same in the evenings, weather permitting. Birmingham and Solihull cinemas were reached by train travel.'

'On Monday evenings we cycled two miles to Fenny Compton to the pictures held in the village hall.'

'In the villages we had to make our own entertainment because of the lack of transport. It was impossible to get home at night. There was a ten o'clock train back to Willoughby about once a week but it meant you had to leave a show before the end. However, as cinemas opened shows were put on from two o'clock onwards so it was possible to go during the day. I remember seeing the first talkie, *The Singing Fool* with Al Jolson and Jack Buchanan in *Goodnight Vienna*. They were wonderful.'

'Once a week our treat would be a visit to the pictures in Coventry.

I remember going to The Grand (later The Regal) on the Foleshill Road and seeing a Charlie Chaplin film. Sometimes we would go to The Roxy (Redesdale) near Cash's Lane or The Brookville in Holbrook Lane. They were our locals. Sometimes we would go to The Gaumont (Jordan Well) where we were entertained by the organ music before the film and during the interval. The organ would appear as if from the depths of the earth with the organist already seated and surrounded with coloured lights. It was called a Wurlitzer organ. The Empire Cinema in Hertford Street, and The Alexandra in Cox Street were always well patronised.

There will never again be pantomimes such as we children were privileged to see and enjoy. Flying ballets – where the dancers flew out and above the audience dressed as butterflies, birds and dragons. The costumes were out of this world, and there was wonderful scenery. The pantomimes usually took place at The Hippodrome in Hales Street, but one which stands out in my memory was *Mother Goose* at the Opera House, also in Hales Street, where a huge goose soared up to heaven (or so I thought) with Mother Goose riding on its back.'

'Alcester's Regal Cinema in the middle of the High Street was housed in the old Corn Exchange, consisting of a ground floor which was not tiered (large hats and tall gentlemen could be a nuisance) and a balcony.

There were two performances every night, at 6.30 pm and 8.30 pm and the programme was changed twice a week. When Sunday opening came about another film was shown for one night. It was a most popular place, especially the back rows; lots of romances started in the cinema and although it was nicknamed the "Flea Pit" it didn't put people off from going often.

The projection box opened straight onto the street and had two projectors, so there was no waiting while the reels were changed. There were very few breakdowns but when there was everyone made cat calls and stamped their feet.

Prices were very reasonable, ninepence and a shilling downstairs, one shilling and sixpence in the balcony. Ice-cream, sweets, etc were sold during the intervals. Sadly it closed in the mid 1960s.'

GOING AWAY

Holidays away from home were not the commonplace they are today. Many men had no paid holiday entitlement from their work, and the difficulty and expense of travel often prevented any thought of family holidays. When we did get away, for a day or for longer, how we appreciated it!

DAY TRIPS TO WESTON

'Studley was on the branch line of the LMS Railway in the 1930s when I was a child. The line ran from Barnt Green to Ashchurch, and Studley shared its station with Astwood Bank.

Although the station was a good mile from the village centre, day trips to Weston were always crowded. They were red letter days in our young lives. We were up and dressed early, wearing our macs. In the cool of the morning we trudged up to the station, each carrying bucket and spade or whatever we thought we needed. The grown ups carried large bags with sandwiches, towels and mackintosh "waders" to wear over our clothes if it was cold. These garments had bloomer-type bottoms and a bib top and protected the child's clothes from Weston's mud and water if they should splash too much or fall. I fell; covered in black sticky mud, I howled. My aunt ran me over to the boat-sailing pool nearby and dunked me in to wash me. I was mortified – all the children laughed.'

THE SUN ALWAYS SHONE

'My father, who worked at Courtaulds on shift work, only had three days holiday in the summer, until I was about nine years old in the 1930s when he was allowed a week. In those days holidays were unpaid, so it was a case of saving up hard all year. I can remember holidays at Blackpool where we went by train, Weston-super-Mare and Skegness (which was reached after spending one night in a boarding house at Leicester as there was not a connection until morning). We once went to Great Yarmouth by charabanc which took hours and hours. As the years went by we made it as far as Cliftonville (Margate was a bit on the common side in those days).

Of course, the sun *always* shone. I remember getting sunburn and having to wear a sunhat made of coloured grass and walking along

233

with a parasol. Ice creams at the seaside were different – delicious, like creamy custard filled with lumps of ice. I can taste them to this day.

Summer also brings back memories of a cousin's party in June each year in a farmer's field, playing in the hay and dining on bowls of strawberries and cream. It *never* rained.'

SUBTERFUGE

'Holidays were practically unheard of in the 1920s. In fact, I was 18 years old before I saw the sea and that was at Torquay with my future wife and in laws. In between times I had made visits to Liverpool to stay with my aunt and uncle, but that was on a tidal river and not the real sea.

To enable me to get to Liverpool from Brinklow a great deal of subterfuge was necessary. In those days the LMS Railway ran day trips to various places on a Sunday for five shillings, and if one was to Liverpool I would travel on the outward journey, stay until such a trip was put on again in the reverse direction and return home after a fortnight or so on a five shilling ticket.'

MEMORABLE OCCASIONS

Royal occasions have been celebrated with enthusiasm by towns and villages throughout Warwickshire. Royal visits, jubilees and coronations brought excitement and patriotic fervour – although the advent of television by the time of the 1953 Coronation was a sign of things to come as more people spent the day indoors, albeit with friends and neighbours.

QUEEN VICTORIA'S JUBILEE

'One of my early memories is of Queen Victoria's Jubilee celebrations at Sutton under Brailes. They were in traditional English village pattern of service in church, then a big meal of roast beef and plum pudding seated in a barn. There followed a cricket match for the men, races and games for the children, with the women sitting around nursing their babies and having a good gossip. Then a communal tea and an evening of song and dance with plenty of beer to loosen things up.'

THE THREE VILLAGES

'Ansty, Barnacle and Shilton are three villages which are a mile distant from each other. Ansty and Shilton are on the Coventry-Leicester road and Barnacle is a hamlet one mile from Shilton.

At the beginning of the century the three villages all joined together to celebrate highdays and holidays and the end of wars, etc but, as the years have passed, they have become more independent of each other and now they usually each hold their own celebrations.

Barnacle and Shilton still have an annual fete and flower show in their own village hall and Ansty has a flower show in the Working Men's Club, which originally started out as their village hall.

Many years ago the idea of holding functions was to get enough money together to build a hall for the villagers to meet in. At one time the only place of any size in the three villages was the school at Shilton. This consisted of two classrooms divided by a folding screen which was pushed back to make one large room. There was no mains water so all water for catering had to be drawn from the pump across the road and carried to the school.

Celebrations for a special event, ie a coronation, jubilee or peace celebrations, usually took the form of a "meat tea", sometimes on a special plate which would be taken home after the meal as a memento of the occasion. The honour of carving the joints of meat would be allocated to people of "high standing" in the village. To be chosen was felt to be a mark of high esteem. The meal would then be followed by entertainment, usually a concert of songs and recitations. In later years dances were held in the school, with the permission of the headmaster.

To begin with money was raised by the three villages jointly for a hall and the first one was built at Barnacle. This was known as Barnacle Memorial Hall and was built as a memorial to the local soldiers who had died in the 1914-18 war. A roll of honour in the hall records the men's names and, after the Second World War, they were joined by the names of the men who had lost their lives in that war. An interdenominational service is held at Barnacle Memorial Hall on the Sunday nearest to Armistice Day every year.

In June 1902 the celebrations for the coronation of King Edward VII and Queen Alexandra were a joint affair between the villages and the special plates had "Anstey and Shilton" on them. In the centre of the plate is a picture of the King and Queen. Over the years the spelling of Ansty has changed and the "e" has been dropped from the name. On the 22nd June 1911 the coronation of King George V and Queen Mary was celebrated. A special plate was issued showing their majesties and, as only the name Shilton appears on the top of the plate, I think that Ansty must have had their own celebrations.

At the end of the First World War as part of the celebrations for the declaration of peace, a procession took place and this made its way through both Ansty and Shilton. The children dressed up and joined in the fun, following the musicians as they paraded through the villages. Florence Bolton of Shilton, the nine year old daughter of Joseph Bolton who was the local carrier, headed the procession portraying Peace. She rode her father's white horse Blossom and was dressed in white, she had her long hair loose and was barefooted. The horse was led by her father who also wore a long white coat and a white hat.

Part of the coronation celebrations in June 1937 was the tea held in Shilton School. Mrs Sarah Rowe was in charge of the catering arrangements and she had the usual committee to help her. A plate was issued showing "Shilton" on the top rim and a picture of King George VI and Queen Elizabeth in the centre and the royal cypher on the bottom rim.

At the end of the 1939-1945 war when peace was declared, food was still rationed. The members of the committee formed to organize the celebration meal went round from door to door in the three villages, asking people to donate small amounts of sugar and tea. Many families had saved ingredients from their rations so that cakes could be made for the children for the tea party held for them at Shilton school. Children from Ansty, Barnacle and Shilton attended the tea and the headmaster gave his permission for a dance to be held in the evening for the adults.

On the 2nd June 1953 for the coronation of Queen Elizabeth II, a "meat tea" was held at Shilton school again served on special plates which were taken home after the meal. The plates had "Shilton" at the top above a picture of the young queen. The children dressed up in fancy dress, had games at the school and each received a gift.

Some of the villagers had been fortunate enough, earlier in the day, to be able to watch the celebrations in London on television. The sets only had a nine inch screen and, of course, the picture was only available in black and white. The curtains had to be drawn so that the picture could be seen more easily. For many people it was the first time they had watched anything on television.'

A GREAT DAY

'One of our great days was when we went to Dunchurch station, walking all the way, and lined the road when George V came to inspect the troops who had been abroad for some years. They afterwards went to France to fight in the Great War and many were killed, so later an avenue of trees was planted along the route they had marched, all the way from the station to Stretton. Some of those trees are standing today.'

THE DUKE OF YORK

'The only Royal visitor we had between the wars at Polesworth that I remember was the Duke of York, afterwards to become George VI, who came to Pooley Hall Colliery. Our schoolmaster took us down to the Square to see the Royal car pass through on its way back to London. Just to see the car was in itself an event in those days.'

The Waine family on an outing in Sutton Park at the time of George V's Coronation in 1911.

237

JUBILEE AND CORONATION

'I was six years old when the Silver Jubilee of George V was celebrated in 1935. A huge towering bonfire was built by the local mine workers at Hurley and a party was held in the field nearby. Food was prepared and eaten off a long table in a marquee and sports were organised for the children. These included apple ducking and trying to eat apples suspended on pieces of string on a frame.'

'In 1935 I was 14 years of age in my last year at school. The occasion uppermost in my mind that year was the Silver Jubilee celebration.

All schools in Leamington took part in a pageant held in the Victoria Park. School children were dressed in white, the girls in white dresses, the boys in white shirts and shorts. There were quite a number of different designs of the outfits but they were all white. The children marched from their various schools, with the leader carrying the Union Jack.

On the green arena there was marching to the brass band, a gymnastics display and country dancing, and singing of patriotic songs. The mayor made a speech which was difficult to hear, but we all clapped our hands enthusiastically at the end.

Each child was given a commemorative badge in blue enamel, with the design of the King's and Queen's head engraved in silver. On the reverse of the medal was the Coat of Arms of the Royal Borough of Leamington Spa. The medal was fitted with a fastener so all the children were able to wear them for the march back to their various schools where refreshments were waiting.

I still have my medal to this day.'

'The 1935 Jubilee was a wonderful day at Lapworth. Celebrations commenced in the morning with the May Queen's procession, and afterwards lunches were served. There were country dancing displays by the schoolchildren, and competitions and races for children and adults. After a tea, the children all received a commemorative mug.

The Coronation of George VI in 1937 was celebrated in a similar way. There was a children's fancy dress competition this time, the entries having to be made from paper. Meals were served and there were races and competitions again.'

'At Ullenhall, the 1935 Jubilee celebrations began with a horse-drawn waggon carrying the Jubilee Queen and her attendants processing from Crowleys Farm down the village to a field at Brook House, where we held sports such as races, barrel boxing and pillow fighting on a pole. There was tea in a marquee, and afterwards children were presented with a commemorative mug by Mrs Barratt from Heath Farm. The celebrations ended with a bonfire being lit on the allotment field. During the day there was also country dancing, the girls wearing dresses made from material provided by Mrs Friend of Crowleys Farm. The sun shone and altogether it was a very happy day.

The 1937 Coronation celebrations were more spectacular, organised by Mrs Peace, who lived at Rose Cottage. There were four horse-drawn waggons; on the first was Britannia with attendants, with peoples of the Empire on the three others. Refreshments were served in the new village hall. The weather was not very kind that year.'

QUEEN ELIZABETH'S CORONATION 1953

'After a meeting in the village hall at Hurley, a committee was formed to plan the celebrations for the 1953 Coronation. A fund was started and volunteers collected twopence weekly from every house in the village for several months. This enabled everyone to have a meal – adults having dinner in the village hall, in three sittings, and the children having a tea party at school. Sports were held in a field opposite the butcher's shop during the afternoon for adults and children.

Every child was given a mug from the school and a hymn and prayer book from the village.'

'Coronation Day was spoilt, not only by the dreadfully cold, wet weather but also with the advent of television. Very few people attended the morning celebrations at Lapworth apart from the organisers and helpers – most were watching television!'

'In 1953 we were one of the few families in our area of Rugby to own a television set so we had a houseful of friends and neighbours in to watch the Coronation in black and white on TV. Everyone brought something to eat and drink and we pooled it all and had a picnic.'

'Many people from Knightcote squeezed into our farmhouse sitting room to watch the Coronation on the nine inch television screen. A meal was held in the farm garage (no village hall) and entertainment was provided by the villagers. I remember we used a wind-up gramophone for the music.'

239

VILLAGE FEASTS AND FETES

All through the year there were holidays and celebrations to be looked forward to, from the closely contested village flower show to the traditional Wakes and Mop Fairs, and always, of course, the great festival of Christmas. Some holidays of the past are now gone for ever, such as Empire Day, once a part of every schoolchild's calendar and a welcome half day's holiday from school.

EMPIRE DAY

'In my first class at a Rugby school, just after the First World War, we sat on little wooden stools at tables. On Empire Day, 24th May, we sang a patriotic song which began: "We have come to school this morning, 'tis the 24th of May, and we join in celebrating what is called our Empire Day." Then we saluted a large Union Jack which always seemed to stand in a corner of the classroom. On the wall was a large picture of the battle of Spion Kop in the Boer War.'

'Empire Day was always celebrated at Willoughby village school in the 1920s. We all stood round the flagpole and the Union Jack was raised with great ceremony as we sang "Britons never, never, never shall be slaves" with great gusto.'

'On Empire Day at Ashorne, the children would line up outside the school while the Union Jack was raised on the flagpole and the National Anthem was sung. Each child was then given a penny and a half day's holiday from school. The penny was duly deposited at the local sweet shop. This went on for several years, and then the penny was gradually stopped.
   Up until the middle 1930s a gentleman in the village used to come up to the school on Empire Day and present the children with a medal and a year after they would get a box to add to it with the date on.'

THE FLOWER SHOW

'Ansley Common Flower Show was special. For weeks before, gardeners would feed, water, talk to and guard their kidney beans, onions, marrows etc. An air of competition was everywhere, with what seemed like the whole village eager to grow the best produce and flowers and be commended as a winner. Quite a few jars of ale were consumed (not by chapel folk, of course) during the long, hot summer day. J H Phillips Esq, the colliery owners, would present the awards and a good time was had by all.'

'The Flower Show at Tanworth in Arden had exhibits of flowers, vegetables and dressed poultry. The Flower Show was far more important than the village fete that was held each year at the Old Vicarage.'

'Ufton & District Flower Show was formed in 1912, and soon became well known in the area. At its peak over 3,000 people paid to go in. Eight large marquees at a cost of £5 each were erected and a band engaged.'

THE MOP FAIR

'I remember the Mop Fair at Alcester between the wars, with its open lamps and roundabouts. My favourites were the Peters Horses, the cakewalk, and Clarkes Motors. The prizes given on the stalls were amazing – tea sets, sets of saucepans, large animals etc. A pig was roasted outside The Red Horse in Henley Street and another one in High Street.'

'The Mop (fair) was another exciting day to look forward to at Studley and we saved our pennies for this occasion. The Mop was held at the end of September in Newlands Fields, off New Road, nearly opposite the Catholic school. Some of the older pupils were asked to help pull on ropes to erect the amusements. I think they were paid with free rides.
   Rocky Herbert's was my favourite stall, selling brandy snaps, humbugs, "troach drops" and other such old-fashioned sweets. Besides bumper-cars (dodgems) there was a cake-walk, swingboats, a helter-skelter, ghost train, shooting, coconut shy, darts etc, and the roundabouts.
   The "little horses" cost only a penny per ride. A man with a hook in place of one hand turned a wheel to make them go tamely round and round. The "big horses" cost twopence per ride. They rose and fell as they revolved.
   Besides horses there were cockerels, or sometimes ostriches. All had names, they glowed with colour and pieces of mirror-glass reflected the hundreds of brilliant lights. Best of all was the jolly music, played by an organ, highly coloured and having little people

who "played" instruments in time. I was amazed to see rolls of strong paper with holes punched in it actually made the organ play.'

THE WAKES

'The Sunday nearest 19th July was the start of the Wakes festival at Sutton under Brailes. Children away from home brought presents to their parents and all went to church together. Next day roundabouts and swingboats were set up on the green together with coconut shies and gingerbread stalls. The latter were owned by a man from the next village who encouraged custom by shouting, "Walk up and buy my ginger snaps, my little virgins!" What were virgins, I wondered? All this cut into our hard-saved pennies, which had been earned by jobs such as picking up stones in the field before the hay was cut or weeding or running errands at the farm.'

'The Polesworth Wakes were a highlight in our lives, coming in September and lasting from the Friday, when the fair started, until Monday at midnight. Being a church school and the Wakes being a religious festival, the Nethersole School always had two days

The coming of the fair, here at Tysoe, was a red letter day in the village year.

242

holiday. The Harvest Festival was held on Wakes Sunday, the church being decorated with sheaves of corn, fruit and vegetables and flowers. Wake Monday was also a popular day for weddings and for families to visit relatives. The streets were lined with stalls and the fair started at twelve noon and went on until twelve midnight.'

'At Blackwell, on 12th June each year we had a Wake. The gipsies brought stalls, swinging boats and the ginny horses etc. As there was no public house in the village, most people made their own wine and entertained their friends. Mother used to make all kinds of wine and she made lemonade and cake for the children. It was a day we looked forward to all year.'

'There was great excitement on Trinity Sunday when the Wake would arrive at Long Itchington for three days. We spent our pennies on rides. Relatives would come on the Wednesday, which was the big day. The village band always played on the village green. In 1932 a great flood occurred when water flowed from one end of the village to the other. The Wake was washed out and lots of houses flooded.'

CLUB DAY

'Each Whit Sunday the Ufton Sick Club held their Annual Dinner. At ten o'clock a band was engaged to parade round the village led by the club officials. Emblems of office were carried to the church for a service (members not attending church were fined one shilling). Then followed a dinner at the school, after which a fete was held on the green. After the Great War the dinner took place in a large marquee in Ufton Fields. The last Club Day was held in 1924.'

'One of the highlights of the year at Ilmington was Club Day held on the first Tuesday in June. It began with a procession round the village to the church for a service. The procession was accompanied by the brass band and an old photograph shows it coming up Back Street with the men wearing the sashes of which some were so proud that they were buried with them. There followed a meal for the men, sports, and a tea for the women and children. The feast was held in a marquee erected for the purpose at varying places, sometimes where Windmill Close now stands. The chosen ground was entered through an arch decorated with "Whitsun Roses" and these are said to have been gathered from a guelder rose tree outside what is now Bevingtons. There is still a tree there. The club owned its own blue and white crockery with silver lustre tea pots. This was stored above what was then the baker's but is now the post office. It was the duty of the baker's daughter to wash it in readiness for the feast. The crockery was sold when the club was disbanded, but the exact date of this is not remembered, possibly just after the First World War.

Exactly what this club was is still uncertain. Some say it was the Oddfellows – a subgroup of the Tysoe branch. This, however, was only formed in 1912. In Tysoe the lodge appears to have replaced an earlier insurance society and such a society had been founded in Ilmington in 1815. The rules of this society have been found at the Birthplace Trust Record Office. It was founded for the purpose of relieving "such members as shall be prevented from working through sickness, lameness or other infirmities; for burying the dead and paying widows or children of the deceased the money owing to them". It had a president, treasurer, two stewards and a clerk of accounts, and was based at The Red Lion. There were 13 rules of which number seven reads as follows: – "No benefit shall be paid to anyone till he has paid into the Society for two whole years. No benefits shall be paid for venereal causes, inoculation for smallpox, immoderate drinking, fighting, wrestling, football playing, cudgelling or any such like malicious exercise." The last rule states that no more than £20 is to be kept in the Box, the rest must be invested. It is the date of the feast day of this club which connects it with "Club Day". In the rule book of this club there is no mention of the blue sashes of which the men were so proud.

A second insurance society, Ilmington Unity Sick and Dividend Club, founded in 1893 also at The Red Lion was disbanded in 1965. In this case payments might begin after two months membership. These records consist largely of the lists of officers and cash accounts for the year. There is one mention of 58 dinners at two shillings each in 1896 and in 1898 "Dinners £6 4s 0d". In 1893 its 38 members received a dividend of £1 1s 10d but there is no further mention of dividends. Its income during the 1950s averaged about £160 a year and its membership ranged from 38 in 1893, 58 in 1895, to 121 in 1953.'

THE MINERS' GALA

'The highlight of the year at Dordon was the Miners' Gala, when there was a carnival, sports and a free tea if your father worked at the pit.

In September, Dad always took us to Polesworth Statutes, which was a funfair with roundabouts powered by huge traction engines.'

HARVEST TREAT

'In the early years of the century, after the harvest, the Marquis of Northampton sent waggons and horses to collect all the children under 14 from the Tysoe area and bring them to Compton Winyates. Nearly all farmers locally were his tenants. Best bibs and tuckers were freshened up and donned, boots polished and buttoned up, tediously, with hooks, knees were scrubbed and faces and hands washed, for this was truly a gala day.

Tea was served in the great hall, consisting of sugar buns, cream cakes, tea and lemonade, and was followed by games of hide and seek, though no one ever found anybody in the secret hideaways and dark recesses of this glorious Tudor house. Prizes were for all, whether they won them or not – bats, balls, skipping ropes and games. *Every* year several children fell in the moat and had to be fished out by the servants. Parents could attend, but only to watch. Finally, all the children left for home, happy but tired, clutching a bag containing sweets, an apple and an orange in their sticky hands.'

BONFIRE NIGHT AND CHRISTMAS

'Guy Fawkes day was an event at Sutton under Brailes preceded by weeks of gathering wood and then making the bonfire in which horse chestnuts were roasted to go off bang. For days after we roasted potatoes in the ashes, and, of course, smokey and black as they were, nothing baked in an oven and served on a plate was half so good.

The highlight of the year was, undoubtedly, Christmas. Directly Bonfire Night was off hand, we began making weird and wonderful presents for parents, grandparents and aunts. We painted cards too and made texts on perforated cards which we filled with cross-stitch. "Stir up Sunday" meant that it was time to do so with the plum pudding mixture and everyone had to take a turn and make a wish. At last *the* day dawned and there was the excitement of finding the stocking we had hopefully hung up filled with trifles the modern child would scorn. White sugar mice with string tails and pink noses, jack-in-the-box, tin whistle, tops, skipping ropes, and an orange maybe, and family jokes remembered. The form in which presents were arranged varied every year. Tied to the brass ribs of the green gig umbrella hung up in the hall was one, in a pork pie of brown paper another, and a snowball of cottonwool are some I remember. They were given out after breakfast with the whole household present – no one was forgotten. Even our beloved dog Dash had his present. It was a puzzle to me how presents came from absent aunts

245

and grandparents and I never suspected our friend the postman of having had any hand in it.

After service in church, where there were often new books bound in sweet-smelling Russian leather to be proudly carried, came the traditional Christmas dinner of roast beef, followed by plum pudding in a blaze of fire made of burning brandy. The great luxury was dessert, composed of fruit, nuts and ginger wine. The iced cake of today had not yet come into fashion. Another Christmas joy was the party and Christmas tree at the rectory given for all the children of the village, but those attending Sunday school had prizes in addition to gifts from the tree. We were not among these.'

'Bonfire Night at Ilmington was a colourful occasion. The bonfire was built on the Upper Green and in the days when faggots were stored for the winter, and the wheelwright's wood was seasoning outside what is now the garage, it was an anxious night for some. The parish council had tried to forbid bonfires in 1900 and their efforts against the taking of timber do not seem to have been outstandingly successful. The wheelwright's family was not allowed to attend the bonfire but had to mount guard over the wood. It was, too, an anxious night for the village policeman. One story is told of an enthusiastic farmer who encouraged people "to fetch more wood where that came from", only to discover the following morning that it had come from his own store.'

'Bonfire Night was always exciting and children saved for weeks to buy fireworks, Jumping Jacks and sparklers. All our garden rubbish was saved for the bonfire for weeks beforehand.

Then it was Christmas. Houses were decorated with home-made streamers and holly, and a bunch of holly often took the place of a Christmas tree, the branches hung with sugar ornaments as well as shiny baubles. Toys, although simple, held a magic for children and shopkeepers would decorate their windows. At Polesworth, we always went to Sunday school and church on Christmas Day, wearing our new gloves, scarves and hats. Afterwards we would be sent out to deliver mince pies, and often a Christmas dinner, to elderly relatives.'

'Christmas eased its way along without any commercialisation. We were not aware of it until perhaps three weeks before the event when we would begin carols at school. The looked forward to event was a trip to Woolworths in Smithford Street, Coventry, to see Father Christmas and on payment of sixpence we would receive a present. The boxes were wrapped in pink and blue tissue paper for girls and boys respectively. The gifts were always of good value. I don't know what the boys received but we girls usually had a doll or golliwog, bricks with pictures on to form a large block, books, or mosaic beads. The tree was dressed a few days before Christmas and the shopping done either at the shop near the General Wolfe hotel (locals would say they were going "up the Wolfe" to shop) or the town and in the market where we could shop until 9 pm on Friday and Saturday nights. The stalls were lit with paraffin lamps which gave a welcoming warm glow. The market hall was a hive of activity and we could purchase anything – cheese, poultry, meat, fruit, sweets, tripe, linoleum, clothes and pets. For us children there was always the penny stall where we could browse until we found suitable items. At the entrance to the Market Hall was a weighing machine – an enormous piece of machinery – where a bearded gentleman officiated and one's weight was *guaranteed* to be accurate. We either walked to town or used the trams for the journey. The price charged was twopence for adults and a penny for children from Courtaulds in Foleshill Road into Broadgate.

Just before Christmas my uncle who lived in Haifa would send a crate made of wood and tied with yellow raffia-type rope which always contained the most mouth-watering, juicy Jaffa oranges. I've never seen such large oranges since, or tasted such fruits. They were certainly a treat. Christmas Day was never accompanied by snow as far as I can recall. On Christmas Eve I hung up my pillowcase and was always delighted with the surprises. Perhaps being an only child I was fortunate as I remember having on various Christmases a doll's pram, doll's house (made by an uncle) and a fairy cycle. Most Christmases in my early childhood followed the same pattern. We would usually have cockerel for dinner (which my father had fattened up) – like most people we kept poultry at the top of the garden. Then my grandparents on mother's side would join us for dinner which my mother had prepared, very much like today's meals with a Christmas pudding made by her, and usually containing in it a silver threepenny bit or sixpence (always wrapped in greaseproof paper for hygienic reasons). After dinner the grown ups would play whist, whilst I played with my toys and we would have the wireless on for entertainment. On Boxing Day we went to my aunt and uncle in Earlsdon. We always walked both ways, so I think the tram drivers were given a holiday then.'

MORRIS AND MUMMERS

'It seems to be impossible at this date to speak with certainty of the tradition of Morris Dancing in Ilmington, as distinct from the revival which occurred led by Sam Bennett. What is quite clear is that Sam Bennett learned his tunes by ear from the father of one of the older inhabitants. This man played the tunes on an old pipe, which is well remembered but now lost. No one now remembers a visit of Cecil Sharp but it seems probable that he did collect from this village. Attempts have been made to ascertain which, if any, dances or tunes were peculiar to Ilmington but so far without success. Shepherd's Hey, Mowing the Barley, and Pitch Pole Jack were mentioned. One man is remembered as dancing a Patten Dance. A member of another old established Ilmington family remembers playing the tabard for Morris dancing. The Christmas broadcast of 1934 introduced from Ilmington referred to the playing of the pipe and tabor, then well remembered. A flute belonging to the family of the old gentleman, who taught Sam Bennett, was dated to 1870 but this is not the pipe which was used. This same family refers to a drum and fife band which long preceded the brass band already described.

Mention of the Mummers' play to members of these two families who have been in the village from at least the 17th century still elicits the spontaneous quotation of some of the lines, though they agree that it has probably not been performed for at least 100 years. Again, Sam Bennett is said to have tried to revive this without success.

Reginald Tiddy collected Mummers' plays in this district before the First World War. His book *The Mummers' Play*, published post-humously in 1929, has been consulted. In it he gives the plays peculiar to Great Wolford, Pillerton, Ilmington and Weston Sub Edge among other villages more remote from Ilmington. Of these, that of Ilmington is much the longest. He believed the Mummers' plays to have a sacrificial origin far back in pagan antiquity, to be deeply rooted in the folk memory of somewhat isolated villages and that there may have been a very late printed version in the 17th or early 18th centuries of which existing forms are garbled versions handed down by oral tradition among largely unlettered folk. By this time many characters had been incorporated in the plays and transformations had taken place, for example St George became King George. Their humour is peculiar to them, and is always topsy turvey patter which he regarded as the garbled survival of magical incantations.'

THE PARTY

'When I was a child the first Saturday after Christmas, other than if it was Boxing Day, was always the day of the Children's Party at Ashorne. It was the highlight of the year and made the Christmas festival last longer.

248

The Saturday was greeted with great excitement. We were quite a large family and lived in a small cottage without electricity or running water. Like most people in Ashorne, we had to bath in the kitchen, where a large copper heated the water, so you were never cold during that process.

We all had our hair washed and trimmed and there were new white hair ribbons for the girls. We girls always wore thin party dresses and little woollen capes and took either ballet-type or black ankle strap shoes to change into when we arrived at "The Hut" as the village hall was called. In my memory it always seems to have snowed.

The Village Hall Committee organised the party. It seems to have been an all male collection with their wives doing the "Women's work".

After tea we played games and then one of the men would cut the presents off the Christmas tree and call out the name on the parcel. Mrs Porteous from Ashorne House presented each child with the gift. She was a dear little lady with quite a squeaky voice and always seemed to be dressed in black. We were always drilled by my mother as to what we had to say and do when Mrs Porteous gave us our present. Girls did a little curtsy and said thank you madam. My brothers gave a Cub or Scout salute and said thank you madam. Mrs Porteous sometimes said a little word to a child, but children in my day were quite shy and were glad to get back to their seat and undo the parcel.

At the conclusion of the party every child was given a bag of sweets, nuts, an apple and an orange to take home, and we went off excited, happy and very full.'

'Every New Year's Day at Alcester, a party was held for all the children of the town, with a visit to the pictures, then tea in the Town Hall with farthing sticky iced buns, and a present of apples, oranges and chocolate.'

MEMORIES OF MAY DAY

May Day held a special magic for many of us. Age old traditions were followed in town and village, with special songs to be sung, a May Queen and King to be chosen and dancing around the maypole.

A GREAT DAY

'May Day in Leek Wootton was traditionally held on 1st May or as near as possible to that date. I personally remember it being held on the 12th May, it being the then vicar's birthday. On whichever date held, two weeks prior there was much activity in the village school, the age range of the boys and girls being five to 14 years.

First the maypole was brought out, the ribbons checked and the maypole songs and dances rehearsed. The May Day traditional songs and country dances were performed until thoroughly mastered. Handicraft lessons were devoted to the making of paper flowers and streamers to bedeck the Queen's coach, throne and garlands, the decorating of which was carried out by the head teacher and the boys the day before. Two "Queens" were chosen, by secret vote, one by the infants with three Maids of Honour, and one by the middle and senior classes, also with three Maids of Honour. The Queens were known as the Big Queen and the Little Queen. All this was taken very seriously, as there was much competition for the honour of being chosen May Queen.

On the day, all the girls were arrayed in white dresses, the Queens wearing short veils under crowns of flowers, for many years made by a local florist in the village, and each Queen carrying a basket of flowers, similarly made and donated. At one stage the Maids of Honour wore mauve sleeping hair nets bought from Woolworths for threepence each. A boy was chosen to play the part of Jack-in-the-Green (a pre-Christian spirit), his clothes being decorated with green foliage.

On May Day morning the children assembled at the school to form a procession for a nine o'clock start. First, the Little Queen followed by her Maids of Honour and the infants, then the Big Queen with her Maids of Honour followed by the rest of the school. The first port of call was the big house nearest the school, where many parents would have congregated to listen to the songs and watch the dancing on the lawn, the music being provided by a teacher on her violin, or by the children's own voices. After this first event the school divided, the infants' procession calling at some of the larger houses in the village to sing and dance, while the seniors proceeded towards Kenilworth, round Rouncil Lane calling at the large houses there, back down Woodcote Lane to Woodcote (now Police Headquarters), from there to Hill Wootton, then to Guy's Cliffe, Wootton Court, other big houses in the vicinity, finally back to school for a short rest. At the end of each performance at all the venues the children made a collection, and refreshments were provided for them at many stops.

When the infants returned to school the procession would reform, the Queens walking in their coach, which was supported by their six Maids of Honour, the senior boys carrying the maypole and the garlands. When all was ready, the procession, led by Jack-in-the-Green, set off for the vicarage (now Wootton Paddox) arriving there at 2 pm. Here the majority of villagers were gathered to watch the time honoured ceremony of "Crowning" the Queens, before which numerous songs and dances were performed. One very pretty and unusual dance was performed by the senior girls, "The Butterfly Dance", the wings being attached at the back of their dresses. The Queen always had white wings with silver stars on them, the rest of the girls different coloured ones, made of pretty coloured muslin. The dance was accompanied by a song beginning: "Butterfly wings, butterfly wings. Airy, fairy, dainty things. Flitting about from morn till night. All in the Garden of Delight etc." The butterflies folded up, re-awakening to perform the rest of the dance – it was very effective. Finally the maypole dances were performed round the actual maypole, beautiful patterns being formed by the intricate weaving of the ribbons. Woe betide any pupil who allowed his/her ribbon to become slack or twisted, spoiling the pattern! Boys did a sword dance. The ceremony here ended with the actual crowning of the Queens, in my day usually by Lord Leigh of Stoneleigh Abbey, but often by a local person of note. Small presents were given to the Queens and Maids of Honour.

The children then processed back to school where sugar buns, chelsea buns and lemonade awaited them. The collection boxes would be emptied, the contents counted and shared between the pupils, the Queens receiving an extra sixpence and the Maids of Honour an extra threepence. The children then wended their weary way home to Hill Wootton, the Woodloes, to far ends of the village to be welcomed home by their proud and loving parents.

A dance was held in the evening for all villagers to attend, with a four piece band. In latter years many old pupils returned year after year, and there was much reminiscing.'

251

'With the coming of Spring and the quickening of life in farm and field, it was natural that Spring's birthday, May Day, should be celebrated. The children of Sutton under Brailes, before the First World War, would be dressed in their best and carry a most beautifully made bower of crossed hoops in which sat the doll May Queen. On the top of this bower was always a bloom of Crown Imperial from the shepherd's garden. With traditional songs, the children visited not only each house in the village, but all the outlying farms which must have totalled many miles. However, after a huge communal tea they still had energy to play vigorous games.'

THE KING AND QUEEN

'One thing I remember at Tredington in the 1920s was May Day, when we danced around a wooden may pole. It was bedecked with all different coloured ribbons and the dances were called "The Spider's Web", "The Plait" and "Dancing Merrily Around".

A May Queen and King were crowned each year on May Day. They were normally chosen from the group of older children due to leave school that year. The Queen was dressed in a long white dress with a sash, she wore a crown on her head and carried a posy of flowers. The King wore a purple satin suit with a sash and a gold cardboard crown.

After the King and Queen had been crowned, we danced in various places around the village. Two of the largest boys would stand on the maypole to keep it from tipping over. All the children would wear their Sunday best, the girls wearing sashes and carrying posies of flowers.

In the afternoon we went to Blackwell on a horse trolley, lent by Mr Wilkes of Manor Farm. The carter came too, to look after the horse. At one farm the farmer offered the King one penny if he would kiss the Queen. The farmer's wife gave us home-made lemonade and cake. After stopping at different locations around the village, to dance, we then climbed aboard the horse trolley and went to dance in Armscote, a neighbouring village.'

'When I was about four years old, before the First World War, I was May Queen at Dunchurch and was pushed around in a mail cart decorated with flowers. The girls sang May songs at all the big houses. I remember my mother made me a white spotted muslin dress and sewed bunches of pink ribbons all over it.'

THE MAY SONG

'At Ufton the May Queen was crowned and the children made a garland of flowers, marching in procession round the village, then on to Stoneythorpe Hall and back through Bascote Heath singing a May song – quite a considerable way. The May song went as follows:
"Good morning, young ladies and gentlemen
We wish you a happy May
We have come to show you a May garland
Because it is May Day
A branch of May have we brought you
Before your door it stands
It's all spread out and scattered about
By the work of our Lord's hands
W have travelled a very long way
And now we must go – good luck to you all
We wish you a happy day." '

'Water Orton celebrated May Day with the schoolchildren dancing round the maypole on the village green, singing:
"Dance round the maypole trit trot trot
See what a maypole we have got
Dressed in ribbons all in a bow
See what a maypole we can show."
Then the children would visit the large houses around the village, singing:
"Maypole day is a very happy day
Please to remember the first of May
Now we have sung our short little song
We can no longer stay
We wish you all both great and small
A happy month of May."
The occupants of the houses would give the children a donation.'

'May Day in Brailes was a great treat for all the schoolchildren. They all met at school at nine o'clock, then processed around the lower end of the village headed by the King and Queen singing May Day songs. Girls usually dressed in white and carried bunches of garden flowers; the boys were in suits or their best coats, complete with caps bearing garlands of flowers. All went home to dinner, then started out again at two o'clock singing around the top end of the village. At four, everyone returned to school for a tea which teachers had prepared, with some parents helping. Afterwards school sports took place, where most children managed to get a prize of twopence, fourpence or sixpence for winning a race. There are many happy memories of this day.'

'May Day was a big event in Stoneleigh. We went around the village singing May songs, particularly "The cuckoo is a pretty bird, he singeth as he flies". After that we would walk up "Jobblees Hill" through the fields to the Abbey to sing to Lord Leigh's family, who were all lined up in front of the Abbey to receive us. We were taken into the main entrance for a drink of milk and a bun. Then we walked back across the fields home. No parents came with us.'

THE MAYPOLE

'The maypole on the green is a main feature of Welford. Children from the village school crowned their May Queen on 24th May, which was Empire Day. The Queen and her Court arrived on a horse-drawn dray, followed by Robin Hood and his Merrie Men (and women!). Other children wore coronets of real flowers, often wild ones, or jester caps with bells. A collection was made by boys on hobby horses. In 1934 the maypole was struck by lightning, but a new one was duly paid for by public subscription.'

'The maypole at Ashorne would be erected in the middle of the village in the meadow called Chapel Meadow close by the Congregational chapel. The children would go round the village with garlands on two poles collecting money to pay for goes on the swingboats, roundabouts and coconut shy – after they had performed the maypole dance.'

'The children at Newbold on Stour danced around the maypole in the school playground. They also danced at nearby Ettington Park for the Shirley family. They carried posies of flowers and, preceded by the decorated maypole carried by the older children, would process around the village.'

'Children at Tysoe spent several weeks practising for the maypole dances earlier this century, and bluebells and primroses were picked to decorate small hand-held poles. On the morning of 1st May, before school, they carried these poles round to people's houses saying, "Please to smell my maypole", expecting in return a treat of sweets or pennies.'

Index

255

256